MARGINALIZED VOICES IN MUSIC EDUCATION

Marginalized Voices in Music Education explores the American culture of music teaching and learning by looking at marginalization and privilege in music education as a means to critique prevailing assumptions and paradigms. In ten contributed essays, authors set out to expand notions of who we believe we are as music educators and who we want to become. This book is a collection of perspectives by some of the leading and emerging thinkers in the profession, and identifies cases of individuals or groups who have experienced marginalization. It shares the diverse stories in a struggle for inclusion, with the goal to begin or expand conversation in undergraduate and graduate courses in music teacher education. Through the telling of these stories, the authors hope to recast music education as fertile ground for transformation, experimentation, and renewal.

Brent C. Talbot is Associate Professor of Music Education at the Sunderman Conservatory of Music at Gettysburg College.

MARGINALIZED VOICES IN MUSIC EDUCATION

Brent C. Talbot

Routledge
Taylor & Francis Group

NEW YORK AND LONDON

First published 2018
by Routledge
711 Third Avenue, New York, NY 10017

and by Routledge
2 Park Square, Milton Park, Abingdon, Oxon OX14 4RN

Routledge is an imprint of the Taylor & Francis Group, an informa business

© 2018 Taylor & Francis

Library of Congress Cataloging in Publication Data
Names: Talbot, Brent C., editor.
Title: Marginalized voices in music education / Brent C. Talbot.
Description: New York ; London : Routledge, 2018. | Includes index.
Identifiers: LCCN 2017021844| ISBN 9780415788328 (hardback) |
ISBN 9780415788335 (pbk.)
Subjects: LCSH: Music—Instruction and study—Social aspects--United States. |
Multiculturalism—United States. | Marginality, Social—United States.
Classification: LCC MT3.U5 M313 2018 | DDC 780.7/073—dc23
LC record available at https://lccn.loc.gov/2017021844

ISBN: 978-0-415-78832-8 (hbk)
ISBN: 978-0-415-78833-5 (pbk)
ISBN: 978-1-315-22540-1 (ebk)

Typeset in Bembo and Stone Sans
by Florence Production Ltd, Stoodleigh, Devon, UK
Printed and bound by CPI Group (UK) Ltd, Croydon, CR0 4YY

This collection is dedicated to those in our communities and around the world who are fighting for recognition, for validation, and for inclusion in our musical imaginary.

CONTENTS

PREFACE

The idea for this project emerged out of the call for proposals for the biennial symposium of the *Society for Music Teacher Education* (SMTE) in 2015, the focus of which was on issues of social justice. While I was conducting fieldwork in Indonesia during a pre-tenure research leave in the fall of 2014, I read the news reports from overseas about our nation's responses to the deaths of Eric Garner, Michael Brown, Laquan McDonald, Akai Gurley, and Tamir Rice. Troubled about these events, I floated an idea on Facebook about creating a national project that would examine our role as music teachers in various forms of oppression. I suggested we take a look directly at people's experiences with marginalization and privilege in our field, and to find a way to elevate and share their stories with our community. The post generated much interest and within hours Sandra Stauffer, Darrin Thornton, Marg Schmidt, Karin Hendricks, Vanessa Bond, Don Taylor, and Colleen Sears among others expressed a desire to share their own stories of marginalization in the field of music education or to collaborate with colleagues and students with whom they knew had experienced forms of oppression in music education. We each proposed individual presentations at SMTE as well as a collective one that drew on themes across each case. The overall goal was to populate the symposium with narratives that are typically muted or left out of the music education imaginary. Our presentations at SMTE were well-received and generated much conversation. Additional interest during and following the conference led to more researchers like Tami Draves, Elizabeth Parker, Amy Spears, Joyce McCall, Deejay Robinson and Sarah Bartolome contributing to our efforts.

The collection of narratives in this book represents only a portion of the diversity that exists within American music education. Our intent is to use the telling of each experience as provocation for discussion on diversity and inclusion in our field, not to define parameters, create a grand narrative of otherness, nor attempt to represent all identity constructions, but instead to reveal patterns of injustice. The result is a book designed to challenge assumptions and to begin conversations in undergraduate and graduate courses in music teacher education. This book is just a beginning and not meant to be a comprehensive collection of marginalization. There are many voices and identity constructions missing from this collection; however, it is our hope that people will draw upon some of the stories and theoretical frameworks presented within these chapters in order to explore—in class discussion or future research—other forms of oppression and marginalization in our field. We hope students and teachers will extend this work and share their own and others' experiences in future collections and journals. As Stauffer (2012) comments, "We have a professional responsibility to help [people] know that they are not alone, and to help them make these stories of music education present in the educational imaginary . . . we should tell stories of self-making, of re-making and replacing ourselves" (p. 11). Through this telling, we strive to disrupt the stories created for others and recast music education as fertile ground for transformation, experimentation, and renewal.

All of the stories presented in this book remind us that there is great diversity that is often muted and unexplored within the field of American music education. Critical storytelling, either autoethnographically or through case study design, was specifically used to help readers grapple with the complexity and nuance of each person's experience (Stauffer, 2014). Although providing a concrete list of implications or answers is not an appropriate result of this type of scholarship, the stories found within these pages do raise many questions about current practices in our field. For example, in what ways do practices in school music programs require students to categorize themselves? How might music educators make it known that they are open to different possibilities? How might we do things so that the scale of measurement is not against dominant norms? How might we re-envision our program requirements, our entrance exams, and how we market and advertise our programs? How might we work toward dismantling the systems of oppression and opening spaces for more equitable and inclusive practices? How can we use music to change our world? At the end of each chapter, the reader will find a list of discussion questions and activities to extend conversation and further thinking on the topics at hand. The objective of this book is to create dialogue around marginalization and privilege and to have music educators consider ways in which we participate in systemic oppression in music, in education, and in society. As Freire (2000) says, "To surmount the situation of oppression, people must first critically recognize its causes, so that through transforming action they can create a new situation, one which makes possible the pursuit of a fuller humanity" (47). As music teachers, we have the power to create new situations, even when we may feel the pressures to conform to the dominating practices of our spaces for teaching and learning. We cannot, to quote Loraine Hansberry (1964), afford to "stand idly by and wait for change to occur," but instead we must develop—as a community of learners—a culture of critical reflection and action that will lead to challenging systemic forms of oppression in education.

References

Freire, P. (2000). *Pedagogy of the oppressed*. New York: Bloomsbury.

Hansberry, L. 1964. *The Black revolution and the White backlash*. Presentation. Forum at Town Hall sponsored by the Association of Artists for Freedom, New York, June 15.

Stauffer, S. (2012, June). *Trading places: Transformation in progress in the lives of music educators*. Paper presented at the MayDay Group Colloquium 24, East Lansing, MI.

Stauffer, S. L. (2014). Narrative inquiry and the uses of narrative in music education research. In C. Conway (Ed.), *The Oxford handbook of qualitative research in American music education* (pp. 163-185). New York: Oxford University Press.

ACKNOWLEDGMENTS

I have been fortunate in my life to continually find myself surrounded by really intelligent and skilled people who challenge and expand my world view. I am not always sure how I find myself standing in the presence of such great thinkers, creators, and performers, but I am certainly happy that these people continue to accept, support, and guide me along my creative journeys. I take pause here to acknowledge their contributions to the very book you are about to read.

First and foremost, I must thank my husband Adam Cordle, as well as my family and close friends, from whom I have robbed countless hours of time in order to edit and write about things that really matter to me. From companionship to intellectual engagement, your love and support is what keeps me going.

I am indebted to the many students over the years who have been excellent collaborators as we strained against and have tried to make meaning from school(ing) and society. The very impetus for this project began in our classroom as we attempted to make sense of various events unfolding in the news and to understand more deeply the root causes of systemic violence, marginalization, and privilege. It was in concert with members of our music education program that I first began to understand, implicitly and then more explicitly, the interrelated but never equivalent positionalities from which we speak and from which we view the world. It was also in conversation with these great music educators, sometimes in close proximity, sometimes on travels together, sometimes over text or email, that I refined the ideas presented here. All current and past students have contributed to this experience in one way of another, but I would like to specifically thank Alice Broadway, Matt Carlson, Eddie Holmes, Kelly Reymann, and Alex Schweizer for our in-depth discussions and research together on such topics.

Mentors have the ability to look ahead at what is often difficult to see and to assist us in navigating the many obstacles that are in our way. Often we find the obstacle to be us: the researcher, writer, and teacher. Two incredibly important mentors in my life assisted with this project and helped review the material submitted for publication. The first is my dissertation advisor, Susan Conkling, who continues to guide and influence my thinking many years later. The second is Deb Bradley, my sage and patient editor in chief at *Action, Criticism and Theory for Music Education*. Both deserve significant recognition for helping shape this project. Their thoughtful critique, their knowledge and attention to theory, and their direct feedback greatly strengthened each chapter and created a cohesiveness across the entire book. The field of music education owes a great deal of appreciation for all the behind-the-scenes work these two gifted women do every day for our profession.

There are tirelessly hardworking people in the world who produce absolutely dazzling scholarship that pushes our field in new directions. Karin Hendricks is one such scholar. From our first days together as visiting professors at the University of Illinois to our continued work on issues of social justice, the compassionate ways in which Karin sees and explains things have powerfully transformed my writing. Similarly, I am thankful for Roger Mantie, who may very well be the smartest person I know. From the moment I met him at the National Association for Music Education (NAfME) biennial conference in St. Louis, I knew we would become powerful conspirators. Collaborating with these two critically and theoretically oriented scholars has dramatically changed my work. Both Karin and Roger's wisdom and advice have helped develop the frameworks and approaches found throughout this book.

One of the benefits of being employed at a liberal arts college is that you work in close contact each week with intelligent people across many disciplines who consistently inspire you. Hakim Mohandas Amani Williams teaches in the Africana Studies and Education departments at Gettysburg College. Our shared interests in critical pedagogy brought us together. Since our very first meeting, Hakim has modeled an urgent, relentless inquiry in the world that demands action and alertness to our most important social and cultural needs. Similarly, McKinley Melton, a brilliant scholar in our English department whose scholarship on James Baldwin has opened my eyes about race in America, has demanded the very best of me as a writer and as a colleague. Additionally, Gretchen Carlson Natter at the Center for Public Service and Robert Natter at the Sunderman Conservatory of Music, who, through many discussions and through collaboration on local, national, and international projects, have contributed to the development of a social justice-oriented music education curriculum at Gettysburg College. The council of each of these great colleagues has shaped the presentation, language, and framing of this project in countless ways.

I would like to acknowledge the hard work of each contributing author of this book: Joyce McCall; Deejay Robinson; Darrin Thornton; Karin Hendricks and Dorothy; Margaret Schmidt and Carlos Castañeda Lechuga; Colleen Sears and Cathy; Sarah Bartolome and Melanie Stanford; Vanessa Bond and Jamey

Petrus; Don Taylor and Zeke; Elizabeth Parker, Amy Spears, Tami Draves, Christopher and Lindsey. Their stories are courageously inspiring and incredibly important in helping create change in our field. Lastly, I would like to thank Clint Randles for introducing me to Constance Ditzel at Routledge, who supported the development of this project from the very beginning; for that, we are all incredibly grateful.

Brent C. Talbot, Ph.D.
April 2017

INTRODUCTION

Brent C. Talbot, Editor

> Culture, like food, is necessary to sustain us. It molds us and shapes our relations to each other. An inequitable culture is one in which people do not have the same power to create, access, or circulate their practices, works, ideas, and stories. It is one in which people cannot represent themselves equally. To say that American culture is inequitable is to say that it moves us away from seeing each other in our full humanity. It is to say that the culture does not point us toward a more just society.
>
> Jeff Chang (2016, p. 56)

In *Who We Be: The Colorization of America,* Jeff Chang claims that cultural changes surrounding the Civil Rights Movements of the 1960s were equally important in transforming American society as legal ones and that both faced a sustained hostile response that continues to this day. According to Chang (2014), the notion of multiculturalism challenged the American identity of who we thought we were and eventually who we were aspiring to become. It was a time when universities debated whether the Western canon should continue to be elevated or imagined outside the politics of racial, patriarchal, heteronormative, gendered, and ableist hierarchies. Over the decades to follow, powerful counterattacks were launched and many understood that the battles being waged over shaping culture were high-stakes.

The events over the past few years in Ferguson, Staten Island, Baltimore, Charleston, and Orlando, to name just a few, the debates surrounding gay marriage and transgender rights, as well as the misogynistic and xenophobic rhetoric that propelled Donald Trump and other world leaders to positions of power, have all contributed to an increased awareness of issues of social injustice. These events and debates continue to shape our perceptions of culture and have helped to expose both the oppressive nature as well as the liberating possibilities of culture. As Chang (2014) writes, "The struggle between restoration and transformation, retrenchment and change, [begins] in culture" (p. 5). So, what is our culture? Who is represented in/through the cultural (re)production experienced in our classrooms? How does (re)presentation, underrepresentation, or misrepresentation undo or reproduce various forms of inequality? Whose voices are elevated? Whose are muted? How does cultural knowledge survive? Who has access to the means of production of culture? Who has the power to shape culture? Who doesn't? Which culture(s) do we embrace, (re)present, and perpetuate as music educators? What cultures are we negating, muting, and silencing as music educators? *Who we be?*

Who We Be?

We turn to a study by Ken Elpus to help provide a look at "who we be." Elpus (2015) examined the demographics of music education by analyzing data from test takers of the Praxis exams. Because nearly all states require this exam for teacher licensure, it serves as one of the most accurate accounts of measuring demographics of certified music teachers in public schools in the United States. Elpus (2015) reported that 56.03 percent of the music teacher licensure population between 2007 and 2012 ($N = 20,521$) identified as female, while 43.97 percent identified as male. In terms of race and ethnicity, 86.02 percent identified as White, 7.07 percent Black, 1.79 percent Hispanic, 1.94 percent Asian, 0.30 percent Native American, 0.32 percent Pacific Islander, and 0.82 percent multiracial (p. 325). Publicly available 2012 US Census data show that the US adult population is, at present, only 66 percent White. According to Elpus, "the music teacher workforce and the pool of potential music teachers represented by Praxis test takers are substantially less racially, culturally, and ethnically diverse than the population of the United States" (p. 330).

This disproportion was not only found in the field of music education, but also reported across arts organizations in the United States. For example, a study by the Andrew Mellon Foundation (2015) reported that 87 percent of American museum leaders, curators, conservators, and educators are White. In another study of over 1,000 New York City arts organizations by the New York City Department of Cultural Affairs (2016), 78 percent of board members and 79 percent of leadership staff in these organizations are White, while the population of New York City is only 33 percent White. These reports point to larger structural problems and raise questions not only about representation, but about access and power. Teachers, like curators and leaders of arts organizations, make daily decisions about which cultural works will be heard/seen, and whose culture(s) and stories will be shared and advanced as part of the broader imaginary. Because we rarely share what we do not know, we must consider whose culture and which cultural works are most likely to be advanced when 87, 86, 79, or even 78 percent of the decision makers are of a particular race/ethnicity? Will the culture of music education point us toward greater understanding and justice, or will it be used as an apparatus to reproduce social injustice and cultural inequity? To quote Battiste (2013):

> Education, like the institutions and societies it derives from, is neither culturally neutral nor fair. Rather, education is a culturally and socially constructed institution for an imagined context with purposes defined by those who are privileged to be the deciders, and their work has not always been for the benefit of the masses. Education has its roots in a patriarchal, Eurocentric society, complicit with multiple forms of oppression of women, sometimes men, children, minorities, and Indigenous peoples. (p. 159)

Researchers in music education have found that marginalized populations encounter barriers in gaining admittance to pre-service music university programs (Elpus & Abril, 2011; Fitzpatrick, Henninger, & Taylor, 2014). Scholars attribute this to the privileging of certain ways of music making and music knowing, mainly the exclusive performance of Western Art repertoire learned through Western notation (Bradley, 2007; Clements, 2009; Koza, 2008; Palmer, 2011; Mantie & Talbot, 2015; Sarath, Myers, & Campbell, 2017; Talbot & Mantie, 2015). Researchers have also found that when marginalized populations do successfully matriculate and gain access to the workforce, they often face feelings of isolation and powerlessness (Bergonzi, 2009; Fitzpatrick, Heninger & Taylor, 2014; Gardner, 2010; Pembrook & Craig, 2002; Talbot & Hendricks, 2016; see also every chapter in this book). The relative homogeneity of the music teacher workforce reported about in-service teachers (Hancock, 2008) and collegiate music teacher educators (Hewitt & Thompson, 2006) along with the demographics of the potential pool of future music teachers (Elpus, 2015) provide strong empirical support to recent calls for the adoption of culturally responsive pedagogy in school music classrooms and ensemble rehearsals (e.g., Abril, 2013; Boon, 2014; Fitzpatrick, 2012; Lind & McKoy, 2016; Shaw, 2012, 2016).

Scholars have offered varied solutions toward closing some of the gaps mentioned in the studies above. Fitzpatrick et al. (2014) suggested earlier intervention in high schools by university and conservatory music programs to assist and support underrepresented populations, something Darrin Thornton also proposes in Chapter 3 of this book. Practitioners have advocated for better training and preparation of pre-service music teachers to work in urban school districts and/or expand pedagogy to include more relevant musical offerings that connect to students' cultural backgrounds (Martignetti, et al., 2013; McKoy, 2012; Shaw, 2012, 2016; see also Chapter 4 in this book by Hendricks & Dorothy, as well as Chapter 5 by Schmidt & Castañeda). Elpus (2015) suggested that better test prep for Praxis II testing may assist in eliminating a barrier for populations who fail the exams more frequently, which include individuals who identify as female, are from lower socioeconomic statuses, and/or are Hispanic or Black.

However, I would argue that better test prep does little to address the findings from Elpus' study, and instead raises serious questions about cultural bias about the Praxis tests and whether the Praxis tests should remain the standard for evaluating readiness and preparation for employment in the field of music education.

Cultural bias influences the characteristics that constitute who we consider to be qualified to teach music and who we feel should become music teachers. It occurs when people make assumptions about conventions of appearance, language, repertoire, notation, ways of learning, ways of transmission, and ways of performing. Cultural bias permeates every sector of the field of music education, from the various cases found in the chapters of this book to the leadership of our national lobbying organizations. For example, in 2016 the executive director and chief executive of the National Association for Music Education (NAfME) expressed to leaders of other arts organizations attending a meeting on diversity arranged by the National Endowment for the Arts that members of the music education profession are not diverse partly because "blacks and Latinos lack the keyboard skills needed to advance in our field" (Cooper, 2016). These culturally biased remarks created a firestorm on social media. Public outcry forced the NAfME executive board to request the executive director's resignation. The executive director's departure came at a time when many sectors of the music and arts industry—from leading orchestras to schools of music—reported a lack of diversity, particularly in the auditioning and hiring of musicians and educators of color. In announcing his departure, NAfME thanked the executive director "for his service to our purpose and mission" and announced that the organization would renew its focus on inclusion and diversity, stating, "Our mission statement is 'music for all,' and we take that very seriously" (ibid).

But does the structure of our music education system allow us to actually teach "music for all" and do we *actually* "take that very seriously"? In *Redefining Music Studies in an Age of Change: Creativity, Diversity, & Integration* by Sarath, Myers, & Campbell (2017), David Myers outlined the model of music education that took hold in the early twentieth century in the United States—a model that reflected "Western European assumptions and practices" and was promoted through the educational missions of Symphony Orchestras of the late nineteenth century, the instrument manufacturers and the competitive band movement of the 1930s through 1950s, as well as the influence of the recording and publishing industries. Similarly, Roger Mantie and I (2015) in Susan Conkling's book, *Envisioning Music Teacher Education*, made explicit the "structure of participation" in what we call (following the work of Weber) "the music education order." By examining programs of study, textbooks, course objectives, the production of "expert knowledge," the terminal degrees of music teacher educators, and the *NASM Handbook*, we came to better understand the ways in which social reproduction occurs in and through the music education order and why it is often so maddeningly difficult to change not only representation in our field, but our practices. Through our work, we showed how social actors, policies, institutions, and various accrediting and credentialing bodies contribute to maintaining and operating within a system that limits who can be defined as "musician" and who can become a "music teacher." Myers' chapter explains how the specialization of performance teaching and conducting at the secondary and tertiary levels has relegated the notion of "music for all" to the early elementary grades and created a curricular structure that almost exclusively supports participation in large ensembles, perpetuation of European musical practices, and privileging of affluence (something echoed in recent op-eds across the globe; see Gill, 2017). Missing from the actual practices of many school music programs (even though most teaching philosophies and mission statements would indicate otherwise) is the value of creativity, life-long amateur music making (Mantie, 2015; Mantie & Smith, 2017; Regelski, 2007), and engagement with diverse styles of music learning, transmission, and performance (Talbot, 2012; Talbot & Mantie, 2015). Echoing Myers, it is problematic that "such a normative music and music education curricular culture, derives *not* from the nature and structure of music and music experience in all times and places, but from a desire to perform and advance classical repertoire among talented students" (Myers, 2017, p. 127). This specialization structure is exclusionary to many identities, cultures, abilities, interests, and ways of musicking (Small, 1987). Music teaching and learning practices for *all* students—ones that "build a continuum of music interest and expertise from amateur to professional, from monocultural to transcultural, and enrich communities on a broad and sustainable scale" (Myers, 2017, p. 127)—could significantly alter our culture, our communities, and our world. In short, music education, with all its potential for naming, decoding, expressing, and addressing social issues, for all its potential for enacting change, for all its opportunity for participation, collaboration, and creativity, chooses to perpetuate an exclusionary system steeped in classism, racism, sexism, heterosexism, genderism, ableism, and ageism.

These structural and systemic issues in music and the arts are a result of the habits of coloniality (Bradley, 2006; Hess, 2015, 2016; Patel, 2016) and have mostly been ignored and/or unrecognized as a problem for decades. Although counter movements like the multicultural music education movement have made some tangible progress for the profession of music education in helping open up spaces for inclusion following the debates of the academy in the 1960s and 1970s (see Kang, 2014; Mark, 1998; and Volk, 1998 for historical overviews), they have struggled to address the larger systemic issues at play in our profession, focusing more on diversifying content than on ways of learning, transmitting, and performing music. Only in light of the recent justice movements and rising cultural activism, from Colin Kaepernick taking a knee during the "Star-Spangled Banner" to Spike Lee boycotting the Oscars to the public outcry against the comments made by NAfME's executive director, have many of the art world's and culture industry's leaders considered the broader systemic problems. The arts and the field of music education are trying to play catch-up, and we are looking for a band-aid to the problem—blaming the causes of inequity on lack of resources, lack of skill development, lack of parental support, and/or advocacy. Advocacy for our field would not be necessary if the broader population felt the work we did as music teachers represented and reflected their identities and daily lives. We need to be fully invested participants in conversations of diversity and inclusion in our schools and in our state and national organizations. We need to listen to how other fields are addressing concerns, listen to those on the margins who have experienced oppression in their artistic endeavors within and outside our field, and make sure those who represent our work at the local, state, and national levels remain at the table of these discussions. Only through consistent engagement with this challenge will change be possible.

Understanding the question *Who we be?* is more than understanding demographics and counting representation. As stated previously, representation is only part of the problem of cultural equity. We must account for access and power, examining both the personalized individual experiences of marginalization and privilege and consider theoretically the broader structural components that contribute to these experiences. We must ask hard questions about the structure and nature of our work and remove the cloak of (color)blindness that allows us to pretend that we do not contribute to oppression. Our work as music educators has the potential to change the world if we are willing to listen to, create, and celebrate our diversity. To evoke the work of folklorist Alan Lomax, arts produced by diverse groups of people are socially valuable; they offer us ideas, approaches, and values that help us negotiate and understand how to live together.

The authors and I offer this book as a rupture to the grand narrative of music education. It is a collection of contrapuntal stories designed to thicken the texture of our music education imaginary and counter the built-up habits of coloniality in our field, habits that trundle us onward toward a false teleological endpoint— a journey only made possible at the expense of others. I proposed and edited this book by asking authors to pay close attention to social, political, and ethical locations, or what Deleuze (1995) calls *assemblages*—the unfixed yet yielding histories and trajectories that incompletely structure what we know and how we know— the referential coordinates from whence we speak. You will find that the authors and I speak from several locations both personally and professionally and I take a moment here to provide a brief gesture of my own set of coordinates. This is done to reveal to the reader an idea from whose perspective you might be glimpsing. This is important because we need to acknowledge that all knowledge is constructed and (re)presented through a situated and ontological lens that comes from somewhere(s) and someone(s) (Patel, 2016).

Who I Be?

I speak to you as a product of a colonial past, as an extension and beneficiary of White European colonization. The United States is a settler colony (Patel,

2016), and while other forms of colonization are also present here, the main organizational structure of people, land, and property is through settler colonialism and a philosophy of ownership (Byrd, 2011)—a distinct part of my family's legacy. The history of my family is one of conquest and exploitation of both land(s) and culture(s). This historic reality is an ironic hypocrisy of people fleeing religious persecution from Europe only to participate in developing a social, political, and economic system built upon the persecution and oppression of others. Or to borrow from Freire (2000), the oppressed become the oppressors by re-inscribing and drawing upon the same apparatuses of violence. With my historical legacy come the socioeconomic advantages of inherited and transferrable wealth as well as the codes of language (Delpit, 1990) and social behavior that help keep power firmly in the hands of the dominant economic class. Although I have learned this history throughout my lifespan, whether at family gatherings, church events, or in classes throughout my education, it was/is always presented as normative and benign—a manifest destiny from which I and others like me are naturally "supposed to" benefit. I recognize now the fallacy of the narrative of this "destiny," but it has taken years for me to unpack and see; years for me to admit to myself that I was born into an unjust system from which I benefit; and yet more years to move beyond the guilt that prevented me from doing anything to counter this injustice.

However, at the same time I speak to you as a gay man who has witnessed and experienced oppression, whether being told I would not be taken seriously or respected as a music teacher, conductor, or scholar; or being told I would never be hired or granted tenure if I revealed I was gay; or being told I played "the card" when awarded a grant; or being told by a colleague that "it is inappropriate to speak about personal relationships or one's sexuality in the class-room" while this heterosexual colleague wore a wedding ring and had a photo of their spouse on the screensaver of their classroom computer; or being told by an administrator I should "tone it down" in front of students and parents; or being trailed down streets by men calling out, "Faggot!"; or being targeted from the rooftop of a fraternity on an afternoon bike ride with my husband; or being told "we'll lose alumni contributions if we fly the rainbow flag on campus"; or being told by a student "my father is going to come beat you up when I tell him you are gay"; or being told by administrators that I am overreacting when I report such incidents; or being recognized for my outfits or my dancing with back handed compliments like, "you're so good . . . but, of course you are"; or being told that "boys will never join your choir because they'll be afraid of being associated with a gay man"; or not being able to travel to particular places in the world with your husband because of anti-gay laws; or feeling you have to constantly look over your shoulder and be hyper alert everywhere you walk; or feeling you need to let go of your husband's hand as people approach you on the street; or always locking your doors even when you are in the house; or having to give your husband a handshake after a performance because you fear his employer might be in the audience; or constantly living with the feeling that you must work harder than everyone around you so that no one can ever use that as an excuse when they try to get rid of you for "other" reasons.

Put simply, I am both oppressor and oppressed. The types of hybridities I represent echo in many of us. They are thoroughly engendered in societal institutions and are *enskilled* in the bodies of the social actors operating in such spaces (Scollon & Scollon, 2003). As Patel (2016) writes:

> Coloniality, because of its pervasiveness, implicates everyone through its ongoing structure of people, land, and well-being. These implications do not mean that anyone's structural location relative to colonization is fixed by virtue of birthplace or social identity, but rather at every juncture there is constant opportunity and responsibility to identify and counter the genealogies of coloniality that continue to demand oppression. (p. 6)

Understanding the complexity of my different locations provides me a lens to consider systemic oppression operating on other coordinates. Though I have not experienced systemic oppression in the same ways other authors in, or readers of, this book may have experienced, knowing how oppression feels and operates in one coordinate of my identity has helped me critique my participation in other forms of oppression. It also has helped me empathize with other people's identities and has moved me to stand in solidarity with justice movements beyond the LGBTQQIAA+ community. In the vein of Gaztambide-Fernandez (2012), specificity offers a more robust potential for solidarity than eliding important differences in social locations. Once I became aware and conscious of my oppression and my participation in systems that oppress others, I found myself faced with the choice to either work toward dismantling and decolonizing oppression in the spaces in which I operate and with the practices and language I employ, or to work toward reinforcing those structures and perpetuating the practices and language of oppression and coloniality. It is a constant struggle and journey for which I will continue to work and from which I will continue to learn.

Each one of us speaks and views the world from multiple locations. In the spirit of Feminism (Savigny, 2014), I offer my own positionality above to not only give voice to my experiences, but to also provide insight to the reader about the positions and views I bring to this work as an editor. As Savigny states, "giving voice to experience is a key mechanism through which feminist and critical theories seek to challenge existing power structures" (2014, p. 798). By speaking out, we render visible and challenge the power structures at play in our field.

Who You Be?

From which location(s) do you speak? What are your *assemblages*? How do they contribute to or challenge power structures? If we wish to truly do the work of making music education an inclusive and representative experience "for all," then we must be willing to take a hard look at ourselves individually and question and examine our own participation in structures of power. We begin this reflexive process by naming and decoding our personal histories, both within our lifespan and the historical legacies and genealogies of our families and communities prior to our existence and, in so doing, understand more deeply the locations from whence we speak. We then examine and consider how we may or may not benefit from these histories. Then we draw upon this knowledge to speak out and act, keeping in mind that to not speak out and to not act once we have gained this knowledge is also a form of speaking and action. These reflexive procedures are just the first steps necessary to begin the process of dismantling the structures and apparatuses of oppression.

I encourage readers of this book to draw upon the various feminist, queer, critical, and anti-colonial theories presented within the following chapters and to use them as lenses for deconstruction and application in our own lives, in our field, and in society. I also encourage readers to read between the lines of the authors' narratives, to consider the authors' assemblages and localities, and to contextualize this book and each narrative as merely part of a long process of decolonizing music education—one that for each of us is located at a different referential point. Each onto-historical concern represented in this book is central to developing understandings of social phenomena in our field. An onto-historical focus on oppression in music education situates it within the relationship between self and society, agency and control, power, and structure. It demythologizes the trappings of scientism and positivism, and argues for understanding knowledge as embedded in the social, cultural, historical, and political milieu in which it is produced—raising questions about current practices and strucutres in music education and ways our field can become a more inclusive enterprise.

Readers will find that each chapter is grounded in theoretical (as opposed to ideological) bases and is both empirical and practical. As Spina (2000) teaches us, "theory and practice are inextricably interwoven. Practice is the basis of theory and theory is the means of changing practice" (26). There are many in our field who think of theory as something beyond our reach unless one is part of the elite (i.e., intellectual, affluent, and white). This way of thinking allows dominant ideology to obscure its role in practice both methodologically and in the generation of knowledge, making it difficult to question the status quo and keeping a majority of Americans at an unjust disadvantage. Theory, on the contrary, helps us analyze the socioeconomic, political, and cultural mechanisms prevalent in society. While ideology reinforces and gives power to the status quo, theory explains relationships and phenomena in order to disrupt and question practice. Each author in this book uses theory to name and decode oppression in our society and to inform a more equitable and inclusive future practice. We do this to expose the ideological frameworks that support structures of power—not so they can be adjusted or tweaked, but so they can be decolonized and fully replaced with more democratically rooted and socially just approaches.

In conclusion, I ask readers to take pause at the possibilities for decolonizing music education. To do so, means that we must disambiguate schooling from learning and foreground questions of what and whom to be answerable (Patel, 2016). Though I am quite doubtful about the likelihood of institutions for music learning and teaching embracing any goal that is not about social reproduction and re-inscribing preferred knowledge—at least not in our current cultural structures—my more specific interests lie in how music education, within as well as beyond school settings, can take on the work of justice. How can our work as music educators rethink our field to be answerable to the diverse ways of learning and teaching music, as well as the needs of social beings? How can we listen to, learn from, open up spaces for, and give power to the diverse voices in our field? How can we provide access to the means of production of culture and positively contribute to shaping culture? How can we expand notions of *who we be* and who we want to become?

References

Abril, C. R. (2013). Toward a more culturally responsive general music classroom. *General Music Today, 27*(1), 6–11.

The Andrew W. Mellon Foundation (2015). *Art museum staff demographic survey*. In R. Schonfeld, M. Westermann, & L. Sweeney. New York: The Andrew W. Mellon Foundation. https://mellon.org/media/filer_public/ba/99/ba99e53a-48d5-4038-80e1-66f9ba1c020e/awmf_museum_diversity_report_aamd_7-28-15.pdf.

Battiste, M. (2013). *Decolonizing education: Nourishing the learning spirit*. Saskatoon, Canada: Purich Publishing.

Bergonzi, L. (2009). Sexual orientation and music education: Continuing a tradition. *Music Educators Journal, 96*(2), 21–25.

Boon, E. T. (2014). Making string education culturally responsive: The musical lives of African American children. *International Journal of Music Education, 32*(2), 135–146.

Bradley, D. (2006). Music education, multiculturalism, and anti-racism—can we talk? *Action, Criticism & Theory for Music Education, 5*(2), 2–30.

Bradley, D. (2007). The sounds of silence: Talking race in music education. *Action, Criticism & Theory for Music Education, 6*(4), 132–162.

Byrd, J. A. (2011). *The transit of empire: Indigenous critiques of colonialism*. Minneapolis, MN: University of Minnesota Press.

Chang, J. (2014). *Who we be: The colorization of America*. New York: St. Martin's Press.

Chang, J. (2016). *We gon' be alright: Notes on race and resegregation*. New York: Picador.

Clements, A. (2009). Minority students and faculty in higher music education. *Music Educators Journal, 95*(3), 53–56.

Cooper, M. (2016, May 12). Music education group's leader departs after remarks on diversity. *New York Times.* https://nytimes.com/2016/05/13/arts/music/music-education-groups-leader-departs-after-remarks-on-diversity.html.

Deleuze, G. (1995). *Negotiations 1972–1990*. New York: Columbia University Press.

Delpit, L. (1990). Language diversity and learning. In S. Hynds & D.L. Rubin (Eds.), *Perspectives on talk and learning* (pp. 247–266). Urbana, IL: National Council of Teachers of English.

Elpus, K. (2015). Music teacher licensure candidates in the United States: A demographic profile and analysis of licensure examination scores. *Journal of Research in Music Education, 63*(3), 314–335.

Elpus, K., & Abril, C. R. (2011). High school music ensemble students in the United States: A demographic profile. *Journal of Research in Music Education, 59*(2), 128–145.

Fitzpatrick, K. R. (2012). Cultural diversity and the formation of identity: Our role as music teachers. *Music Educators Journal, 98*(4), 53–59.

Fitzpatrick, K. R., Henninger, J. C., & Taylor, D. M. (2014). Access and retention of marginalized populations within undergraduate music education degree programs. *Journal of Research in Music Education, 62*(2), 105–127.

Freire, P. (2000). *Pedagogy of the oppressed.* New York: Bloomsbury.

Gardner, R. D. (2010). Should I stay or should I go? Factors that influence the retention, turnover, and attrition of K–12 music teachers in the United States. *Arts Education Policy Review, 111*(3), 112–121.

Gaztambide-Fernandez, R. A. (2012). Decolonizing and the pedagogy of solidarity. *Decolonization: Indigeneity, Education, & Society, 1*(1), 41–67.

Gill, C. C. (2017, March 27). Music education is now only for the white and the wealthy. *The Guardian.* Retrieved from: https://theguardian.com/commentisfree/2017/mar/27/music-lessons-children-white-wealthy.

Hancock, C. B. 2008. Music teachers at risk for attrition and migration: An analysis of the 1999–2000 Schools and Staffing Survey. *Journal of Research in Music Education, 56*(2): 130–144.

Hess, J. (2015). Decolonizing music education: Moving beyond tokenism. *International Journal of Music Education, 33*(3), 336–347.

Hess, J. (2016). Balancing the counterpoint: Exploring musical contexts and relationships. *Action, Criticism & Theory for Music Education 15*(2), 46–72.

Hewitt, M. P., & Thompson, L. (2006). A survey of music teacher educators' professional backgrounds, responsibilities and demographics. *Bulletin of the Council for Research in Music Education, 170*, 47–62.

Kang, S. (2014). The history of multicultural music education and its prospects: The controversy of music universalism and its application *Update: Applications of Research in Music Education, 34*(2), 21–28.

Koza, J. E. (2008). Listening for Whiteness: Hearing racial politics in undergraduate school music. *Philosophy of Music Education Review, 16*(2), 145–155.

Lind, V., & McKoy, C. (2016). *Culturally responsive teaching in music education: From understanding to application.* New York: Routledge.

Mantie, R. (2015). Liminal or lifelong: Leisure, recreation, and the future of music education. In C. Randles (Ed.), *Music education: Navigating the future* (pp. 167–182). New York: Routledge.

Mantie, R., & Smith, G. D. (2017). *The Oxford handbook of music making and leisure.* New York: Oxford University Press.

Mantie, R., & Talbot, B. C. (2015). How can we change our habits if we don't talk about them?. *Action, Criticism & Theory for Music Education, 14*(1), 128–153.

Mark, M. L. (1998). Multicultural music education in the United States. *The Bulletin of Historical Research in Music Education, 19*(3), 177–186.

Martignetti, F., Talbot, B. C., Clauhs, M., Hawkins, T., & Niknafs, N. (2013). You got to know us: Music education in urban environments as a hopeful model for the profession. *Visions of Research in Music Education, 23.*

McKoy, C. L. (2012). Effects of selected demographic variables on music student teachers' self-reported cross-cultural competence. *Journal of Research in Music Education, 60*(4), 375–394.

Myers, D. E. (2017). Wider ramifications of the manifesto. In E. W. Sarath, D. E. Myers & P. S. Campbell (Eds.), *Redefining music studies in an age of change: Creativity, diversity, and integration* (pp. 127–141). New York: Routledge.

New York City Department of Cultural Affairs (2016). In R. Schonfeld & L. Sweeney, *Diversity in the New York City Department of Cultural Affairs community.* New York.

Palmer, C. M. (2011). Challenges of access to post-secondary music education programs for people of color. *Visions of Research in Music Education, volume 18.* Retrieved from http://users.rider.edu/~vrme/.

Patel, L. (2016). *Decolonizing educational research: From ownership to answerability.* New York: Routledge.

Pembrook, R., & Craig, C. (2002). Teaching as a profession: Two variations on a theme. In R. Colwell & C. Richardson (Eds.), *The new handbook of research on music teaching and learning* (pp. 786–817). New York: Oxford University Press.

Regelski, T. (2007). Amateuring in music and its rivals. *Action, Criticism & Theory for Music Education, 6*(3), 22–50.

Sarath, E. W., Myers, D. E., & Campbell, P. S. (2017). *Redefining music studies in an age of change: Creativity, diversity, and integration.* New York: Routledge.

Savigny, H. (2014). Women, know your limits: Cultural sexism in academia. *Gender and Education, 26*(7), 794–809.

Scollon, R., & Scollon, W. S. (2003). *Discourses in place: Language in the material world.* London: Routledge.

Shaw, J. (2012). The skin that we sing: Culturally responsive choral music education. *Music Educators Journal, 98*(4), 75–81.

Shaw, J. (2016). "The music I was meant to sing": Adolescent choral students' perceptions of culturally responsive pedagogy. *Journal of Research in Music Education, 64*(1), 45–70.

Small, C. (1987). *Musicking.* Middletown, CT: Wesleyan University Press.

Spina, U. (2000). *Smoke and mirrors: The hidden context of violence in schools and society.* Lanham, MD: Rowman & Littlefield.

Stauffer, S. L. (2014). Narrative inquiry and the uses of narrative in music education research. In C. Conway (Ed.), *The Oxford handbook of qualitative research in American music education* (pp. 163–185). New York: Oxford University Press.

Talbot, B. C. (2012). *Finding a way: Discourse analysis of music transmission in Gamelan Eka Sruti Illini and implications for music education.* Saarbrücken, Germany: Lambert Academic Publishing.

Talbot, B. C., & Hendricks, K. (2016). Including LGBTQ voice: A narrative of two gay music teachers. In L. N. Littleford, C. Alexander & S. Fraser-Burgess (Eds.) *Diversity Research Symposium 2014: From Research to Action.* Muncie, IN: Ball State University Press.

Talbot, B. C., & Mantie, R. (2015). Vision and the legitimate order: Theorizing today to imagine tomorrow. In S. Conkling (Ed.), *Envisioning music teacher education* (pp. 155–180). Lanham, MD: Rowman and Littlefield.

Volk, T. (1998). *Music education and multiculturalism: Foundations and principles.* New York: Oxford University Press.

1

SPEAK NO EVIL

Talking Race as an African American in Music Education

Joyce M. McCall

Introduction

The goal of this chapter is to awaken the consciousness of the music education profession by sharing my own personal stories, illustrating how specific structures and social actors (i.e., professors, peers, and colleagues) in our profession perpetuate and "legitimize an oppressive social order" (Brown & Jackson, 2013, p. 18). I believe these endorsements contribute to the social realities encountered by people of color, including negotiating institutionalized Whiteness (the practice of racism in social and political institutions), questioning one's value and sense of belonging in the profession, and grappling with the probability of "selling out"—trading one's experiential truth in exchange for social and professional acceptance.

For centuries, African Americans have communicated their journey toward achieving equity and social justice in America by displaying their stories in their art, dance, literature, and song. Using these cultural artifacts as instruments to construct their lived experiences, African Americans were able to survive by combating racial attitudes and behaviors (Delgado, 1989). Hale Aspacio Woodruff, African-American artist and teacher, painted a collection of murals portraying "the Amistad incident" in 1839, during which African slaves revolted against their White captors and were later recaptured and placed on trial in America (Appiah & Gates, 2004). These paintings also included illustrations of the slaves being returned to Africa after winning their trial. In 1900, William Edward Burghardt (W. E. B.) Du Bois, sociologist, civil rights activist, and educator, challenged inaccurate scientific claims and popular racial caricatures of Blacks by exhibiting approximately 363 photos of young affluent African Americans at the Paris Exhibition (Bini, 2014). Alvin Ailey, African-American choreographer and activist, choreographed dances that not only included ornaments of ballet, jazz, and modern dance, but also thematic elements reflective of African-American culture and identity (Appiah & Gates, 2004). Phillis Wheatley, former slave and the first published African-American female poet, disseminated artistic descriptions of the Black slave experience in America through literary works such as "On Being Brought from Africa to America" (Appiah & Gates, 2004). She illustrated how religious dogma was used to mask the implications of colonialism (the practice of domination over another person or groups of people). Framing African Americans' conflict with that of "the American dream" and their reality of being Black, Langston Hughes, famous African-American Harlem Renaissance poet, playwright, and anthologist, composed "Mother to Son." This poem depicted the resistant capital African-American parents passed on to their children, urging them to never surrender to adversity. As early as the seventeenth century, Black slaves sang Negro Spirituals such as "Steal Away" and "Follow the Drinking Gourd" to protest the actions and ideals of their White oppressors and to also navigate their way to freedom. Through the use of four highly evocative vignettes, Simone (1966), pianist, singer, and civil rights activist, articulated the hardships of four African-American women in her song titled "Four Women." These are just a few examples of how African Americans were able to not only counter a narrative dominated by White voices, but also to emancipate themselves.

Most of the published stories of people of color in music education have been constructed by White scholars of social justice and antiracist work. In "Listening for Whiteness: Hearing Racial Politics in Undergraduate School Music Programs," Koza (2008) discussed how the perpetuation of inequality and inequity gaps in K–12 music programs, as well as admission and audition practices in higher education music programs, present challenges for students of color, often resulting in what she refers to as "the access conundrum" (p. 146). Centering on ways to increase and maintain healthy representations of minority students and faculty in higher education music programs, Clements (2009) suggested that institutions work toward finding reliable ways to recruit and retain minority students and faculty, and provide nontraditional minority students access to alternative curricula and outreach music programs. Clements included that the latter could provide students additional music career choices outside of becoming "orchestral performers, conductors, opera singers, or college music professors" (p. 55). Using an antiracist lens, Hess (2015) suggested that the profession considers how (White) privilege and other devices such as Charles Mills' depiction of society's preservation of privilege and power, "the racial contract," impact and maintain dominant structures in society as well as music education. Moving beyond the university music classroom, music education researchers have also begun to interrogate racial injustices in our society and how the profession could endow cultural, musical, and social transformations in the classroom as well as the community. Following the 2015 mass shootings in South Carolina where nine African Americans were murdered in a church by a 21-year-old White supremacist named Dylan Roof, Talbot (2015) took to pen and paper, urging those in the music education profession to rethink their positions as not only educators, but also creative activists.

He insisted that music educators become more politically involved in their communities through cultivating a climate of activism in the classroom and by facilitating music-making reflective of all social issues of our times, locally, and globally.

In her article titled "The Sounds of Silence: Talking Race in Music Education," Bradley (2007) highlights several obstacles standing in the way of the profession's ability to engage in conversations about race. These obstacles include our struggle to confront colonialism, institutionalized Whiteness, and the profession's tendency to further sideline issues of race and racism within pluralistic platforms such as multiculturalism and social justice. She asserts that in confronting these obstacles in our music spaces, we will enable greater opportunities to engage in purposeful discussions about race. In Bradley's articulation of colonialism, she discusses how, despite music education's best efforts to create more inclusive musical spaces by integrating popular music courses into our curricula, a majority of the curricula is saturated by a Western musical canon, which in many cases reflects a space dominated by White bodies. While the music education profession must come to recognize obvious depictions of inequality in the core of what we teach, we must realize the untouched template of Whiteness—a modern permutation of "us" and "them" (Pinder, 2010, p. 46). In particular, Bradley (2007) emphasizes that Whites must be willing to call out their Whiteness by recognizing that their Whiteness affords them certain privileges and dispensations that are not accessible to people of color. Whether or not they are aware of it, Whites are automatically positioned at the pinnacle of a cultural hierarchy, despite socioeconomic status, education, and political associations. Acknowledging and confronting their Whiteness will not only allow Whites to acknowledge the presence of *other* and their social realities, but it will afford them a better understanding of how racial minorities are forced to see themselves through what Du Bois (1903/2003) refers to as "double consciousness."

Failure to carefully articulate race and racism within pluralistic frameworks such as multiculturalism, social justice results in disastrous misunderstandings. Bradley asserts that while multiculturalism is often modeled as a gesture of inclusion of music outside the western canon, paradoxically this action also places race and racism into a generic box of otherness which lessens meanings and distinctions unique to marginalized populations. In addition, Bradley adds that Whites regularly employ diversion strategies to suppress discomfort in discussions regarding race. Tactics include diverting from race topics toward issues they believe identically align with racism (e.g., gender, LBGTQ, and religion). In 2013, #BlackLivesMatter, a rhetorical device, surfaced as a response to the racial disparities of the twenty-first century, particularly George Zimmerman's acquittal of the murder of Trayvon Martin (Orbe, 2015). Almost immediately following, #BlackLivesMatter was "reconfigured, co-opted, and/or replaced with the more inclusive and racially neutral alternative, #AllLivesMatter" (p. 90). While it is certainly plausible that some Whites employ the latter device as a way to express commonness among all victims of racial discrimination, it also allows Whites to conceal their racism and maintain a post-racial strategy of colorblindness or "historical amnesia" (p. 94). In addition, #AllLivesMatter negates the social reality of African Americans in the United States, while consenting to a dialogue devoid of race. These approaches toward race talk contradict the intended purposes of such conversations. While I do not discredit or dismiss the voices and efforts of my fellow White colleagues, I believe that they are not able to fully articulate the social realities that people of color encounter because of their position of privilege.

Storytelling

Using the *storytelling* rationale (shared accounts of people of color) of critical race theory (CRT) as a means of sharing my experiences of speaking race as an African American, I illuminate how structures within the music education profession and some of its social actors silence particular voices while applauding others. According to Delgado and Stefancic (2001), CRT is a conceptual framework used to examine dominant structures that situate people of color, particularly African Americans, as recipients of discrimination (institutional, unconscious, and cultural) and racism. The foundational premise of CRT is based on several rationales[1]. Storytelling is referred to by many names: "voice-of-color" (Delgado & Stefancic, 2001), "chronicles" and "counter-narratives" (Brown & Jackson, 2013, p. 18), "naming one's reality" (Delgado, 1989), and "the voice" (Ladson-Billings & Tate, 1995, p. 58). Despite nomenclature, theorists and educators alike have and continue to employ stories of the racially marginalized to make clear just how entrenched racial biases are in "the unstated norms of American law and culture" (Brown & Jackson, 2013, p. 19). The power in storytelling lies in its ability to destroy mindset—"the bundle of presuppositions, received wisdoms, and shared understandings against a background of which legal and political discourse takes place." According to Delgado (1989), storytelling allows "outgroups" (the marginalized) to bring to the fore their narratives in efforts to subvert those of the "ingroup" (the privileged) (p. 2412). For instance, Derrick Bell, noted father of CRT, used counter-narratives to inform and deactivate preexisting narratives of his White law students at Harvard University (Ladson-Billings & Tate, 1995). In regard to how storytelling is employed, Brown and Jackson (2013) state the following:

> CRT scholars use chronicles, storytelling, and counter-narratives to undermine the claims of racial neutrality of traditional legal discourse and to reveal that racism and racial discrimination are neither aberrant nor occasional parts of the lives of people of color. Rather racism and racial discrimination are deep and enduring parts of the everyday existences of people of color. (p. 19)

In the section that follows, I share my story of speaking race as an African American in music education, detailing my experience of negotiating a profession whose structures and social actors attempted to silence my voice. Last, I illustrate how my story contributes an authentic dynamic to Bradley's (2007) articulation of those obstacles that get in the way of race talk.

My Story

Prior to starting my doctoral program at Arizona State University (ASU), I had a good idea of what I wanted to research—music programs at Historically Black Colleges and Universities (HBCUs) and Predominantly White Institutions (PWIs). Several experiences contributed to my inquiry, including early experiences of negotiating predominantly White music spaces as an African American, as well as interactions with other African Americans from HBCUs during my tenure as a college music student at a PWI and as a music professional. While I lived in a predominantly Black neighborhood in the south, I attended predominantly White schools, where I participated in school band during my middle and high school years. Although I grew accustomed to moving from one cultural and racial extreme to another, something didn't sit well with me. I, in some way, accepted the fact that I was one of the few African Americans in my band program, but my African-American peers and I couldn't understand why predominantly Black band programs never participated in the band competitions and festivals in which we participated. I recall asking our White band directors why we never saw those bands at competitions. Their reply was always, "Well, their band programs aren't very good" or "They didn't have very good teachers." At the time, I guess I accepted it. After all, the directors were the experts. I later learned that the predominantly Black bands in my area did participate in competitions, but they were always competitions that only Black bands and Black people attended. My observations led to the following questions: Are predominantly Black band programs *that* bad? Why are band programs and the communities that support them segregated—if it's illegal?

I also remember speaking with my friend, Jamal, an African American male who was an amazing jazz saxophonist with great insight on jazz. He transitioned from an undergraduate music program at an HBCU in the south to a large graduate music program at a PWI in the Midwest. While Jamal was excited to start a master's degree in jazz performance in his new place of residency, he found quickly that his previous college experience did not equip him with the type of information that would allow him to comfortably settle into his graduate coursework. He stated that because he was behind his peers academically, he had to take extra classes to catch up and, at times, it seemed like that wasn't enough. In addition, Jamal informed me that because he was one of the few or the only African American in many academic and social settings, he felt alone, out of place, as if he didn't belong. Jamal wasn't the only African-American friend or colleague who encountered similar issues of transitioning from an HBCU to PWI. There were others. While working on my masters of music education degree at The University of Southern Mississippi, a PWI in the south, I noticed that some Black graduate students who previously received their undergraduate music degrees from HBCUs also struggled. I understood what it was like to be one of the few or the only African American at a PWI, but I did not comprehend how or why African Americans from HBCUs were experiencing so many difficulties. Jamal's and other African Americans' experiences of transitioning from an HBCU to a PWI prompted me to ask the following: Why are individuals like my friend, Jamal, encountering difficulties during their transition from an HBCU to a PWI? Are HBCUs preparing their students for graduate study? What aspects of students' experiences of transitioning from an HBCU to a PWI influence their degree perseverance?

After receiving a master's degree in music education, I moved to the Southwest to teach high school band for two years, as one of the two assistant band directors. During my teaching experience, we hosted three student teachers from local HBCUs. We noticed that the student teachers largely used rote teaching and the oral tradition as instructional strategies. While these teaching approaches were appropriate in some instances, they were not always received well by the students. Also, the student teachers were often late and overwhelmed, largely because they were working on assignments that are typically completed before student teaching. I was curious as to why these student teachers were struggling and why they weren't able to connect with our students. Was it that HBCUs and PWIs are really *that* different, specifically in music and how they engage students?

It seemed as though wherever I went, despite my position—student or music professional—the music profession portrayed African Americans as inadequate. I wanted to know why. Given that I planned someday to pursue a doctorate in music education, I started recording my research ideas and questions on a small Sony digital voice recorder I purchased at a local BestBuy. I invited fellow music educators and close friends to engage in conversations about my research interests, particularly in regard to HBCUs and PWIs. Most of our conversations focused on the various types of academic and racial challenges students encountered during their transitions. There was one thing that was obvious to me that I knew I would have to consider—race and racism.

I also shared my ideas with former White music professors. I explained to them that I wanted to apply to a music education doctoral program and seek to understand why so many inequalities existed between HBCUs and PWIs. I included that perhaps many of those inequalities were a direct result of issues of race and racism. Many of them were overjoyed that I wanted to pursue a doctorate, but some were not enthused that I wanted to investigate race and racism. It was interesting because all of these professors were significant contributors to my success as a music educator, and they were very supportive of equal rights and equity—

so it seemed. My professors' rationale included that I would be perceived as "the one who only talks about race," that I would ruin my chances of finding employment in higher education, and that I would make my doctoral experience difficult because no one talks about these things, especially focusing them into a dissertation. They advised me to wait until I was established in the field or until I had tenure. I was angry and very disappointed because my professors were individuals whom I respected and, in many ways, aspired to become. It felt like they were suggesting that I research *anything* but race, an important factor that I believed made my experience of society and the profession much different than their own. How could they support social justice efforts on a broad spectrum yet discourage the illumination of issues that threaten social justice within their own profession? Bonilla-Silva (2010) asserts that Whites often subscribe to a "colorblind" script, supporting "almost all the goals of the Civil Rights Movement in principle," but "object[ing] in practice [to] almost all the policies that have been developed to make [such] goals a reality" (p. 131). He further adds that subscriptions to colorblindness, as the new racial ideology, reinforce White privilege.

I recall speaking with an African-American male friend who, at the time, was teaching high school band in Alabama. After learning of my research interests, he stated, "Joyce, you know, you're going to tick some people off. You are going to have to call out HBCUs *and* PWIs. Plus, you're going to have to talk about race. Those White folks don't want to hear that!" While he knew that I would continue to pursue this topic, I think his interjection was his way of warning me, letting me know what I would be up against—that if I wanted to talk about race and racism I would have to pay a price. There were other close friends who warned me of similar encounters. Their rationales included that I would not be taken seriously because I was a minority speaking race, and that my commentary would be perceived as that of an "angry Black woman." Another African-American male friend informed me that, although my research interests were important and should be a focal point in music education, the music profession would not appreciate my perspective. He also suggested that I consider eventually leaving the profession and seeking out other areas such as instruction and higher education. I believe my friend's suggestion of me leaving the profession to seek out what he perceived to be more inclusive employment opportunities was a "fight or flight" reaction to how embedded institutionalized Whiteness really is in music education. I think he wanted me to leave before the profession could "break me." Sometimes institutionalized Whiteness can leave one feeling quite powerless. I think that many racial minorities are sometimes forced to make similar choices—whether to stay or go—and to be honest, I've considered the latter a few times.

In the fall of my last year of teaching in the Southwest, I applied to the music education doctoral program at ASU. I was skeptical about applying. After receiving an email that ASU was considering me, I was asked to visit the campus for an interview. I was really excited but very nervous, largely because I knew they were going to ask me about my research interests. All I could think about were the comments and concerns of some of my professors and friends. This question sat in the back of mind, "Should I tell them what I think they want to hear or should I tell them the truth?" I remember going into the interview, and there were the music education faculty, four smiling faces, waiting to meet me. While I'm not 100 percent sure, they seemed a little excited—at least that's what I would like to believe. If my memory serves me correctly, I distinctly remember being asked in the interview, "Well, Joyce, tell us about yourself!" After that question, I don't recall them asking me anything else because I talked the whole time. I told them about my background, my teaching experience, military career, and what I hoped to accomplish during my time at ASU and beyond. Once I began to discuss my research interests, I completely forgot the negative commentary I received prior to the interview. I think it was because I was passionate about my interests and serious about contributing to the efforts of solving issues in the music education field. I didn't care at that point. I wanted to be honest. Later that day I learned that they wanted me to attend their school and be a part of their program. I informed the ASU music education faculty that I would be honored to attend.

At the start of my first year as a doctoral student at the largest four-year public institution in the United States, I was a bit intimidated because I was no longer at a school whose student and population seemed manageable. I was also a first-generation college student, and I was one of the few African Americans in the school of music, and always the only one in all of my classes. It was rare that I saw anyone who looked like me. During my first and second years at ASU, I sometimes found it difficult to speak up in class, especially on issues of race and racism, largely because in past experiences I found it difficult and, at times, impossible to explain racism or my encounters with racism to Whites. In those moments, I anticipated needing someone who looked like me with similar histories in my corner, backing me up—someone who could chime in and say, "Oh, yeah! That happened to me too! The struggle is real!" It sometimes felt as though it was me against "them." I don't know . . . I thought that no one would really understand my perspective. There were times when some of my peers and professors did not understand, but that did not discourage them from learning, questioning their position in society, and asking questions. They would often tell me that I was the expert in my research area in the school of music and they were excited to learn alongside me. While some people might say, "Oh, they said that because you're Black and they assumed that you would know about racism—that's why they deemed you as the expert"—I don't believe that. I honestly believe that they really wanted to learn, with a genuine intent to change.

After completing my coursework, comprehensive and oral exams, and the first three chapters of my dissertation in two and a half years, I began to dive deeper into my research. I read anything and everything that I could get my hands on that related to my topic. I was a machine—at least I would like to believe so. My dissertation was titled *Degree Perseverance Among African Americans Transitioning from Historically Black Colleges and Universities (HBCUs) to Predominantly White Institutions (PWIs)*. Throughout my tenure at ASU, I made an effort to focus all of my required papers for my classes around my dissertation. I used multiple theoretical lenses including cultural capital model (Bourdieu, 1977), community cultural wealth theory (Yosso, 2005), CRT (Delgado & Stefancic, 2001), and double consciousness theory (Du Bois, 1903/2003) to investigate how academic, cultural, social, and racial aspects influenced degree perseverance among African Americans moving from an HBCU to a PWI. Data revealed that while participants encountered academic, social, and cultural challenges, issues of race and racism were, by far, the most significant influences toward degree perseverance. Participants shared that some of their White professors and peers viewed their racial identity as well as their education from HBCUs as inferior.

Dr. Margaret Schmidt was my dissertation advisor and committee chair. She was amazing and given her patience, research interests, and background in social justice issues, I would say that she was a perfect match. Every piece of literature that I read for my dissertation, she also read. We had weekly conversations about my research. It was nice to be honest about the whole "race thing" in front of a White person without her getting mad. Dr. Schmidt never appeared to be uncomfortable. If anything, she welcomed challenges and sought to understand. Too, I think she understood that while I wanted to research HBCUs and PWIs and investigate issues of race and racism, in some ways, I was uncomfortable with talking about race in a predominantly White setting. My professors in other classes were also very supportive and empathetic.

Now, while I knew that writing a dissertation was supposed to be challenging, for me, it was both agonizing and informative—agonizing because I was grappling with speaking my truth about race and racism from my perspective as an African American, and informative because I began to understand how academia and the academic system perpetuate racism. But I could not stop myself from thinking about all of the warnings I received from close friends and former professors. It was very debilitating. Often, the conversations I had with close friends and former professors about race and racism replayed in my head. Sometimes, I would find myself second, third, and fourth guessing everything I wrote in my dissertation. There were times I even considered starting over with a new topic. While I knew that choosing something else was an option, I didn't want to be in school longer than I had anticipated, and I didn't want to quit. I'm not a quitter. But, again and again, I reverted back to whether or not what I was doing was right and would help or hinder my connections in the music education profession. There were times when I would silently cry because although I knew just exactly what I wanted to say and what I wanted the profession to hopefully understand, my hands were tied.

I remember writing my discussion chapter and calling Dr. Schmidt to inform her that I didn't know what to say. I mean, I knew what to say, but I didn't want to appear as if "I'm going off" on the profession or that I was *the angry Black woman.* But, I was! I was angry, Black, and a woman, but angry for good reason. My conversation went sort of like this, "Dr. Schmidt, I don't know how to say what I really want to say." I thought the theoretical frameworks would help me out. If I am to be honest here, I thought that the frameworks would provide me some capital in discussing race and racism. "I thought they would help me get to the core of the feelings of the participants' of my study—what it feels like to be Black in a PWI or music space. It's frustrating because I don't know how best to articulate how it feels to be Black." She replied by saying something like this, "Joyce, I understand. Just say what you feel. Only you know what's in your head. It's okay that you're angry. You should be. We all should be. You write it and we'll figure out how best to get your point across." While her comments made me feel good to know that I had her support and guidance, I continued to grapple with speaking race. But, now that I think about it, I think those theories got in the way of what I really wanted to say.

By the end of my fourth year of my doctoral experience, I was preparing for my dissertation defense, the crown jewel of every Ph.D. hopeful. While I knew absolutely everything I was going to say about my topic, findings, and other topics related to my research, I was very nervous in my defense because I had baggage, burdens that I carried with me throughout my doctoral experience. While it can be argued that those burdens were not manifestations of my own actions and that they had been present in society long before I was born, they were still my burdens to carry. So, I held back in my defense. Despite my professors and peers at ASU ensuring me that I was in a safe place, I didn't believe it because I knew that outside of the ASU, society viewed my voice differently, and that the profession did not want to hear what I had to say. These were my perceptions. There was a point in my defense where one of my professors asked me, "Joyce, why don't you tell it like it is? You wrote a section that was brilliant, exposing the profession for its negligence. This paper needs more of that!" In Chapter 8, I wrote:

> African Americans, along with other minorities and their musical tastes, languages, backgrounds, and types of knowledge, should be acknowledged and recognized. Participants reported experiences that clearly exhibit a different scenario. Participants felt discounted not only by their peers, but also by professors occupying positions of authority and power to influence students' perception of themselves and of those around them. It is imperative that PWIs recognize that, within their spaces, issues of race and racism still exist and are perpetuated by ignorance, superiority, and uninformed attitudes. Unless PWIs decide to take an aggressive stance toward inappropriate racial attitudes and ideals, the inclusive and diverse spaces they often illuminate may appear to minorities as a hypocritical message—the status quo is enough.
>
> (McCall, 2015, p. 270)

Recently, I have gone back to that chapter, taking notice of the dynamics of my voice, of how I pushed the boundaries, and also of how I cautiously argued.

> While many graduate music programs want to hire more minority faculty, relatively few African Americans hold doctoral degrees. I suggest that PWIs not only employ and recruit more African American professors and students, but also immediately reflect on how their environments, decisions, and actions may devalue or discount Africans Americans.
>
> (McCall, 2015, p. 281)

My words were sometimes cautious and apologetic, while in other moments they were clear, bold, and courageous. I believe that these instances are vivid testaments of my indecisiveness, concern, and psychological grappling with speaking race. I wanted to tell the profession that we are not fulfilling our goals of inclusiveness and diversity. I wanted to tell them that we were failing people of color. But . . . I felt I couldn't go too far. I had to silence myself. I had to mute my voice and/or dial it back a few clicks. I remember being asked "Is there any reason why you pull back?" I recall readjusting my seat in the small conference room and looking down. I said something to the effect of, "Well, I am concerned that I might get in trouble. I want to get hired!" My committee immediately told me that I should speak up and call it for what it really is. While I knew their words to be honest and true, I also knew other truths—beyond the walls of ASU and the music education department there were bodies of people and ideals that viewed me differently—*and* my professors were all White. They could be unapologetically honest and bold because speaking race as a White person has far fewer consequences.

After successfully defending my dissertation, I discovered that other African-American doctoral students across the country were also grappling with speaking race. I received phone calls and emails from students whom I had never met. They were elated that someone finally spoke up and that someone finally told their stories because, unlike me, they were never given the chance to write about it. Apparently, some of them presented their professors with similar ideas, but were quickly denied or pushed to write about things that they were not interested in or that were related to their professor's research. Similar to what some of my professors told me, their professors also suggested that they hold off and wait until they were established in the field. So, not only does the profession regulate *which* voices are heard, but also *when* they are heard. Dei states:

> The most important question today is not who can do critical race work or antiracist work, but rather, whether we all are prepared to assume the risk of doing so. Not everyone who speaks race is heard. In fact, racial minorities speak race all the time but are heard differently. . . . In order for

certain issues about the experiences of racism to be accepted in public consciousness, they must be raised by a dominant body.

(Dei, 2006, p.15)

Today, as a postdoctoral resident scholar/visiting assistant professor at one of the most celebrated music schools in the country, I continue to grapple with speaking race in music education. While attending conferences within the last year, a few professors from other institutions shared with me that they encourage their doctoral students and newly minted professors to talk about "less interesting things" because it would make their path to tenure easier. I believe that perhaps these professors and others in the profession deny the integration of race talk into their spaces because they would eventually have to "face the music." They would have to recognize that the very spaces that they promote as inclusive and diverse are actually spaces that also reinforce and perpetuate the status quo. They also would have to acknowledge their perpetuation and harboring of institutionalized Whiteness. I am not sure that I will ever transcend this state of being. Perhaps I will continue to wrestle with the possibility that my voice as an African American speaking on issues of race and racism will negatively influence my career and reputation. However, I wonder if any of my White colleagues whose voice articulates issues of race and racism were ever told to "speak no evil."

Commentary

As Bradley (2007) highlighted, several obstacles contribute to the difficulty of speaking race, including colonialization, institutionalized Whiteness, and managing pluralistic platforms. The latter of the three often diminishes the reality of racism's impact on certain individuals and groups of individuals. Further illuminating the challenges of speaking race, using the storytelling rationale of CRT as a platform to share my story, I underlined some of the challenges associated with speaking race as an African American in music education. My attempts to speak race in the profession were intersected by projected fear, oppositional attitudes and behaviors of former professors, colleagues, and close friends, double consciousness, and a culture dominated by White bodies. While these encounters did not sideline my efforts to further expose issues of race and racism, they certainly positioned me into a peculiar state of mind, causing me to question my voice and the supposedly inclusive spaces that music education promotes. While I believe that some of the responses to my research interests stemmed from a genuine concern for my success in the profession, others manifested from a position of self-preservation to assist in legitimizing and maintaining the social order. No matter the rationale, both manifested social realities that I had to negotiate. My experience of dealing with the fear of not knowing if my actions would result in being perceived as *the angry Black woman* or as someone whose research is too narrowly focused presented me with the following questions: Why does my own profession wish to silence me? Are these opposing voices acts of terror to dis-courage minority voices from contributing authentic pieces that would threaten a narrative dominated by White voices? Is my voice not important? These were questions that I attempted to answer during my time at ASU. While I have taken steps toward speaking race in music education, these questions have not been completely resolved.

I urge the music education profession and its occupants to not just simply rethink and integrate ways of discussing race and racism, but to also lift restrictions on all scholarly work essential to truly understanding the mechanics of race and racism and their impact on society and education. Doing so means embracing stories of the marginalized. Despite awkwardness and discomfort, the profession must be willing to assume the position as both the listener *and* learner. Between the storyteller and listener, there are benefits, moments that give us pause to realize our humanity, heal, and reconcile our shortcomings. However, to achieve these things, we must be willing to acknowledge our individual biases as well as those obstacles encountered by people of color. In other words, we must make every effort to understand the unique challenges encountered by others by situating our view squarely behind "the spectacles" of others, allowing us to consciously "wipe off" the lenses from which we view the world and start anew (Delgado, 1989, p. 2440).

While I understand and even resonate with Dei's (2006) observation that a dominant voice must be raised in order for subordinate voices to be heard, I echo the African proverb "Until the story of the hunt is told by the lion, the tale of the hunt will always glorify the hunter." I know my story. No one knows it quite like me. I would like the option to speak race to not only liberate myself, but others as well. The music education profession must make every effort to break the silence in our music spaces to illuminate those voices that encounter racism and other injustices daily. No one voice or collection of voices should be silenced or held hostage at the expense of their truth, no matter who, how, or when they choose to speak race.

Discussion Questions and Activities

1. As a member of the music education community, have you encountered challenges associated with voicing your interests and/or concerns toward issues of social justice?
   a. How might you negotiate these challenges?
   b. How might other social actors (i.e., yourself, peers, and professors) assist you and others in negotiating these challenges?
2. In what way(s) does the music education profession endorse and harbor racism?

3. How does the profession regulate *who* and *how* certain individuals speak about race?
4. How are social actors, including yourself, situated in the music education profession and how might this positionality contribute to and perpetuate the legitimization of "an oppressive social order?"
5. How might we consciously position ourselves to understand the experiences of those who are often allocated to the margins?
6. In combating a narrative dominated by White bodies, the author suggested the music education profession "lift restrictions on all scholarly work essential to understanding the mechanics of race and racism and their impact in society in education." What might this look like if this was to become a reality?
7. Purposefully engage in conversations with individuals from racially marginalized populations, noting their challenges of negotiating structures dominated by White bodies and the suggestions they might offer to the profession in efforts to further provoke positive change.

Note

In addition to storytelling, the foundational premise of CRT is based on the following rationales: (1) ordinariness, racism is not "aberrational," but real (Ladson-Billings, 2013, p.37); (2) interest convergence, directed concessions of the dominant group toward a particular minority group only when their interests align with their covert goals; (3) social construction thesis, racism is a product of race-based categorization; and (4) intersectionality, no individual or groups of individuals subscribe to the same loyalties and subscriptions (Delgado & Stefancic, 2001).

References

Appiah, K. A., & Gates, Jr., H. L. (2004). *African: Arts and letters: An A-Z- reference of writers, musicians, and artists of the American experience.* Philadelphia, PA: Running Press.

Bini, E. (2014). Drawing a global color line: "The American Negro exhibit" at the 1900 Paris exposition. In G. Abbattista (Ed.), *Moving bodies, displaying nations: National cultures, race and gender in world expositions: Nineteenth to Twenty-first Century* (pp.39–65). Trieste, Italy: EUT Edizioni Università di Trieste.

Bonilla-Silva, E. (2010). *Racism without racists: Color-blind racism and the persistence of racial inequality in the Unites States.* Lanham, MD: Rowman & Littlefield Publishers, Inc.

Bourdieu, P. (1977). *The field of cultural reproduction.* New York: Columbia University Press.

Bradley, D. (2007). The sounds of silence: Talking race in music education. *Action, Criticism & Theory for Music Education, 6*(4), 132–162. Retrieved from: http://act.maydaygroup.org/articles/Bradley6_4.pdf.

Brown, K., & Jackson, D. D. (2013). The history and conceptual elements of critical race theory. In M. Lynn & A. D. Dixson (Eds.), *Handbook of Critical Race Theory in Education* (pp. 9–22). New York: Taylor & Francis.

Clements, A. (2009). Minority students and faculty in higher music education. *Music Educators Journal, 95*(3), 53–56.

Dei, G. J. S. (2006). Introduction. In N. Amin & G. J. S. Dei (Eds.), *The poetics of anti-racism* (pp. 14–23). Halifax, Nova Scotia, Canada: Fernwood Publishing.

Delgado, R. (1989). Storytelling for oppositionists and others: A plea for narrative. *Michigan Law Review, 87*(8), 2411–2441.

Delgado, R., & Stefancic, J. (2001). *Critical race theory: An introduction.* New York: New York University Press.

Du Bois, W. E. B. (1903/2003). *The souls of Black folk.* New York: Fine Creative Media.

Hess, J. (2015). Upping the "anti": The value of an anti-racist theoretical framework in music education. *Action, Criticism & Theory for Music Education, 14*(1), 54–84. Retrieved from: http://act.maydaygroup.org/articles/Hess14_1.pdf.

Koza, J. (2008). Listening for whiteness: Hearing racial politics in undergraduate school music. *Philosophy of Music Education Review, 16*(2), 145–155.

Ladson-Billings, G. (2013). Critical race theory—What it is not! In M. Lynn & A. D. Dixson (Eds.), *Handbook of critical race theory in education* (pp. 34–47). New York: Taylor & Francis.

Ladson-Billings, G., & Tate, W. (1995). Toward a critical race theory of education. *Teachers College Record, 97*(1), 47–68.

McCall, J. M. (2015). Degree Perseverance Among African Americans Transitioning from a Historically Black College and University (HBCU) to a Predominantly White Institution (PWI). (Doctoral dissertation. Retrieved from ProQuest Dissertations and Theses.

Orbe, M. (2015). #AllLivesMatter as post-racial rhetorical strategy. *Journal of Contemporary Rhetoric, 5*(3/4), 90–98).

Palmer, C. M. (2011). Challenges of access to post-secondary music education programs for people of color. *Visions of Research in Music Education, volume 18.* Retrieved from: www-usr.rider.edu/~vrme/v18n1/.

Pinder, S. O. (2010). *The Politics of race and ethnicity in the United States: Americanization, de-Americanization, and racialized ethnic groups.* New York: Palgrave MacMillan.

Simone, N. (1966). Four women. *Wild is the Wind* [CD]. United States: Phillips Records.

Talbot, B. C. (2015). "Charleston, Goddam": An editorial introduction to ACT 14.2. *Action, Criticism & Theory for Music Education, 14*(2), 1–24. Retrieved from: http://act.maydaygroup.org/articles/Talbot14_2.pdf.

Yosso, T. J. (2005). Whose culture has capital? A critical race discussion of community cultural wealth. *Race Ethnicity and Education, 8*(1), 69–91.

2

BLACK KEYS ON A WHITE PIANO

A Negro Narrative of Double-consciousness in American Music Education

Deejay Robinson & Karin S. Hendricks

I don't feel noways tired.
I've come too far from where I've started from.
Nobody told me the road would be easy;
I don't believe He's brought me this far to leave me.

Introduction

My earliest memory of being in awe of music was listening to the Gospel Choir sing those lyrics. I remember watching tears stream down my grandmother's face as she sang in the choir and gently swayed side-to-side like a pendulum on a grandfather clock. I was no more than five or six at the time, and the image of a strong Black woman being moved to a seemingly different universe is still etched into memory.

I grew up in a big Southern city where church was the center of life. Gospel music was always around me. I sang in the church Gospel Choir on the first Sunday, the Young Adult Choir on the second Sunday, the Youth Choir on the third Sunday, and the Mass or Combined Choir on the fourth Sunday. Even on Monday evenings, my grandmother, Rosa Marie Lasiouxx, or "Granny," and I rode to choir practice in Mister Freddie Lee's red pick-up truck. I often heard Granny's voice above the aroma of candied yams, hickory-smoked BBQ chicken, green beans, and butter biscuits when I came home from school. I had always wondered through all of the singing that was around me, what was it about music that caused eyes to well up with tears and people to jump up and shout as if there was fire shut-up in their bones.[1]

The music evoking transcendence that I observed in Granny fascinated me. I believe I wanted to study music in order to understand what was it about singing that could transport one from the natural world to a supernatural world and, second, was it possible for me to be similarly moved by music.

My quest to uncover the transformative power of Gospel music led me to musical theater. I auditioned and landed roles in school productions, local community theaters, and eventually the states' leading professional theater companies. Theater gave the opportunity to take on another character and experience life through the character's perspective. For me, acting was a bridge between the natural and the supernatural worlds; however, something was still amiss. I never thought my grandmother and others in the church congregation were acting when music, speech, praise, and worship seemingly engendered transcendence. Still feeling empty, I joined the high school Gospel Choir for a sense of community and to continue to understand how music moves people.

The high school Gospel Choir was well known within the school and local community. While joining the choir, I expected to identify with the Black students who shared a love of Gospel singing. I also hoped that the choir would connect me with others who could have experienced the transcendent power of song that I observed in my church community. I felt a sense of belonging from the very first rehearsal when the conductor, a community leader, taught us to sing a four-part song entitled "He Has Done Marvelous Things, Praise the Lord!" The song engendered a praise and worship like I had never seen before among young high school students. The energy in the room was palpable. I was in awe and felt like I was at church, even though I was in an urban high school chorus classroom. As I looked around I noticed that everyone looked like me. I witnessed how my counterparts felt the music and sang every note with their entire being, as if we were a professional choir led by Kirk Franklin. Feeling secure in my new high school environment helped me to branch out and audition for the spring musical.

The audition for the high school musical ran like all other auditions I had previously experienced. There was a diversity of students, singers, actors, and dancers from the campus. After the audition, the choral director, Mr. Abrams, asked me to audition for a coveted spot in the elite Chamber Chorus. I remember Mr. Abrams asking me about my background and commenting on the power of my voice, for he believed my tenor voice would be an asset to the chorus. For the chamber audition, Mr. Abrams informed me that I should come prepared with a song to sing, classical preferred, and be expecting to sight-read rhythms and a melody. I was horrified.

I was terrified and intimidated at the Chamber Chorus audition because everything that was familiar was now unfamiliar. Except for me, no one auditioning for the chorus was Black. I felt inadequate and inferior to my White counterparts because all the White students had great voices, could read music, and sang in a different language. I felt isolated from the White students who were singing songs in Italian and German, while I prepared to sing "If You Believe" from The Wiz with my 16 bars marked as I had been taught for musical theater auditions. In essence, I was an anomaly because my upbringing required me to learn music in a different manner than the White students I observed auditioning. In one fell swoop, the Chamber Choir audition brought into consciousness the innate difference between learning music in the Western European classical tradition of studying music theory, and the Southern Gospel tradition of learning songs through call-response, rote, and being immersed in the feeling of music. Moreover, the audition highlighted the advantage afforded to my White counterparts simply because White European culture and traditions were expected as the standard. Any deviation from those teachings was considered inferior purely based on racialized negativity that determines what is and is not music (Bradley, 2006; Gaztambide-Fernández, 2011; McLaren, 2011; Koza, 2008; O'Toole, 2005). The tension between my blackness and the whiteness of the other students immediately made me feel less like the confident gospel-singing musician that I knew I was. Contradicting feelings of inadequacy were feelings of admiration and awe. I somehow concluded that I needed to be in Chamber Chorus if I wanted to be considered a serious musician. Furthermore, perhaps the secret to understanding transcendence rested in the ability to read and understand the language of music. Why was I willing to uproot my beloved high school Gospel Choir community and conclude that singing in the Gospel Choir would not prepare me to be a musician?

The Race Gap in American Music Education: Encountering Blackness in Curriculum

American music education has a significant racial inequality abyss. Authors have previously analyzed the demographic profiles of pre-service music teacher candidates and have concluded that music education is significantly over-represented by Whites and significantly underrepresented by Asians, Blacks, and Hispanics (Elpus, 2014, 2015; Rickels, et al., 2013; Elpus & Abril, 2011). Rickels and colleagues (2013) surveyed 250 high school seniors auditioning for admittance into American university music education programs and concluded that the racial demographics of the 250 respondents were 80.8 percent Whites, 5.2 percent Blacks, 9.2 percent Hispanics, 2.8 percent Asians, and 1.2 percent unidentified.

Elpus (2015) further exposed the racial inequality within music education through a comprehensive analysis of the demographic profiles of pre-service music teacher Praxis II scores in the United States. In this causal comparative study, Elpus analyzed 20,521 Praxis II test scores from 2007 through 2012. Tests scores were first separated and analyzed into two data sets of pass and fail. Then Elpus compared the results to the entire population of teachers in the United States as well as the US population as a whole. Elpus found that White candidates were significantly overrepresented among those who passed, whereas Black, Asian, and Hispanic candidates were significantly more likely to fail the Praxis II test.

Applying Koza's (2002) assertion that "Black prospective music education majors face inordinate obstacles to college admission and that teacher licensure exams may be an additional barrier preventing those Black perspective music teachers who gain college admissions from entering the music teacher workforce" (p. 5, as cited in Elpus, 2015), Elpus postulated that there may be a "leaky pipeline to music teacher licensure that excludes potential music teachers systematically by race and ethnicity" (p. 4). Elpus's analysis of the Praxis II music test scores is, to date, the most recent and comprehensive nationwide demographic profile of music teacher licensure candidates.

Previous literature on the demographic profile of in-service music teachers has suggested that marginalized populations of students that do matriculate in pre-service music education programs face feelings of isolation and powerlessness (Bergonzi, 2009; Fitzpatrick, Henninger, & Taylor, 2014; Gardner, 2010; Pembrook & Craig, 2002). Fitzpatrick et al. (2014) interviewed six participants who were accepted into music education university programs across the United States. The participants identified as Black and Latino/x and three of the six self-identified as homosexual. The purpose of the case study was to examine the experiences of marginalized students in regard to admission and retention in pre-service music education programs. Each participant was interviewed once for 1–2 hours in a semi-structured interview format. Common themes that emerged from the six participants were lack of understanding of the expectations of the audition process, isolation due to dissimilar background and experiences from White classmates, the importance or role models in maintaining retention and creating a sense of belonging, and the power of personal resiliency to overcome obstacles. Deejay's narrative resonates with the findings of Fitzpatrick and her colleagues. Deejay felt disconnected because his blackness and background in Gospel singing and musical theater placed him as an outcast and thus he felt inferior and invisible to his White counterparts who were classically trained.

Researchers have analyzed the demographic profile of the field of music education and used the data to conduct case studies to suggest that marginalized populations may encounter barriers after gaining admittance to pre-service music university programs. Authors have offered extrinsic solutions to ameliorate the race gap by suggesting better test prep for Praxis II testing (Elpus, 2015) and earlier intervention in high schools from university and conservatory music programs (Fitzpatrick, et al., 2014). Within music education, practitioners have advocated for better training and preparation of pre-service music teachers to work in urban school districts and/or expand pedagogy to teach multicultural music (McKoy, 2013). In a more explicit example, Deborah Bradley organized a graduate seminar in which her all-White students examined their Whiteness in contrast to the majority Black students they teach. The course was designed for students

> to analyze how racially coded cultural meanings are produced, interpreted, legitimated, and/or rejected in educational settings . . . and [consider] how race has been investigated and taken up in/through sociology, cultural studies, and studies of education and schooling, analyzed through a lens of anti-racism pedagogy and practice.
>
> (Bradley, Golner, & Hanson, 2007, p. 294)

Each of the aforementioned articles examined how individual music educators engaged in the work of multicultural music teaching and learning. Arguably, the multicultural music education movement and its goal to offer inclusivity by providing an alternative to the Western European classical canon is music education's most tangible internal solution to eliminating race disparities within music teaching and learning. However, the recent statistical data by Elpus (2015) may suggest that the multicultural music education movement has lost traction, is extremely isolated, and/or is not addressing the root cause of the race gap in music education.

The purpose of this chapter is to situate Deejay's story and position his experience of being a voice from the margins in music education within past research. Using the theoretical lens of Du Bois's (1903) theory of double-consciousness, we offer a perspective on how Deejay, as a significantly underrepresented Black male in a significantly overrepresented White-male field, came to understand his legitimacy in music education. Du Bois's framework of double-consciousness has been used as a lens to understand how Black people in a White-dominated society view themselves in relationship to the world they encounter. Although double-consciousness theory has been applied to analyze the experiences of marginalized populations in psychology and in the field of education (Banji & Prentice, 1994; Fiske & Taylor, 2013; Markus, 1977; Markus & Kitayama, 2010), the theory has not yet been applied to suggest how Black music education students may view themselves in a White-dominated field. In conclusion, we will suggest how double-consciousness permeates within music education in order to offer implications for how the theory may be useful in understanding marginalized populations in music teaching and learning.

Due to misunderstandings and imbalances of the Black and White power dynamic in our field (the very essence of which we discuss here), we believe it is especially critical to be transparent about the process by which we co-authored this chapter. The project began as a shorter paper Deejay wrote for a university class he took with Karin, after which we worked together regularly over the course of a second semester to expand the manuscript into a full book chapter. Deejay wrote the narrative entirely on his own and also took the lead in authorship of the supporting literature review. The process of writing and refining together became an optimal opportunity for two music educators—from two vastly different backgrounds—to engage in critical conversation about race, power, and privilege in American music education.

Our aim is not to generalize the experiences of all marginalized populations within the field; instead, the goal is to offer a means by which we as teachers, researchers, and advocates of music education can inquire about the race gap within the field and, secondly, to attach a lens by which we view the issues of access and retention of marginalized populations in music education. Understanding the forces that may deter Blacks from matriculating and completing a program of study is just as important as the methods by which the field tries to recruit Black and other minority populations. Failure to take into account the forces that prevent Blacks and other minorities from becoming music teachers can be likened to a pianist mindlessly playing the black keys on the piano but not understanding how flats and sharps alter melodies and chords and thus act as essential functions of tonal harmony. In a US society that is increasingly becoming aware of institutional systems that perpetuate and maintain racism and amidst the growing #BlackLivesMatter movement, music education may risk being deemed as yet another institution that systemically discriminates against Blacks and other minority groups if the present race gap is not critically analyzed and abated.

I left the South to attend a small private liberal arts university in the Midwest. I believe that I was admitted to the vocal performance program solely based upon my vocal talent and not my ability to sight-read melodies and rhythms. My studio teacher, Mark, had a keen understanding of my past as a Gospel singer and musical theater performer, in addition to my limited exposure to European classical music. Mark was tenacious in his belief that I had talent and that my skills would grow with proper training and guidance. My studio teacher exposed and imposed upon me Western European art songs with the utmost care. As the director of the Opera Department, Mark encouraged me to audition for the spring opera L'incoronazione di Poppea. I was double-cast as Ottone, the leading tenor of the opera. Mark believed that Sebastian, the other Ottone, would be a great mentor for me to learn beside because Sebastian was a talented singer and pianist, and we could therefore support one another while learning the role.

The first full cast sing-thru of Act I came after a couple of weeks of coaching. I remember looking around the room full of White vocal performances majors, many of them in their second, third, or fourth years. I witnessed singer after singer stand up and perform their part with confidence over the basso-continuo accompaniment. Soon it was my turn to sing. I stood up and felt as if the floor beneath me had swallowed my stomach. The music director played the chord and I began to sing, but feelings of isolation and loneliness were all that I could think of. I struggled to make it through the rehearsal determined to not be embarrassed in front of my peers. At the end of the rehearsal I burst into tears. I sobbed saying, "I can't do this. This is not for me!" Mark quickly pulled me aside and reassured me that we would get through it together.

Mark was like a father figure who supported me; however, not all of my professors were as supportive and responsive. I often sat in classes feeling isolated and marginalized and in some instances berated for being behind the learning curve of White classmates. I struggled through music theory, foreign language diction, and art song classes. In music theory classes, the expectation was that I could quickly identify pitches, read and notate rhythms, hear chord progressions, and harmonically analyze music. I would receive my tests and see red ink all over my paper and looked around to see my predominately White colleagues with less ink and higher grades on their papers. Even singing—the area I thought was my greatest strength—became a weakness in art song repertoire classes. I felt lonely as I listened to my White classmates perform songs in Italian, German, and French that they had received the previous week. Professors often became frustrated and irritated when I mixed up foreign language diction idiosyncrasies or could not hold the melody against the accompaniment.

My collegiate experience left me feeling marginalized because I was different. I was different because I had not been steeped in Western European classical music like my colleagues, who had likely taken private instrument/voice lessons or played in youth ensembles from an early age. I was an anomaly because I was the only Black person in most of my music classes. I felt even more isolated in less theoretical classes such as music history and music education because they too exposed how different my music background was from those about whom I read in history or method books. I was drawn to study music because of the transformative power of Gospel music that I observed back home in the South and for my own professional development to be seen as a musician. In many ways I hoped that studying music would help me understand the uniqueness and transformative power of Black Gospel music. Conversely, I found myself studying the uniqueness of Whiteness and the superiority of White ingenuity. Instead of feeling like a musician, I began to feel like a problem and became aware of the inherent difference between my White counterparts and me.

Encountering Double-consciousness in American Society and Educational Settings

"How does it feel like to be a problem?" asked Du Bois (1903, p. 7). He continued:

> The Negro is sort of a seventh son, born with a veil, and gifted with second-sight in this American world—a world which yields him no true self-consciousness, but only lets him see himself through the revelation of the other world. It is a peculiar sensation, this *double-consciousness*, this sense of always looking at one's self through the eyes of others, of measuring one's soul by the tape of a world that looks on in amused contempt and pity. One ever feels his two-ness—an American, a Negro; two thoughts, two unreconciled strivings; two warring ideals in one dark body, whose dogged strength alone keeps it from being torn asunder. (p. 9)

Double-consciousness is theorized as the psychological feeling that African Americans experience in viewing oneself as both African American (Black) and European American (White). The weight of being African American is deeply embedded in the social context of American "slavery, segregation, and fueled by contemporary racial disparities and the ongoing experience of prejudice, discrimination, and inequality" (Brannon, Markus, & Taylor, 2015, p. 586). At the root of double-consciousness is an internal struggle. The internal struggle is a contradiction between the self-consciousness, how one views oneself, and self-realization, how one is ultimately viewed by society (Reed, 1997, as cited in Ciccariello-Maher, 2009, p. 20). Sociologists have conclusively demonstrated that White value systems, culture, and traditions are revered in American society (Desmond & Emirbayer, 2009; Lewis, 2003; Omi & Winant, 1999); thus, African Americans experience double-consciousness due to the imbalance of Black culture and traditions against the presumed superiority of White culture and traditions.

Brannon et al. (2015) studied both independent and interdependent schemas in African-American college students in order to observe how double-consciousness affects African-American students in educational settings. Schemas are organized patterns of thought that influence a person's actions. For example, a Black student preparing to take a test may carry negative stereotypes that Black people are bad test takers. Negative thought patterns can influence one's performance and thus lower the student's test score. Independent and interdependent schemas are widely held beliefs that guide one's or a group of people's thoughts and behaviors. *Independent* schemas encourage a person or a group of people to view social contexts through a singular or narrowly focused lens. Conversely, *interdependent* schemas encourage a person or a group of people to view social contexts as an extension of the self, "connected and related to others" (Brannon et al., 2015, p. 587).

We have adapted the language and use the term "forces" rather than "schemas" for the purpose of this discussion. Force, by definition, is the push and/or pull resulting in an interaction. While most individuals are able to organize thought patterns and freely respond according to their thought and belief systems, African Americans as a minority demographic—especially in the context of American society—are forced to continually alter their thoughts and actions and are not always permitted to respond freely due to fear of judgment and in some instances dire consequences (Coates, 2015). The burden of having no true self-consciousness and continually measuring oneself based on the revelation of the other is an internal push and pull bestowed upon African Americans.

The weight of independent and interdependent forces of Figures 2.1 and 2.2 determines the weight of the scale. Figure 2.1 is weighted toward African-American culture because of the experience of discrimination (interdependent force) that becomes a lens through which Blacks view American society.

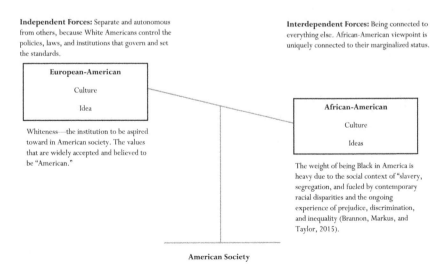

FIGURE 2.1 A Weighted Scale of Double-consciousness in American Society

Encountering Double-consciousness in American Music Education

The elevation of Western classical music is an interdependent force within American music education in two ways. First, scholars have noted the intentional and unintentional ways in which the dominant class silences and erases a multitude of diverse music experiences by continuing to place emphasis on the re-creation of Western European classical music (Kindall-Smith, McKoy, & Mills, 2011; O'Toole, 2005). Second, Eurocentric classical music not only dominates multicultural music curricula, but also serves as the lens through which all other music is viewed, making the multicultural music education movement another means of perpetuating White hegemonic culture (Hess, 2013, 2015).

The teaching and learning of multicultural music has been purported to be a window to reveal the beauty and indigenous characteristics of a particular culture's music (Style, n.d.; Glazier, 2005). Instead, the window through which we view indigenous music from a White perspective is grossly tinted when we simplify music of other cultures to Western European standards or appropriate another culture's music and claims it as their own. We have often observed this white-washing of cultural music when choral teachers consult and teach the International Phonetic Alphabet for accurate pronunciations of Western European art songs, but fail to consult the African-American Vernacular English (AAVE) when teaching African-American Spirituals.

White cultural hegemony continues to pervade the multicultural music education movement. For example, Feay-Shaw (2002) completed a thorough analysis of the quantity and quality of Mexican-American and Latin-American music in scholarly music education periodicals (e.g., *Music Educators Journal*), resource books (e.g., *The New American Songbook*), and curriculum textbooks (e.g., Silver Burdett). Four salient points emerged in Feay-Shaw's research:

1. Between 1935 and 1942, no publications on Mexican-American music were found.
2. In 1966, one article published highlighted how Spain forced music traditions on Mexico.
3. Between 1970 and 1980, Music Educators National Conference (MENC) published an article entitled "Minority Concerns Concern Us All" and held sessions at the 1980 conference that addressed the inclusion of multicultural music in school curriculum.
4. In 1980, collections of Latin-American folk songs were included in numerous textbooks; albeit, "Latin folk songs were so often reworked for school use that they lost both their authenticity and their validity as cultural representations" (p. 97).

While Feay-Shaw's (2002) survey of repertoire focuses on Latin-American music, we would imagine that the findings would be similar if one conducted an analogous search controlling for African-American music, Arab-American music, or music of any other marginalized population.

Independent forces lift the right side of Figure 2.2 toward African-American traditions. African-American traditions in music curriculum are left aloft because of the scarcity of the African-American demographic and perspective within American music education, leaving Blacks to be a mostly silent and lonely voice within their music education programs. The continued psychological questioning and encountering of one's blackness in a White-dominated field may become the force that pushes Blacks away from entering or completing a program of study in music education.

Blacks may feel isolation due to the discordance between interdependent forces that weigh Blacks down in American society and the independent force that isolates Blacks in American music education programs. Black music students might lack self-consciousness due to the absence of historical African and African-American music perspectives in comparison to the omnipresent historical European and European-American music perspectives. In society, Blacks are likely to find others who share similar backgrounds and experiences; however, Blacks may find no one with whom they identify in American music education programs.

While in music education programs, Black music students may bring with them perceived negative cultural stereotypes when surrounded by predominately White peers and professors. Black music students may be asking, "Will my professors think I have a poor work ethic because I sometimes get bad grades?" "Why do my peers seem to be learning information faster than I do?" "Why do I look around the classroom and only see White composers? Were there no Black people

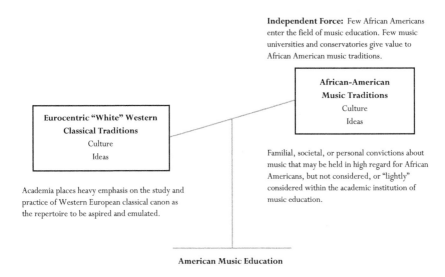

FIGURE 2.2 A Weighted Scale of Double-consciousness in American Music Education

who composed great music to be revered as well?" These existential questions could be among the many that reflect Du Bois's (1903) depiction of "two souls, two thoughts, two unreconciled strivings; two warring ideals in one dark body" (p. 9) and illustrate ways in which Black music students feel different from their colleagues. How do Black students first encounter the psychological state of double-consciousness that forces them to ask such existential questions?

(Re-)Encountering Double-consciousness: *Nigrescence*

If double-consciousness is the psychological awareness of one's Blackness in a White society, then nigrescence is the exact moment in which one realizes that the definition of Black is synonymous with inferior. Du Bois recounted a story from his childhood in which he, as a Black boy from Great Barrington, Massachusetts, realized that he was different than the other students in class. While in school, the boys and girls had an idea to make and exchange greeting cards to welcome a new student. Du Bois, being the only Black student in class, recalled having a pleasant experience until a new student from the South refused to accept his greeting card. At the moment of the refusal, Du Bois immediately realized that he was an anomaly and that he might be viewing the world differently than his White counterparts (1903, p.8).

We propose that the activation of double-consciousness lies within the inciting incident of nigrescence. Once Blacks become awakened to the inferiority of their blackness, then they begin to see how skin color and racism are deeply embedded in the social, political, and economical arenas of American society (Hochschild & Weaver, 2007). In addition to the absences of the Black perspective in education, Blacks face discrimination during the application process for employment due to racialized stereotypes simply because of their name (Bertrand & Mullainathan, 2003). The rise of the #BlackLivesMatter movement that captivated the media and America during the Ferguson and Baltimore protests has promulgated the stereotype of Black people as "gangsters" and "thugs" while simultaneously exposing discriminatory practices of law enforcement that target Blacks and other minorities. Figure 2.3 indicates that, while nigrescence may elicit double-consciousness, Blacks will perpetually (re)encounter and (re)experience the inferiority forced upon them simply because of their Black skin.

William Cross's *nigrescence*, the psychology of becoming Black, provides one answer to why Deejay chose the predominately White chamber chorus over the all-Black Gospel Choir. Cross (1994) defined *nigrescence* as the processes by which Black children develop an awareness of their racial identity. The first two stages of Cross's theory of *nigrescence* are *pre-encounter* and *encounter*:

- In the *pre-encounter* stage, the personal and social significance of one's racial group membership has not yet been realized and racial identity is not yet under examination (Cross, 1994, p. 122). Deejay was operating in the

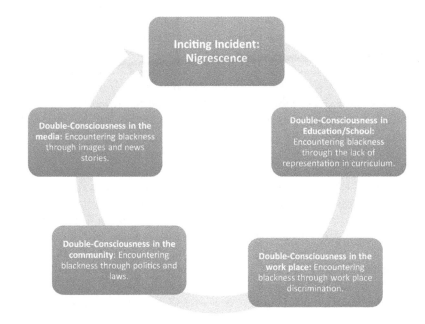

FIGURE 2.3 Circular Representation of the Many Encounters of Double-consciousness

pre-encounter stage before the chamber chorus audition because he had no prior reasons to question his music aptitude.

- "When the environmental cues change and the world begins to reflect his blackness back to him more clearly" continued Cross, "[the adolescent] will probably enter the *encounter* stage" (Cross, 1994, as cited in Tatum, 1997, p. 55). Deejay's inability to sight-read made him feel like an aberration, and those feelings were intensified because he was the only Black student auditioning; thus, witnessing his White counterparts' abilities to read rhythms and sing melodies made him feel inferior.

- "While wrestling with his blackness, the black child absorbs many of the beliefs and values of the dominant White culture, including the idea that it is better to be White" (Tatum, 1997, p. 55). Cross's theory suggests that Deejay left the all-Black Gospel Choir because he saw the benefits of having a great voice, reading music, and singing in a different language, all of which were afforded to his White counterparts.

Departing from the all-Black Gospel Choir and joining the predominately White chamber chorus was the only choice by which he could see himself becoming a "legitimate" musician. This incident examines just one encounter of double-consciousness in Deejay's life; however, additional encounters have occurred in his workplace, professional community, and in the media.

I guess all I have ever wanted from my educational experiences—inside and outside of the classroom—is to be valued and accepted as an equal. I know that I will never be seen as equal because conscious and unconscious biases about my dark skin are always lurking. I came to my current teaching position at an affluent private school after leaving my position as a K–5 general music teacher for an urban public school district. I decided to leave the public school system because I felt helpless and alone in addressing systemic barriers within that space—barriers that continually tell "Black and Brown boys that their educational attainment [will] come last to Whites and Asians" (Miranda et al., 2014; Robinson, 2016, 2017).

My decision to accept a position at a private school came after witnessing an affinity lunch on the school's campus.[2] It was then that I knew I wanted to be a part of a school where people intentionally create spaces for the fellowship of students and faculty of color. In this new work environment I have found a seat at the table for student-centered diversity programming (e.g., diversity assemblies and concerts), however, the discomfort continues for me as I am now a hyper-visible voice on the margins—the voice of a Black male teacher grappling with the legitimacy and worth of his perspective and identity in and out of school. I often witness a willingness to address certain issues of diversity in my workplace, while issues surrounding race continue to be ignored. For example, the school has made tremendous progress in supporting our LGBTQ students and families, moving beyond banal classroom discussions and into the realm of praxis by removing single-sex bathroom signs and participating in days of silence. Yet, when I suggest similar awareness and action-driven initiatives regarding institutional racism, bigotry, and issues students and faculty of color face, I am met with fear, resistance, and silence.

I witnessed similar diversions in the broader field of music education after Michael Butera, the former CEO and President of the National Association for Music Education, stated that "Blacks and Latinos lack the keyboard skills needed for this field" and intimated that music theory is too difficult for us as an area of study (McCord, 2016; Rosen, 2016). Butera's comments made national news and many of our field's systemic issues surfaced across various media. In the heat of the debacle, I publicly burned my membership card to the organization and called upon others to speak out. Professional music education organizations wrote (re-)commitments to diversity and reaffirmed values of inclusion; however, little to no actionable changes were made. Meanwhile, that same year an entire music teacher education conference was relocated to another state when many professors took issue with the event being held in North Carolina—a state engulfed in national outrage over the passage of an anti-LGBTQ bill. Where was this type of unilateral action when NAfME's CEO made bigoted and racist remarks? As James Baldwin once said, "Not everything that is faced can be changed, but nothing can be changed until it is faced." I wonder when will we as teachers and citizens come to terms with our inhumanity around race?

Discussion

Deejay's story is unique to him and cannot be used to generalize the experiences of all African Americans within music education. Instead, we offer a lens of double-consciousness as a way to contextualize Deejay's narrative within the literature and to use this theoretical framework as a tool for which teachers, researchers, and advocates of music education can investigate why there is a significant race gap within the field. Double-consciousness theory may be one lens through which the field can view the issues of access and retention of marginalized populations in music education. Further inquiry into how double-consciousness manifests in music education is necessary in order to (a) uncover why there is a lack of minorities within music education, and (b) examine the success of minorities that complete music study and are successful teachers, professors, and/or professional musicians. For example, a music-specific application of Logel et al.'s (2009) study of double-consciousness during high-stakes testing situations in women who study mathematics might be useful in understanding how the activation of negative thoughts can affect individuals' cognitive ability to perform at their best in music. Could the activation of negative thoughts decrease cognitive function and thus lower test scores of Blacks on the Praxis II music exam? Could stereotype threat also lower performance when students are assessed in juries, auditions, and other high-stakes performance situations? Applying Logel and colleagues' study to music education could expose similar or different results that may be helpful in understanding the racial gap in music education and prompt music practitioners to rethink current practices such as high-stakes performance assessment.

As mentioned previously, Brannon et al. (2015) investigated both independent and interdependent schemas in Black college students in order to observe how double-consciousness affects Black students in educational settings. The findings revealed that university settings could bolster the academic performance and persistence in mathematical and verbal assessments when campuses leverage interdependent schemas. If a music-related application of the study revealed a coloration between the percentage of Blacks becoming music educators and university curricula shifting away from the heavily dominated Western European classical canon, then this could lead to important implications for our field. Our profession may need to consider rigorous and implicit restructuring of pre-service music education curricula and licensure programs—a risky but audacious process for those willing to take to challenge and interrogate institutional hegemonic privileges.

Conclusion

The veil of double-consciousness is not completely negative. As Du Bois (1903) remarked, it is "dogged strength alone" that keeps "two souls, two thoughts, two unreconciled strivings; two warring ideals in one dark body . . . from being torn asunder" (p. 9). The strength and resiliency of African Americans is what keeps the soul of Black folks from being shattered.

My collegiate and graduate school years were tedious, however; the unwavering belief in my voice, my perspective, and the voice of Granny praying for a better world for her grandson continues to propel me forward today. Fitzpatrick et al. *(2014) concluded that marginalized students in music education are not only resilient, but also benefit from mentors who guide them through program study. I am certain that I would not have completed any of my degrees without the support from Mark, my undergraduate voice teacher, and many other graduate school professors who encouraged me to tell my story.*

In writing this chapter, I have found empowerment as a Black man in a significantly White field by applying the theoretical lens of double-consciousness to my experience. It is through the recognition of the veil that I have come to better understand why music, an art form that originally mesmerized me, produced feelings of inadequacy and isolation. In accordance with Ciccariello-Maher (2009), I have found that the realization of double-consciousness can lead to liberation, but more importantly activism. I am now empowered to continue in the field of music education and join my voice in the chorus of those singing for the elimination of the opportunity-, achievement-, gender-, and race-gap in music education.

> I don't feel noways tired.
> I've come too far from where I've started from.
> Nobody told me the road would be easy;
> I don't believe He's brought me this far to leave me.

Discussion Questions and Activities

1. Reflect on your music education experiences from elementary school to the present and identify moments in which you may have received an advantage because of your race, ethnicity, gender, and/or sexual orientation.

2. Reflect on your music education experiences from elementary school to the present. Identify moments in which you felt as if you were at a perceived disadvantage because of your race, ethnicity, gender, and or sexual orientation. Write down the experience as you remember it. Try to capture the emotions you felt when you realized you were being unfairly disadvantaged.

3. Activity: Choose one person in class and share your responses for question two. Each person should take turns. Then, draw a Venn diagram and record similarities and differences. Choose one to two observations to share with the class.

4. Although some teachers have taken action to dismantle race disparities in music education, as a whole, this narrative argues that the field has not addressed the root cause of the racial abyss. What do you think are factors that contribute to the continued overrepresentation of Whites in American music education?

5. Considering that most music teachers have autonomy over curricula, name three action steps you can take to make your curriculum more just and equitable (e.g., consult the AAVE when planning and rehearsing spirituals for concerts).

Notes

1. Musicologist and ethnographer Glenn Hinson (2000) described the transcendent phenomenon of Gospel music in his book *Fire in My Bones*. Hinson studied a Southern Gospel group and the unique link between singing, speech, prayer, testimony, and worship. He found that Song helps to focus one's thoughts acting as a kind of cognitive lens that encourages singers and hearers alike to link lyrics with life experience, a process that believers say invariably leads to praise. The praise initiates the supernatural conversation, thus opening the mind's doors to transcendence (p. 2).
2. An affinity lunch is a gathering where members of the same race discuss topics and issues relevant to their lived experiences as a marginalized member of society. This practice is common among the National Association of Independent Schools (NAIS).

References

Banaji, M. R., & Prentice, D. A. (1994). The self in social contexts. *Annual Review of Psychology*, *45*(1), 297–325.

Bertrand, M., & Mullainathan, S. (2003). *Are Emily and Greg more employable than Lakisha and Jamal? A field experiment on labor market discrimination* (No. w9873). National Bureau of Economic Research.

Bergonzi, L. (2009). Sexual orientation and music education: Continuing a tradition. *Music Educators Journal*, *96*(2), 21–25.

Bradley, D. (2006). Music education, multiculturalism, and anti-racism—can we talk? *Action, Criticism & Theory for Music Education*, *5*(2), 2–30.

Bradley, D., Golner, R., & Hanson, S. (2007). Unlearning whiteness, rethinking race issues in graduate music education. *Music Education Research*, *9*(2), 293–304.

Brannon, T. N., Markus, H. R., & Taylor, V. J. (2015). "Two souls, two thoughts," two self-schemas: Double consciousness can have positive academic consequences for African Americans. *Journal of personality and social psychology*, *108*(4), 586–609.

Coates, T. (2015). *Between the world and me*. New York: Spiegel & Grau.

Ciccariello-Maher, G. (2009). A critique of Du Boisian reason: Kanye West and the fruitfulness of double-consciousness. *Journal of Black Studies*, *39*(3), 371–401.

Cross, W. E. (1994). Nigrescence theory: Historical and explanatory notes. *Journal of Vocational Behaviour*, *44*(1), 119–123.

Desmond, M., & Emirbayer, M. (2009). What is racial domination? *Du Bois Review*, *6*(2), 335–355.

Du Bois, W. E. B. (1903). *The souls of black folk*. Chicago, IL: A.C. McClurg and Co.

Elpus, K. (2014). Evaluating the effect of No Child Left Behind on US music course enrollments. *Journal of Research in Music Education*, *62*(3), 215–233.

Elpus, K. (2015). Music teacher licensure candidates in the United States: A demographic profile and analysis of licensure examination scores. *Journal of Research in Music Education*, *36*(3), 1–22.

Elpus, K., & Abril, C. (2011). High school music ensemble students in the United States: A demographic profile. *Journal of Research in Music Education*, *59*(2), 128–145.

Feay-Shaw, S. (2002). The music of Mexican-Americans: A historical perspective of a forgotten culture in American music education. *Journal of Historical Research in Music Education, 24*(1), 83–102.

Fiske, S. T., & Taylor, S. E. (2013). *Social cognition: From brains to culture.* Thousand Oaks, CA: Sage.

Fitzpatrick, K., Henninger, J., & Taylor, D. (2014). Access and retention of marginalized populations within undergraduate music education degree programs. *Journal of Research in Music Education, 62*(2), 105–127.

Gaztambide-Fernandez, R. A. (2011). Musicking in the City: Reconceptualizing Urban Music Education as Cultural Practice. *Action, Criticism & Theory for Music Education, 10*(1), 15–46.

Gardner, R. D. (2010). Should I stay or should I go? Factors that influence the retention, turnover, and attrition of K–12 music teachers in the United States. *Arts Education Policy Review, 111*(3), 112–121.

Glazier, J., & Seo, J. A. (2005). Multicultural literature and discussion as mirror and window? *Journal of Adolescent & Adult Literacy, 48*(8), 686–700. doi:10.1598/JAAL.48.8.6

Hess, J. (2013). Performing tolerance and curriculum: The politics of self-congratulation, identity formation, and pedagogy in world music education. *Philosophy of Music Education, 21*(1), 66–91.

Hess, J. (2015). Decolonizing music education: Moving beyond tokenism. *International Journal of Music Education, 33*(3), 36–347.

Hochschild, J. L., & Weaver, V. (2007). The skin color paradox and the American racial order. *Social Forces, 86*(2), 643–670.

Kindall-Smith, M., McKoy, C. L., & Mills, S. W. (2011). Challenging exclusionary paradigms in the traditional musical canon: Implications for music education practice. *International Journal of Music Education, 29*(4), 374–386.

Koza, J. E. (2002). Corporate profit at equity's expense: Codified standards and high-stakes assessment in music teacher preparation. *Bulletin of the Council for Research in Music Education, 153*(1), 1–16.

Koza, J. E. (2008). Listening for Whiteness: Hearing racial politics in undergraduate school music. *Philosophy of music education review, 16*(2), 145–155.

Lewis, A. (2003). Everyday race-making. *American Behavioral Scientist, 47*(3), 283–305.

Logel, C., Iserman, E., Davies, P., Quinn, D., & Spencer, S. (2009). The perils of double consciousness: The role of thought suppression in stereotype threat. *Journal of Experimental Social Psychology, 45*(1), 299–312.

Markus, H. (1977). Self-schemata and processing information about the self. *Journal of personality and social psychology, 35*(2), 63–78.

Markus, H. R., & Kitayama, S. (2010). Cultures and selves: A cycle of mutual constitution. *Perspectives on Psychological Science, 5*(4), 420–430.

McCord, K. (2016). Why we must have inclusion, diversity, and equity in the arts: A response to the National Association for Music Education. *Alternate Roots.* Retrieved from https://alternateroots.org/why-we-must-have-inclusion-diversity-and-equity-in-the-arts-a-response-to-the-national-association-for-music-education/.

McKoy, C. (2013). Effects of selected demographic variables on music student teachers' self reported cross-cultural competence. *Journal of Research in Music Education, 60*(4), 375–394.

McLaren, P. (2011). Radical Negativity: Music Education for Social Justice. *Action, Criticism & Theory for Music Education, 10*(1), 131–147.

Miranda, H., Mokhta, C. Tung, R., Ward, R., French, D., McAlister, S., & Marshall, A. (2014). *Opportunity and equity: Enrollment and outcomes of Blacks and Latino males in the Boston Public Schools* (Center for Collaborative Education, Anneberg Institute for School Reform at Brown University). Retrieved from http://bostonpublicschools.org/cms/lib07/MA01906464/Centricity/Domain/24/Executive%20Summary_final_pages.pdf.

Omi, M., & Winant, H. (1999). Racial formations. In C. Gallagher (Ed.), *Rethinking the color line: Readings in race and ethnicity* (pp. 9–17). New York: McGraw-Hill.

O'Toole, P. (2005). Why don't I feel included in these musics, or matters. In D. J. Elliott (Ed.), *Praxial Music Education: Reflections and Dialogues* (pp. 297–307). New York: Oxford University Press.

Pembrook, R. G., & Craig, C. (2002). Teaching as a profession: Two variations on a theme. In R. Colwell & C. Richardson (Eds.), *The New Handbook of Research on Music Teaching and Learning: A project of the Music Educators National Conference* (pp. 786–817). New York: Oxford University Press.

Reed, A. (1997). *W.E.B. Du Bois and American political thought: Fabianism and the color line.* New York: Oxford University Press.

Rickels, D. A., Brewer, W. D., Councill, K. H., Fredrickson, W. E., Hairston, M., Perry, D. L., & Schmidt, M. (2013). Career influences of music education audition candidates. *Journal of Research in Music Education, 61*(1), 115–134.

Robinson, D. W. (2017). A labor of love: A rational and second grade general music curriculum for a more just and equitable world. *TOPICS.* Manuscript in press.

Rosen, J. (2016). League president and CEO comments on recent controversy surrounding diversity meeting. *League of American Orchestras.* Retrieved from http://american orchestras.org/news-publications/public-statements/league-president-comments-on-diversity-discussion.html.

Style, E. (n.d.). Curriculum as window and mirror. *The national SEED project.* Retrieved from http://nationalseedproject.org/about-us/timeline/26-latest-articles/41-curriculum-as-window-and-mirror.

Tatum, B. (1997). *Why are all the black kids sitting together in the cafeteria?* New York: Basic Books.

3

WHY JUST ME (OR FEW OTHERS) IN MUSIC EDUCATION

An Autoethnographic Point of Departure

Darrin Thornton

Introduction

In 2010, I started my first full-time position in higher education as a music teacher educator. Several years preceding my return to full-time graduate work, I began attending mainstream and specialized interest group conferences in music education. I was consciously aware of the lack of diversity in general, and specifically alarmed by the absence of Black men as leaders, presenters, and even conference attendees. Although underrepresented groups have seen growth in our profession over time, the case for Black men has remained seemingly unchanged, especially within the instrumental music education specialization. Recent research indicates large racial disparity between those being fully credentialed for state teaching licensure in music education (Elpus, 2015). This type of inequality within the public school workforce is but one ripple within the larger US educational landscape that contains racial achievement and attainment gaps at every juncture of the educational access pipeline from preK–12 schooling through doctoral study. I consider this underrepresentation to be problematic as we endeavor to be more inclusive as a profession and it has led me to question and examine ways this can be changed.

I explore the phenomenon by framing my own experiences journeying to and through the field of music education as a point of departure toward better understanding the problem (Baxter & Jack, 2008). I utilize autoethnography to view myself as the phenomenon, focusing on my own academic, professional, and personal life. The purpose of this investigation is to understand myself as a Black man intersecting with the cultural and historical context(s) of the music education academy (Ellis, 2004). Through retrospective selection, I highlight *epiphanies* along my journey "that stem from and are made possible by being part of this culture" (Ellis, Adams & Bochner, 2011, p 276). These *epiphanies* narrate my lived experiences and are accompanied by *narratives* and *vignettes* that highlight my understanding of educational access. I title and number each epiphany in relation to the broader contextual themes of my journey, i.e., *Epiphany 1—Place Matters*. I title and number each narrative in relation to an experience that helps explain the larger theme, i.e., *Narrative 4—A Visit to the College Counselor*; and I title and number each vignette in relation to an important moment related to educational access, i.e., *Educational Access Professional Vignette 1—McNair Scholars Program*. I later draw upon the vignettes to help inform a pipeline access program that I propose at the end of this chapter.

Early Childhood

I was raised by two college-educated Black parents who grew up through the 1940s–1950s and completed their undergraduate education in the early 1960s. The social-political climate at that time in American history situates their approach to parenting throughout my formative years. My father grew up in inner city Cleveland, Ohio, the youngest of three boys with working parents who migrated to the North from Georgia when he was young. His father worked in a Ford plant after serving in the military, and his mother was a private nurse for the majority of her working years. My mother grew up in inner city Columbus, Ohio, the fourth child of ten. Her father worked construction and her mother cleaned houses for a living. Her mother migrated north from Alabama, and her father grew up in the Columbus area.

My parents met during their undergraduate studies and were married in 1966 directly after graduating with degrees in pharmacy (father) and elementary education (mother). They moved to Washington, DC, to pursue employment. A few years after their move, I joined the family, and my father returned to school to pursue dentistry. One of my brothers was born just before my father finished school, and after successful completion of his degree we moved back to Cleveland, Ohio, where my father began working in a public dental clinic.

Epiphany 1—Place Matters

My parents decided to buy a home in Shaker Heights (Shaker), Ohio, a neighboring suburb east of Cleveland, Ohio. Shaker is considered to be one of the first integrated neighborhoods in the country (1960s), and the school system student population was roughly 70/30 White to Black when I started attending in 1974. The property taxes in this area were relatively high, and there were other viable communities in the greater Cleveland area that would have also offered a strong education. However, my parents specifically chose Shaker for the education system and the opportunities it would afford their children.

This decision did not come lightly, as it put a financial strain on young parents with what would become four children. However, they understood the advantage they would provide by allowing us to grow up in this particular neighborhood. The strong school district was one factor, but there were other benefits of going to school in a diverse setting that did not become apparent to me until much later in life.

Growing up with people from different racial, economic, and religious backgrounds was tremendous preparation for life in general, but also academically and professionally. During my elementary school years I remember seeing difference, but not noticing it in any particular way. In the adolescent years, the racial and socioeconomic lines became more pronounced. However, the opportunities to interact with all kinds of people as friends, classmates, teammates, and music-mates provided wonderful interpersonal learning experiences.

My mother taught me how to act in public so as not to draw negative or otherwise unwanted attention to myself. This training began at a very early age, starting first with what I would call obedience training and then finishing school. My mother would insist on proper grooming and always looking presentable when going to school or other formal places. Once I was home, she required me to change out of those good clothes and into play clothes. Perceptions, especially first impressions, were a big deal, and my mother felt it was important for a Black boy in society to give himself every chance to be seen as a polite, respectful person who then had a chance of being taken seriously.

At an early age, this established a sense of duality between how I would behave and operate within the home/family context and how I would operate in the world in which I lived most of the time at school and professionally. In the Cleveland area, I lived in close proximity to extended family, and there were frequent occasions to gather for holidays and special events. My cousins all lived in more homogenous suburban and urban communities and their experiences, and to some degree their outlook on life, were far different from my experience growing up in the integrated community of Shaker. The following narrative illustrates aspects of these differences:

Narrative 1—Why Do You Talk That Way?

> *Family members (and some Black friends within my own community) would often ask me why I talked "White" because I spoke what they called "perfect" English, on the other hand White friends would ask me why I did not "sound Black" for the same reason. This duality was cultivated naturally as I coded between these aspects of my reality.*

Communicating in "both" worlds became natural, but I saw it more as one world with many dialects (Delpit, 1990). I quickly learned to "talk-the-talk" and "walk-the-walk," although always at the fringe of either community. This was mostly by choice so as not to draw attention or be noticed; however, it was also because I felt tolerated, perhaps even accepted in both communities—but did not feel a full-fledged member of either. This fringe thread would be an essence within the phenomenon of being the *only one* in most professional and academic settings later in my life.

My race is not easily identifiable on paper by my given name or by the sound of my voice on the phone; only a face-to-face meeting reveals my race at first glance. It was my mother's intent to train me to be conversant within any setting in which I might find myself, so that I might be judged more by the "content of my character" (King, 1963) than the stereotypes she feared would guide judgments of me at first glance.

The aforementioned school district racial demographic breakdown was White and "minority," which included everything considered non-White. However, what is not as commonly known about Shaker Heights, OH, is the wide social economic status (SES) disparity ranging from lower middle class to the wealthiest sector of the economic range as this narrative illustrates:

Narrative 2—The Untold Story

> *The communities within the city are divided by the electric cable car commuter rail systems that run through town. There are two sets of tracks and the SES breakdown is stratified by where the domicile is located in relation to these tracks. The southernmost section (the other side of the other tracks) was the lowest SES; between the tracks was just that—the middle-range SES (new money); and the northernmost section (above the tracks) was the old money: "Shaker"—the highest SES section of town. I grew up in the southernmost section, which happened to also be the most diverse section of this "integrated" community.*

K–12 Schooling Years

Epiphany 2—High Expectations

This SES stratification often played itself out in relation to aspects of schooling within Shaker. As the oldest child of parents who were active participants in our educational process, I realized this phenomenon more fully passing through the system. During the elementary years, my parents established the foundations of their expectations relative to my educational goals.

They expected me to be a good citizen in school, focusing on my studies by applying myself to the best of my abilities. However, the best of my abilities was often "influenced" by my mother, who held the bar rather high and always wanted me to be challenged, reaching for more, and not necessarily comfortable. This approach engrained an expectation for high achievement academically and the sense that anything less than that should not be accepted by myself or anyone else in the teaching/learning situation.

My parents expected the school district to provide instruction that was challenging for me and often had to push the system to employ high expectations of my learning achievement and personal conduct. This proved to be problematic on several occasions along the way, where the district's expectations were not congruent with my parents'; thus they needed to intervene. In elementary school, it was a matter of getting teachers to understand that "doing ok" was not good enough; they should expect me to be doing well, and if I was not doing well they wanted teachers to sound the alarm and provide suggestions on the areas where I could improve, so they could work with me on those concepts at home (and they did).

Epiphany 3: The Tracking System—Systemic Discrimination/ Racism

It was middle school/junior high where this disparity became most prevalent as the district academic tracking system kicked into full gear in every subject. Stratification by race and SES seemed to occur even at the beginning years of junior high school. Further, this stratification seemed to match the geographic SES distribution pattern relative to the electric train tracks.

Parents who "knew better" flexed their advocacy muscles and worked with the school to ensure their children were placed in the track that provided the appropriate level of challenge. There were four tracks at the junior high level that resulted in advanced, high regular, regular, and remedial instruction. The remedial track classes were predominantly Black (not minority but Black) enrollment, the regular tracks were more diverse, but the higher regular track was less so; and the advanced track was predominately White and few other (mostly students of Asian descent, with very few Blacks). This next narrative chronicles the process my parents went through to advocate for appropriate course placement:

Narrative 3—Playing Catch Up

> It took significant energy and effort for my parents to convince the school to put me in the advanced-level classes in certain subjects. The recommendations from elementary school were not convincing enough to place me in the advanced level, and I was (and still am) an average test taker, although my grades in all elementary areas were the highest level given. However, my parents insisted I be allowed to try the advanced levels in social studies, math, and science, and stay in upper regular English where placed. This did not happen until halfway through the first year of junior high (seventh grade in this district at the time).
>
> Needless to say, I had some catching up to do and the differences between classes were stark. I had much to prove to some teachers that were reluctant to allow me to try (though some were very supportive). I again felt very much like an outsider or

"fringe" member of this learning community, since the routines had already been established and I didn't feel I "belonged" yet, even though I was accepted and tolerated. Once this tracking placement issue was settled, I was on a trajectory that placed me safely into college-prep courses or above for the remainder of my time in the district.

This was the first time I strongly experienced this "why just me" essence of the phenomenon within the academic setting. However, there was further academic stratification at the high school transition, with the addition of Advanced Placement (AP) courses. These courses attracted the highest achievers into small classes, leaving high-attaining students in the advanced level. The regular levels were divided into college prep and regular, and then there were remedial levels. I learned right as I was graduating that there was also a "school-within-a school" track for students electing a vocational or GED (General Educational Development) track. These classmates would often come to school for part of the day and then go for vocational training elsewhere in the greater Cleveland area.

This tracking system allowed Shaker to accommodate the diverse levels of academic achievement within the integrated community, while still maintaining very high academic standards for achievement and college placement. Well decorated with national merit scholars and prestigious college placements, the district attracted families like mine, interested in providing one of the best public school educations possible in the area within a diverse environment (on paper). However, the social justice issues embedded in this tracking practice created egregious gaps of access that negated the potential advantages of diversity. This academic stratification often created racial tensions that went unaddressed by the district.

College Transition

The academic counseling office at Shaker advised students through the college, vocational training, and workforce transition. The following narrative describes my junior year experience meeting with an academic counselor:

Narrative 4—A Visit to the College Counselor

Prior to this meeting, I discussed options with my parents and also with fellow classmates and friends. I came prepared with a list of schools to consider. After looking at my list, the college counselor started to "manage my expectations" by suggesting a different set of schools, saying the schools on my list were a bit of a "stretch." I was savvy enough at this point to know not to challenge the college advisor on the spot but, as students do, I conferred with classmates, and they reported that their lists (which were very similar to my own) were not questioned by the college advisor as being a stretch if they were White, and the few other Black students in advanced classes received similar "advice" to choose a more reachable list of schools.

I relayed the exchange to my parents and they scheduled an appointment with said advisor to express their disappointment in the lack of expectation for an honors student in their district. My parents had decided to move into this district because they wanted the best educational opportunities for their children. Yet they had to actively advocate for their children's academic well-being in every sector of the system. By doing so, they did achieve the goal of positioning me and my siblings to have choices and opportunities after high school.

Co-curricular Enhancements during K–12 Schooling

Epiphany 4: Opportunities—Unwritten Access

While providing the best public education they could afford, my parents also supported my musical interests through private lessons outside of school. They also supported my interest in sports and thus spent many an hour shuttling me to practices, rehearsals, performances, and games.

In the same vein, they insisted while I was a developing adolescent that I have a job to "learn the value of a buck." I started delivering the local newspaper in fifth grade and had a route until I passed it off to the next neighborhood kid just before leaving for college. This practical education provided me the opportunity to manage my own affairs, to hone people and problem-solving skills, and to be independent in ways many of my colleagues did not have the opportunity to experience.

They also sought out summer enrichment opportunities to expand my skill-set without overloading me during the school year. For example, they insisted I take a typing class (which was not required for high school graduation) during the summer session, along with other math exploratory courses. They found out about the INROADS program whose mission was to "develop and place talented minority youth in business and industry and prepare them for corporate and community leadership" (www.inroads.org).

This was the first mentoring/enrichment type program I experienced geared toward grooming students from underrepresented populations for college and beyond. My parents knew this type of program would be advantageous even though they had already invested a great deal in living in a very fine school district. I attribute these insights to their experiences as college graduates. Another hidden benefit of participating in the INROADS program was studying and working with other people of color who were high achievers academically and looking for a professional future beyond high school and college. This program groomed adolescents for a future in the corporate world by stressing college readiness and providing standardized test prep instruction, foreign language instruction, math enrichment courses, and communication/presentational skills instruction. INROADS also provided practical experiences via access to college students who had been through the high school program, summer internships with companies in the area that agreed to mentor high school students, and various types of etiquette experiences including interviewing, eating at fancy restaurants, attending the symphony, and other formal events.

Alongside these formal enrichment opportunities, my parents also made sure we had strong ties to extended family. Knowing they had willingly moved into a community that catered toward the dominant culture, it was important to them that their children be grounded in who they were and how they were connected through family and the larger Black community. I consider these co-curricular opportunities to be privileges that have helped me along the way at various points on my journey.

College Years

Epiphany 5—Buppie (Black Urban Professionals) Goal Orientation

One ramification of this "goal orientation" is the subservience of "enrichment activities" like music participation as great enhancements that are not considered to be viable professional goals, but rather markers of refinement and quality education. This teleological mindset became a problem for me when picking a major in college because my parents did not see music as a reasonable field of study. Furthermore, they felt music education was something I could study anywhere, meaning I could move home and study music at a local/regional school, versus the private out-of-state school I was attending. The goal of college, for them, was gainful employment that allowed you to adequately provide for yourself and your family. At least that is how it felt to me at the time.

This caused me to explore various majors, starting with Pre-Med, Pre-Business, Spanish, and Communications, and finally landing within the College of Education in a newly formed degree program entitled Human Development and Social Policy with an emphasis in Organizational Behavior. Although that is a mouthful, the degree satisfied my interest in the sociological/educational/psychological aspects of education situated within the context of learning and teaching in America. This line of intellectual inquiry set me up well for a future thread of interest leading me ultimately "back" or into the field of music teaching and learning.

During my junior year, I applied for a research experience via the Summer Research Opportunity Program (SROP), which was designed to introduce and prepare underrepresented undergraduate students for graduate study, particularly the Ph.D. I had the pleasure of working with a professor in sociology who allowed me to work with him on a public school reform effort with the Chicago Public Schools and a then corporate-sponsored demonstration school project.

Epiphany 6: Mentoring (The Unwritten Curriculum)

Through SROP, I was introduced to the world of research and how systematic inquiry informs practice as well as decision-making in various contexts. The experience also provided beginning research methods training, graduate entrance examination preparation courses, research presentation and writing classes, and opportunities to interact with fellow research colleagues and faculty mentors in various fields.

Working with my faculty mentor opened my eyes to personal possibilities as an academic, which was previously not on my professional radar. Although this was my second experience participating in this type of mentoring/preparation/ training program, it was the first time being mentored one-on-one with a faculty member within a field of particular interest, who also happened to be a Black male. This type of learning enhanced my sense of self-efficacy and made research and the world of college teaching via the Ph.D. seem more accessible, as did being surrounded with other scholars of color for the first time in my under-graduate experience (i.e., not being "the only one" or "one of few"). Being brought up in a very practically oriented framework, this blend of theory and practice also helped me see the direct value of research and the type of impact it can have on policy, practice, and thus individual lives.

The doors opened during this mentoring relationship illustrate the opportunities, serendipitous and purposeful, that occur during the mentoring process. These opportunities are often not planned and are only available to those fortunate enough to be part of the mentoring process. This theme of access is a prevailing, almost guiding, principle in my professional work because of the profound effect of this SROP experience.

Although my course of study landed me solidly within the education realm, I was steadily involved in the music area participating in ensembles, taking lessons when allowed, and being active as a leader in the marching band. I was able to maintain my performance skills at least at some level, and kept music as a dear avocation.

Graduate School and Early Professional Life

I carried this interest directly into graduate school after graduating with an undergraduate degree in education and social policy. I entered a Masters in Arts in Teaching degree program, endeavoring to be an elementary school teacher because there were not many male teachers at that level, and I considered the elementary years to be the most formative for the academic futures of students. While studying at a teacher's college (formerly a normal school) devoted to social justice through education, I worked as a teacher's aide in one of the wealthiest school districts in the country. Top-notch professionals in their field mentored me, while I learned practical pedagogical teaching skills, which was very valuable to my development as a teacher. These two fifth-grade teachers allowed me to plan and deliver lessons to small groups of students and the entire class. These experiences prepared me well and also opened my eyes to the large disparities of educational opportunity based on SES and race based on my experiences to that point.

Epiphany 7—Finding/Doing Your Passion: Music Is My Subject Area

After finishing the teaching pedagogy courses, I found myself in the middle of my student teaching practicum semester at odds with my experience. I was placed in a diverse neighborhood much like Shaker with a very gifted cooperating teacher. She was a fantastic model and nurtured my growth in wonderful ways during the experience. However, my heart (and gut) was tied up in knots. Although I was doing very well in the third/fourth-grade split classroom setting, I was not enjoying teaching in this environment as a "regular classroom" teacher.

I had a passion for the students in the setting but did not share the same passion for teaching the five separate subjects covered in the elementary setting (reading, writing, math, science, and social studies). I could see, however, enjoying teaching music at any level in the schools or elsewhere. Therefore, after much consultation with everyone involved, I removed myself from the experience and switched my degree from the M.A.T. program to the M.Ed. program, focused on a thesis project involving educational program design and curriculum development within the curriculum and instruction emphasis.

Alongside my pursuit and development within the field of music education, I have lived a parallel career focused on various aspects of educational access programs, as shown by this first vignette:

Educational Access Professional Vignette 1—McNair Scholars Program

In my first full-time professional post, I served as the coordinator of the Ronald E. McNair Post-Baccalaureate Program (McNair Program). This grant-funded program is still sponsored by the US Department of Education as part of the group of grants known as TRIO, established as part of the Higher Education Act of 1965.

The Federal TRIO Programs are Federal outreach and student service programs designed to identify and provide services for individuals from disadvantaged backgrounds. TRIO includes eight programs targeted to serve and assist low-income individuals, first-generation college students, other individuals underrepresented in undergraduate and graduate education, and individuals with disabilities to progress through the academic pipeline from middle school to post-baccalaureate programs . . . the McNair Program prepares (undergraduate) participants for doctoral studies through involvement in research and other scholarly activities. Institutions encourage participants to enroll in graduate programs and then track their progress through the successful completion of advanced degrees. The goal is to increase the attainment of Ph.D. degrees by students from underrepresented segments of society. (Ronald E. McNair Program)

In this position I was able to practice my curriculum development and program design skills as I created and coordinated a workshop/lecture series for promising undergraduates. I also utilized my counseling and teaching skills to develop co-curricular learning modules related to the graduate school application process during the academic year. In the summers, I coordinated research internship placements along with a continued Ph.D. prep/lecture workshop series. I also drew on my previous experiences with the SROP program and felt fortunate to be on the other side of the mentoring equation for this moment in time.

While working with the McNair Program, I began taking graduate courses in different areas as I considered Ph.D. programs. I took a few courses within the human development department and enjoyed continuing in the developmental psychology vein. However, after the second course, I realized more firmly that my desired subject area was still music. Since I was very active in the graduate education scene on campus, I was aware of the fellowship opportunities available for graduate study. I explored applying for a Ph.D. fellowship to study music education. However, during the process, I learned from the faculty that I would not be eligible to study in their area without a conferred music degree and a few years teaching music in the public schools. This posed an obstacle to my intended goal of studying at the doctoral level.

Epiphany 8—Persistent Lifelong Learning

Faced with this closed gate, I decided it was time to take bold steps in a different direction academically and pursue a degree in music. I explored various options within the School of Music and chose to explore the Masters in Music degree in conducting with an instrumental focus. I auditioned into the program and was accepted with a host of music prerequisites to fill in the gaps I did not have as an undergraduate (music theory, music history, and juries in a performance studio area). These prerequisite courses amounted to an extra year of study, which at that point in my career was a price I was willing to pay. Once admitted to the program, I then applied for and was granted a Masters fellowship and progressed through the program as prescribed. This opportunity changed the course of my professional life by allowing me to "right the ship" regarding studying music. Throughout my music studies, I did not encounter many other people of color.

While studying toward this degree, I directed two different summer educational access programs and, after graduating, I worked as a recruiter for the Graduate School as described in this vignette:

Educational Access Professional Vignette 2—Professional Summer Programs and the Graduate School

The first was a summer internship/readiness program for underrepresented undergraduate students interested in medical school. These students were recruited primarily from HBCUs and spent the summer on the predominately White campus where I studied and was employed. The second was a similar program geared toward students (same population) interested in attending Veterinary School.

I provided guidance in the design of the overall academic programming surrounding and connecting the specific science and medicine/veterinary coursework and program leadership. I hired and trained all summer program staff and guided the development of co-curricular activities including test preparations, etiquette training, related graduate science rotation workshop series, and faculty/graduate student mentor-mixers. These activities provided participants with opportunities to fully explore the educational offerings at a comprehensive research institution both within their desired professional degree, along with the other research areas that influence that profession. These opportunities kept my hands and feet in this type of work and allowed me the chance to continue this generative process of mentoring.

After graduating with a Masters in Conducting, I was hired at the same institution into a joint appointment within the Graduate School and the School of Music. In this post, I primarily served as the director of graduate recruitment and retention, while teaching conducting courses to undergraduates and conducting one of the concert bands within the School of Music. Within this institution, overall recruitment was a somewhat decentralized effort, whereas recruitment of underrepresented groups was an effort spearheaded by the central office of the graduate school. As director of these efforts I had the opportunity to interact with prospective students, individual department faculty, and administrators related to issues of recruitment and retention of all graduate students, but specifically those from underrepresented backgrounds. This position furthered my knowledge base and experience working with educational access programs.

After my partner completed her doctorate, we relocated to another state in a different part of the country. The position I applied for and negotiated within that institution fell through and I arrived in the area jobless. The inner-city public schools were looking to hire music teachers late in the summer. I was not certified at the time but I turned in my materials and received an immediate call from the supervisor of music. I was offered a job to restart a band program at one high school and one middle school in the district that had not had a program in 10 years. Although I was working with many more teachers of color than ever before, I was the only instrumental music teacher of color in this large urban school district. Why, I wondered.

I was granted permanent certification by this state after a successful first year of teaching and taught three more years in the state, working in urban and rural settings before making another out-of-state move. The following vignette outlines the third set of professional parallel experiences I had prior to my current post on faculty:

Educational Access Professional Vignette 3—Upward Bound and Office of Fellowships and Awards

I arrived on my current campus as a trailing partner. My first position on campus was directing the Upward Bound Math Science program, another TRIO grant-funded project. This program aims to "help students recognize their potential to excel in Math and Science and to encourage them to pursue postsecondary degrees . . . and ultimately careers in the Math and Science profession" (Upward Bound Math Science). Administering a high school to college bridge program was not unfamiliar territory given my past experiences. This experience provided further tangible experience with the educational access gap at this point in the education pipeline.

I then transitioned to another post directing the Office of Fellowships and Awards in the Graduate School of this same institution. This position gave me a different vantage point on the graduate school matriculation process. I was also on the giving side of the fellowship and scholarship coin as well, which enabled me to influence policy and practice to best meet the goals of each funding program, including funding for underrepresented populations.

Epiphany 9—Why Just Me?

After a year back on a university campus, I began taking graduate courses to help determine which direction I would take my doctoral studies. I debated the merits of the Music Education Ph.D. and the D.M.A. in conducting, with the ultimate goal of moving into the university faculty ranks. After weighing the options, I decided to pursue the Ph.D. in Music Education because it most represented my full professional self. I chose to study at the current institution and continue working part-time for a few years, since my daughter was expected the fall after I applied. I later resigned from my position in the graduate school and finished the degree full-time.

Upon completion of the Ph.D., I was hired onto the faculty at the same institution. As previously stated, during my doctoral studies and the years since, I have actively attended professional conferences and wondered "why just me" or "so few others" in regard to people of color in general and Black men specifically? When I drill down further to consider my specific area of instrumental music education at the higher education level (and band within that), the absence is even more pronounced.

I have witnessed and experienced many of the disparities in the areas of educational access and professional opportunity built into the competitive (Kohn,

1992) and racist nature of American culture (Bonilla-Silva, 2003; Ladson-Billings, 1996, 1998; Ladson-Billings & Tate, 2009). As I compare my opportunities and advantages to other relatives in my own family, the differences are very clear. Students in different social economic areas of the country have starkly different educational experiences (Lareau, 2003; Lewis-McCoy, 2014). I have yet to see a great equalizer for racism—not even financial privilege or educational attainment eradicates the effects of systemic racism.

Being the child of two first-generation college graduates, who successfully negotiated college and graduate school, gave me advantage. College graduates represent 19.1 percent of the US population over the age of 25 (Aud, Fox & Kewal Ramani, 2010). Within the US Black population over the age of 25, 13.6 percent have attained an undergraduate degree, and Black males represented 36 percent of Black students enrolled in undergraduate degree programs in 2008 (p. 123).

Standardized test scores play a very important role in the gatekeeping process. Black students score the lowest of all racial groups on AP exams with a mean score of 1.91 out of five (p. 77). In 2008, Black test-takers scored the lowest average (430/800) of all other racial/ethnic groups in both the critical reading and mathematics sections of the exam (p. 82). A small percentage (3 percent) of Black ACT test-takers scored high enough to meet the college readiness benchmark on all four exams (p. 86).

The graduate school statistics illustrate a similar disparity with the minority population in general and the Black male population specifically. Out of the total US population, 7.5 percent have attained masters degrees and 2.8 percent have attained doctorate/professional degrees (Aud et al., 2010, p. 141). Within the Black population over the age of 25, 1.3 percent held doctorate or professional degrees. The gender gap is most pronounced within the Black population with Black females representing 71 percent of Black graduate enrollments in 2008 (p. 125).

The undergraduate application process in Music Education privileges classical studio performance areas, as well as ways of music-making and music-knowing (Mantie & Talbot, 2015; Talbot & Mantie, 2015). These privileged practices, by nature, prefer certain musical backgrounds and experiences to others (Bradley, 2007; Clements, 2009; Koza, 2008; Palmer, 2011). Though none of this is new, it frames the "why just me" discussion in an empirical fashion that cannot and should not be ignored.

I am convinced my parents exerted the advocacy effort to ensure I was provided the type of education that would give me access to post-secondary educational opportunities, because they knew firsthand what it would take. Furthermore, they knew there were opportunities outside the schooling setting I needed to have in order to be groomed, as best they could, for the widest range of future opportunities after high school (Lareau, 2003). These factors in part lead to the "why just me" phenomenon, as it is not hard to see how few parents of Black boys/men hold college degrees in comparison to their majority counterparts (Lewis, Diamond & Forman, 2015).

Although I did not run into many other Black men in my school or professional experiences, I have met up with a few as fellow students in the undergraduate setting and as students in my current higher education setting. Obviously these Black men made it through the gateways of admission into a School of Music, and thus demonstrated the skills and backgrounds in the preferred music-making styles and practices (Koza, 2008). However, few of these men chose to enter, or persist in, the music education program.

Although I have hypotheses as to why that may have happened, I would like to do further research with this population to explore why so few choose music education as a professional route within the music profession. This autoethnographic exploration has afforded me the opportunity to organize my lived experiences into personal understandings I now wish to use as a framework for (a) further exploration into this phenomenon by probing the experiences of other Black men both within the field of music education (to the degree they exist) and in other higher education fields of study to further test the framework and (b) propose a pipeline mentoring/development program that could hopefully begin to bridge the important gaps for Black men (and other underrepresented groups) interested in pursuing music education careers in the academy.

Pipeline Access Program

The educational and professional access illustrated in the vignettes lead to my firm belief in access programs. Many of the required professional skills are often not taught inside the classroom. Those with privilege and access often gain these experiences as a natural part of living their lives (Lareau, 2013). However, for the "dis-privileged" (underprivileged), these professional skills are often serendipitously learned along the way by benevolent mentors or via the school of hard knocks.

I have personally witnessed access programs aid in closing the access gap for underrepresented groups, however I have not yet seen such a program developed for the purpose of addressing the access of underrepresented populations in the field of music education in general or within the academy in particular. To that end, I propose the following outline for a pipeline access program. I openly admit, it is designed to address access, retention, and success through the current racist system at play in the academy. Ideally, the academy will begin to employ more equitable and inclusive practices as demographics become more diverse at all levels, including leadership.

Pipeline to the Music Education Academy Proposal Outline

As with most professions, pathways to the music education academy vary, but there are certain benchmarks that must be reached in order to gain a seat at the academy table. Therefore, it is necessary to address every juncture of the pathway (pipeline) to provide entry and continued access to the profession. I see the junctures in music education to be: preparedness for undergraduate admission, undergraduate degree completion/gainful employment within the field, preparedness for graduate admission, doctoral completion/placement, and retention through tenure/promotion.

I. **College Readiness Program:** designed to (1) develop strong academic skills in the full range of subjects, (2) develop performance skills in at least one conservatory-accepted studio area, (3) develop non-performance musical skills in theory, history, and composition, and (4) provide exposure to a broad range of musical opportunities both through school and outside of school (e.g., summer music camps, regional and all-state groups, travel abroad, etc.). The college readiness program would start no later than grade nine (ideally in elementary school) targeting former middle school participants from backgrounds historically underrepresented in undergraduate programs.

    It would include:

    a. Private studio lessons
    b. Music theory classes
    c. Tutoring for academic classes—or enhancement classes offered in required college courses (math, science, English, foreign languages, etc.)
    d. College bridge program—would happen the summer after ninth and tenth grade, bringing students to a college campus for a comprehensive summer music camp experience. During these experiences, students would also visit other college campuses for tours and gather information from various Schools of Music.
    e. College admissions coaching for the student and the family starting at the end of tenth grade:

        i.   Admissions selection guidance
        ii. Coordinating campus visit (providing funding if necessary)
        iii. Assisting with financial aid, and funding applications
        iv. Coaching with portfolio items: audition recordings, videos, etc.

    f. Scholarship support for participation in prestigious summer camp programs (e.g., Interlochen, Blue Lake) geared toward the summer after junior year but would be eligible to younger students able to audition into such opportunities

II. **Music Education Scholars Program:** designed to identify promising underrepresented undergraduate students and groom them for the "future faculty" pipeline within music education. Ideally some of the high school students from the college readiness program would continue to participate.

    a. Early research experiences
    b. Academic advising with academic enrichment if needed

        i.   Musicianship classes (theory, history, and piano)

        ii. General education courses outside of music

  c. Summer internship experiences

        i.   Teaching

        ii. Research

  d. Test preparation

  e. Teaching job placement coaching

        i.   Developing resume

        ii. Building teaching portfolio

        iii. Strategizing a good match between district and student's strengths

  f. Faculty/graduate student mentor (depending on what is available)

III. **Future Faculty in Music Education Program:** designed for graduate students as a systematic enculturation into the current campus culture and the music education academy.

  a. Early research collaborations with program faculty

        i.   Encourage full engagement within the department.

        ii. Build research competencies specific to the field.

  b. Support for strategic conference attendance

        i.   Attend a variety of conferences, both the large mainstream conferences and the specific area conference.

        ii. Actively share research projects.

        iii. Seek off-campus collaborations with other like-minded graduate students and faculty within the research community.

  c. Networking opportunities on campus and off-campus with fellow graduate students and faculty

        i.   Connection with faculty and graduate students of color on campus.

        ii. Opportunities to mentor undergraduate students.

  d. Professional placement coaching

        i.   Build curriculum vitae and teaching/performance video samples.

        ii. Strategize approach and timing for applying.

        iii. Develop teaching presentations and provide opportunities for students to practice them with current undergraduates.

IV. **Faculty Mentoring Program:** designed for junior faculty members in music education as a systematic enculturation into the specific department, school, college, and university culture.

a. Assigned faculty mentors—meet regularly to discuss progress, problems, general guidance, etc.

    i. Within the department
    ii. Within the larger unit (college or school)
    iii. Faculty of color within the university
    iv. Faculty of color within the field (off-campus)

b. Assistance with dossier preparation for tenure review formative and summative process
c. Networking opportunities with other new faculty in the college/university

Discussion Questions

1. In the *Early Childhood* section of the chapter, the author mentioned that his grandparents migrated North when his father was a young child. Listen to the following National Public Radio program (www.npr.org/templates/story/story.php?storyId=129827444) interviewing Pulitzer prize winning author Isabel Wilkerson about her book: *The Warmth of Other Suns—The Epic Story of America's Great Migration.* If you were able to ask three questions to someone who migrated North during this period of American history, what would they be and why?
2. In Narrative 1 – *Why Do You Talk That Way?*, what does it mean to talk White or sound Black?
3. In Narrative 2 – *The Untold Story*, what do you think contributed to this type of racial and SES zoning segregation within this integrated community?
4. How would you define systemic racism?

    a. Can you describe examples of systemic racism you have witnessed or experienced in your academic journey?
    b. Was there an academic tracking system in your school district?
    c. If so, were you aware of when it started?

5. What explanations would you provide for the difference in expectations demonstrated by the high school guidance counselor in Narrative 4 – *A Visit to the College Counselor*?
6. The author titles Epiphany 4 *Opportunities—Unwritten Access.* Why do you think he uses the term unwritten access there?

References

Aud, S., Fox, M., & Kewalramani, A. (2010). *Status and trends in the education of racial and ethnic groups* (NCES 2010–015). U.S. Department of Education, National Center for Education Statistics. Washington, DC: U.S. Government Printing Office.

Baxter, P., & Jack, S. (2008). Qualitative case study methodology: Study design and implementation for novice researchers. *The Qualitative Report, 13*(4), 544–549. Retrieved from http://nova.edu/ssss/QR/QR13-4/baxter.pdf.

Bonilla-Silva, E. (2003). *Racism without racists: Color-blind racism and the persistence of racial inequality in the United States.* Lanham, MD: Rowman & Littlefield.

Bradley, D. (2007). The sounds of silence: Talking race in music education. *Action, Criticism & Theory for Music Education, 6*(4), 132–162.

Clements, A. (2009). Minority students and faculty in higher music education. *Music Educators Journal, 95*(3), 53–56.

Delpit, L. (1990). Language diversity and learning. In S. Hynds & D. L. Rubin (Eds.), *Perspectives on Talk and Learning* (pp. 247–266). Urbana, IL: National Council of Teacher of English.

Ellis, C (2004). *The ethnographic I: A methodological novel about autoethnography.* Walnut Creek, CA: Alta Mira Press.

Ellis, C., Adams, T., & Bochner, A. (2011). Autoethnography: An overview. *Historical Social Research/Historische Sozialforschung, 36*(4 (138)), 273–290. Retrieved from http://jstor.org.ezaccess.libraries.psu.edu/stable/23032294.

Elpus, K. (2015). Music teacher licensure candidates in the United States: A demographic profile and analysis of licensure examination scores. *Journal of Research in Music Education, 63*(3), 314–335.

INROADS. (2015, May 15). Retrieved from http://inroads.org/.

King, M. L., Jr. (1963). *I have a dream.* Speech delivered at the Lincoln Memorial on August 28 in Washington, DC.

Kohn, A. (1992). *No contest: The case against competition* (Rev. ed.). Boston, MA: Houghton Mifflin.

Koza, J. (2008). Listening for whiteness: Hearing racial politics in undergraduate school music. *Philosophy of Music Education Review, 16*(2), 145–155.

Ladson-Billings, G. (1996). "Your blues ain't like mine": Keeping issues of race and racism on the multicultural agenda. *Theory into Practice, 35*(4), 248–255.

Ladson-Billings, G. (1998). Just what is critical race theory and what's it doing in a nice field like education? *International Journal of Qualitative Studies in Education, 11*(1), 7–24.

Ladson-Billings, G., & Tate, W. F. (2009). Toward a critical race theory of education. *The critical pedagogy reader* (pp. 167–182). New York: Routledge.

Lareau, A. (2003). *Unequal childhoods: Class, race, and family life.* Berkeley, CA: University of California Press.

Lewis, A., Diamond, J., & Forman, T. (2015). Conundrums of integration: Desegregation in the context of racialized hierarchy. *Sociology of Race and Ethnicity, 1*(1), 22–36.

Lewis-McCoy, R. L. (2014). *Inequality in the promised land: Race, resources, and suburban schooling.* Stanford, CA: Stanford University Press.

Mantie, R., & Talbot, B. C. (2015). How can we change our habits if we don't talk about them? *Action, Criticism & Theory for Music Education, 14*(1), 128–153.

Palmer, C. M. (2011). Challenges of access to post-secondary music education programs for people of color. *Visions of Research in Music Education, volume 18.* Retrieved from http://users.rider.edu/~vrme/.

Ronald E. McNair Postbaccalaureate Achievement Program. (2016, March 25). Retrieved from http://ed.gov/programs/triomcnair/index.html.

Talbot, B. C. & Mantie, R. (2015). Vision and the legitimate order: Theorizing today to imagine tomorrow. In S. Conkling (Ed.), *Envisioning music teacher education* (pp. 155–180). Lanham, MD: Rowman and Littlefield.

4

NEGOTIATING COMMUNITIES OF PRACTICE IN MUSIC EDUCATION: DOROTHY'S NARRATIVE

Karin S. Hendricks & Dorothy[1]

> Our communities of practice ... become resources for organizing our learning as well as contexts in which to manifest our learning through an identity of participation. What is crucial about this kind of engagement as an educational experience is that identity and learning serve each other.
>
> (Wenger, 1998, p. 271)

Dorothy entered an unfamiliar music teacher preparation program, far from home, already with several strikes against her. A black, low-income, female from an inner-city neighborhood, Dorothy moved to a university in a conservative, rural area devoid of people who looked like she did, with scarcely anyone who shared her musical values or interests. Her aspiration upon leaving her family, friends, and everything she had known was to obtain a music education degree and then return home to create a better world for herself and others in her community. In reality, however, she came to understand that much of the music education world was impenetrable to her because of where she came from and who she was.

As Dorothy moved from secondary school to university coursework and student teaching, she encountered boundaries of many kinds. In addition to crossing geographical boundaries, Dorothy also ran up against educational boundaries as she strove as a first-generation college student and nontraditional instrumentalist to obtain a degree and certification in music education. The difficulties she faced were further exacerbated by social boundaries, as she dealt unremittingly with inequities due to her race and socioeconomic status. This narrative describes Dorothy's often-frustrated attempts to cross boundaries from one world to another, yet also illustrates her remarkably unfailing resilience and optimism that she might be able to "escape the cycle of things" and make a better world for those whom she would teach.

Boundary Crossing

The marking of material and symbolic boundaries is a natural part of human experience. Whether establishing our own territorial domain or striving to gain entrance into an existent social space, our awareness of how we are situated within, between, or outside of marginal lines helps us to understand our place in the world.

Boundary crossing has taken on multiple meanings in scholarly literature. One is in reference to learning, as one progresses in expertise to become a fully participating member of a particular knowledge community (Akkerman & Bakker, 2011; Andersson & Andersson, 2008; Lave & Wenger, 1991; Wenger, 1998). The concept of boundary crossing has also been used to describe the breaking of barriers that restrict access to social privilege and power (Edwards & Fowler, 2007; Lamont & Molnár, 2002).

In their discussion of learning and knowledge attainment, Lave and Wenger (1991) utilized the idea of bounded social spaces (viz., "communities of practice") to challenge the traditional notion of master-apprentice pedagogy. According to their concept of legitimate peripheral participation, development and change take place as we interact and negotiate within and between social worlds. Learning occurs as a community "newcomer" observes, then participates, and eventually absorbs (and becomes absorbed in) a community's activities, shared resources, and discourse. This process of negotiated entry has the potential to change both individuals as well as the communities they join.

Boundary Objects

Boundary crossing occurs through the exercise of *boundary objects*, or artifacts (either abstract or concrete) that exist within multiple social spaces and serve to translate meanings between social worlds (Star, 2010; Star & Griesemer, 1989; Wenger, 1998). A boundary object's efficacy for translation is realized by nature of its rigid individual identity, juxtaposed with its ability to adapt to different viewpoints or interpretations. According to Wenger (1998), boundary objects can provide a point of reference based on prior meaning within a group, while also serving as a potential resource for the negotiation of new meaning between social worlds:

> This is true of linguistic and nonlinguistic elements, of words as well as chairs, ways of walking, claim forms, or laughter . . . All have well-established interpretations, which can be reutilized to new effects, whether these new effects simply continue an established trajectory of interpretation or take it in unexpected directions.

Examples of boundary objects in music teacher education might include a portfolio that travels with a student through the course of their preparation and is used in job applications, or a musical instrument that a student performs to gain entrance into the program and later uses to teach other students. Envisioning boundary objects as a tool for negotiation between divergent communities of practice, Star and Griesemer (1989) described how boundary objects, in contrast to people, can exist comfortably within multiple and diverse social spaces:

> For people, managing multiple memberships can be volatile, elusive, or confusing; navigating in more than one world is a non-trivial mapping exercise. People resolve problems of marginality in a variety of ways: by passing on one side or another, denying one side, oscillating between worlds, or by forming a new social world composed of others like themselves. However, management of these . . . objects—including construction of them—is conducted . . . only when their work coincides.
>
> The objects thus come to form a common boundary between worlds by inhabiting them both simultaneously. (p. 412)

By virtue of their existence in multiple worlds (even housing varied interpretations and meanings within those worlds), boundary objects can, then, provide boundary crossers with a frame of reference, a point of negotiation, and/or a potential means of legitimization as they step from one social world into another. Boundary objects may simply allow newcomers access into certain social spaces or facilitate increased levels of participation, but may also—depending on the interactions and power dynamics that take place between the newcomer and the community—lead to shifts in understanding and meaning-making for both individual and community.

Boundary Crossing in Teacher Education

Teacher education scholars have used the concept of boundary crossing to better understand the transitions experienced by pre-service and novice educators. For example, Andersson and Andersson (2008) surveyed and interviewed newly qualified teachers in Sweden to inquire about conditions for boundary crossing among who were transitioning from their teacher education program into their first year of teaching. Their findings challenged theory-driven teacher education courses with a minimal practical component, and highlighted the need for interactions and collaborations with more experienced mentor teachers.

Citing Lave and Wenger (1991) and Vygotsky (1978), Andersson and Andersson (2008) emphasized the importance of preparing "teachers for the boundary crossing by enabling them to gain experience from dialogues with more competent others like mentors related to classroom work, lecturers within the academy, and also with fellow students during their education" (p. 650). Although the authors posited that this dialogic enabling would require adequate preparation for pre-service teachers in learning how to navigate social spaces and conversational settings, their discussion does not address the compounded difficulties that pre-service teachers from a differing race or socioeconomic status might face in gaining the social awareness necessary to engage in this social space.

Issues of Access and Marginalization

Fundamental to one's ability to learn and develop within a community of practice is the granting of legitimacy from the group (Lave & Wenger, 1991; Wenger, 1998). This legitimacy might be attained in various ways (e.g., having a sponsor, being perceived as useful, speaking the community's language, etc.). As Wenger (1998) explained, "only with enough legitimacy can all their inevitable stumblings and violations become opportunities for learning rather than cause for dismissal, neglect, or exclusion" (p. 101). In a community of practice where individuals are welcomed and easily incorporated into the community, newcomers eventually become practice-perpetuating "old-timers" as they gain full participation and as the community itself transforms through developmental cycles of negotiation.

Other scholarly discussions of boundary crossing have highlighted human diversity in order to bring awareness to and/or deconstruct the social margins through which some individuals must cross to gain access to power and/or privilege that are enjoyed by those more situated in an established social center (Edwards & Fowler, 2007; Lamont & Molnár, 2002). Intersections of social class, boundary crossing, and learning were discussed by Gallacher, Crossan, Field, and Merrill (2002), who addressed the need for working-class adults at risk of social exclusion to reconstruct identities to support their engagement in further learning (FE) colleges in Scotland. These authors emphasized the importance of viewing learning identities as "fluid or even fragile, rather than fixed and unidirectional" (p. 493).

Unsurprisingly, however, access and support for full participation in social circles cannot be assumed for newcomers. The periphery is a nebulous space of movement and flux and, depending on power relations, peripherality can either be empowering or disempowering. Lave and Wenger (1991) raise concern about potential restrictions that may be placed on newcomers in some communities of practice:

> For newcomers, their shifting location as they move centripetally through a complex form of practice creates possibilities for understanding the world as experienced. Denying access and limiting the centripetal movement of newcomers and other practitioners changes the learning curriculum. This raises questions—in specific settings, we hope—about what opportunities exist for knowing in practice: about the process of transparency for newcomers. (pp. 122–123)

The difficulty, then, comes when a community of practice holds to rigid, inflexible boundaries and does not readily honor the legitimacy of newcomers' skills and ideas and the boundary objects they bring with them. This often appears to be the case in music education, particularly in director-led or teacher-centered music learning settings at various levels of instruction that favor tradition, uniformity, and efficiency over creativity and/or student autonomy. As Carlisle (2009) has argued in the case of secondary school music, programs that are set up for what she refers to as factory-level efficiency do not fully honor the cognitive, social, and emotional needs of students, and posits that "these institutions must [change to] become a function of the children they serve" (p. 141).

Similar to the negotiations that take place within a community of practice, Carlisle suggests that socially just practices in music education require flexibility from teachers who are responsive to the interests and needs of students and make music learning relevant to them, thereby also preparing them to interact in future social circles:

> The phenomena and experience [teachers] cultivate also is dependent upon how well [they] enable students to interact with, develop, and determine their present and future relationship with the world outside of school. When we create the conditions for social justice within interdependent contexts in learning institutions, we are preparing our children and adolescents for resilience and responsibility in a challenging and interdependent world. (p. 142)

As stated previously, growth and learning take place in a community of practice when newcomers are granted legitimacy. Because music teacher education programs are the catalyst for change in the next generation of music classrooms, we argue that flexible practices and legitimization of newcomers' skills must start here.

Lave and Wenger (1991) remind those who observe learning through a lens of communities of practice that any "ambiguity inherent in peripheral participation must . . . be connected to issues of legitimacy, of the social organization of and control over resources" (p. 37). The focus of this paper is upon such issues of legitimacy and organizational control, as experienced by Dorothy, an undergraduate pre-service teacher within a music teacher education program.

In Karin's Voice: Narrative Approach

I contacted Dorothy within two weeks after her graduation from college, inviting her to participate in a study in which she could share stories of marginalization and differential treatment that she experienced while working toward her undergraduate degree in music education. Over the course of the next four months, she and I exchanged multiple emails discussing the project's purpose and intended audience. We also engaged in a 90-minute, recorded phone conversation to discuss general frustrations that she had experienced as a black, female, low-income student whose primary musical instrument was the harp—a musical instrument that, as her story shows, was on the periphery of legitimacy in the music education program at this institution.

As we interacted, Dorothy and I engaged together in reflexive practice regarding the content, conceptual framework, and method for this study, and eventually came to recognize two things. First, Dorothy's learning experiences reflected the experiences of social boundary crossing and boundary objects as described above; therefore, these theoretical concepts could provide a lens through which to frame the project. Second, we decided that Dorothy's story should exist in a narrative form: Our intent was to give place for Dorothy's words to speak for themselves, allowing her to communicate directly with music teacher educators who might have opportunity to reconsider the power dynamics that charge their own interactions.

My part, then, became to recognize and even capitalize upon my vantage point as a privileged white, suburban, middle-class, music teacher educator. While Dorothy's narrative would illustrate and explain her experiences, I would frame the narrative to help our intended music teacher educator audience (with individuals who typically look more like me than they look like Dorothy) conceptualize the discrimination she experienced. I would do this by noting and highlighting those points of her story that caused me to experience stirrings of anger, shock, and empathic or projected regret as I read them. We hoped thereby to enhance the catalytic validity (Lather, 2003; Reason & Rowan, 1981) of our joint venture, first by providing Dorothy a place to honor and reframe her experiences in a way that could empower her voice, and second by highlighting my own "a ha" experiences as I read Dorothy's words.

After three months of email exchanges and the completion of our recorded phone conversation, I emailed Dorothy a brief description of boundary crossing and boundary objects, and asked her to write a narrative based on these themes. She also gave me access and permission to study artifacts she had from her 4 years of schooling and semester of student teaching (e.g., journals and lesson plans). Dorothy chose to keep her identity confidential, selecting a pseudonym to honor Dorothy Ashby, a black, female, jazz harpist. Upon receipt of her narrative, I edited it to clarify minor points and to remove identifying information, while also adding a few poignant issues from the artifacts and from comments she had made during our audio-recorded conversation. Finally, I sent the narrative to a black teacher-educator colleague to gain further insights regarding how to high-light these markers of marginalization. Dorothy read the final document, offering further suggestions and ideas and clarifying her meaning and intent.

I wrote the final section of the narrative in order to highlight three boundary objects (i.e., harp, books, and repertoire) that I noted from her narrative as having an ironic twist, particularly regarding how what they promised to offer Dorothy in terms of gaining legitimacy in a new community of practice did, in fact, create the opposite effect. This narrative highlights Dorothy's struggles and accomplishments as she navigated each boundary.

In Dorothy's Voice: A Story of Boundary Crossing

I had always dreamed about going to college. From a young age, I'd made up in my mind that it was something I was going to do. I didn't need the probing of parents, siblings, teachers, or other family members to convince me it was beneficial; neither did I receive it. It's not that they discouraged me from going to college; it was just never presented to me as an advantageous option for me given my parents' ability to get by without it (my father never graduated from high school and my mother only made it to her junior year of college—she dropped out when she married my father).

Consequently, that's the kind of life we lived. We did just enough to get by. My siblings and I attended public schools that had little funding, "learning" from teachers that didn't teach. As long as we didn't fail any classes, we were okay in our parents' eyes. I don't believe that my parents were negligent because they allowed us to do what it takes to simply survive; I believe they are victims to what they have always known and seen. It's a cycle that I believe goes through impoverished, black communities.

My neighborhood consisted of only black families and we all knew each other. Most of the children attended poor black neighborhood schools but my family was fortunate enough to be bused to schools on the south side of the city. Southern city schools are economically better because more white (most likely educated) people live in the area and are required by law to pay taxes that then contribute to the neighborhood schools. Southern schools are visually indicated as being beyond the Boulevard. The Boulevard is the street that separates the blacks from the whites in the city, although there are no segregation laws in existence.

One side of the Boulevard has upscale mansions and ritzy shopping venues; the other side has abandoned buildings, numerous fried chicken food chains, and an abundance of black people. I am from the latter of the two sides. I was born and raised in an all-black neighborhood [north of the city]. I grew up around gangs, drugs, violence, and prostitutes, and watched many people I know become victims of it all. My parents grew up around these influences as well but they always lived an honest life before us even if that meant simply working at a dry cleaner to provide for us. My parents couldn't afford for us to live in a better place, but they sheltered us for the most part by making us come in early and monitoring who we talked to.

The Road to College

In high school, there came a point in time where going to college had to become more than a dream for me. At that point, I began reading pamphlets and magazines about getting into college. I joined afterschool programs to build my resume and went to college preparation classes on Saturdays and in the summer. My parents supported me through all of this but never made me do any of it.

The only thing my mom made me do was continue to play the harp. The harp was something I stumbled upon in middle school. For my first 2 years of playing the harp, I loved it but once it was time to go to high school, where more practicing was involved and less of my friends were interested in staying in the class with me, I wanted to quit. Unfortunately, my mom made me audition as a harp major at the high school and I was accepted. On my first day of harp class, I was surprised to find that the harp class and the strings class were combined. I was even more shocked that my harp teacher wasn't there. After a week of having no harp teacher, the strings teacher told me I could learn one of the other stringed instruments; I ended up playing the viola.

Learning the viola was something I realized I couldn't stay with because the strings teacher decided he would rather be in his office on Facebook than teach. My sophomore year of high school, I was forced back into harp because no other arts classes that I liked were available. I hated playing the harp so I tried to quit again. The same exact scheduling problem happened to me my junior year and I was stuck back in harp class, but this year harp became fun again. I enjoyed practicing and was invited to join a summer music program. While playing at different venues through the summer program, I was told that playing the harp would get me a lot of scholarships because I was black and good at it. I really took that to heart and started taking the harp seriously. I hoped that playing harp would be my way into college for free.

In my academic classes, I was always one of the brightest students because I enjoyed reading and I played music. Where students in my class had trouble simply paying attention, I sat unchallenged and unprepared for the reality of college academics. I had never written a paper in high school; it was never required. We read abridged versions of novels out of a textbook and answered the corresponding questions. The only reason I believe I was able to write my personal statement for college, let alone any paper in college, was because I read so much on my own and I knew how good prose sounded.

I also attended an excellent summer program that helped me learn how to write at a higher level. Since math instruction in high school was subpar at best, I failed math twice and withdrew from it once while I was in college. I finally passed on my fourth time taking the class. I also failed a political science class while in college simply because I didn't have the resources to get a book. When taking the music theory placement test for becoming a music education major, I did not pass until the third time taking the test. Ironically, I went to a visual and performing arts high school. The combination of all of these failed attempts in college depicts the kind of education I received up until college. I had never failed a class in high school, but I was never prepared for the challenge of college.

Studies in Music Education

I was accepted into the music education program only after three attempts to pass the theory placement exam, and then I faced many more challenges. I was the only black person in my class and one of the few in the music education program. Up until that point, I had only attended mainly poor black schools. As a result, my experiences were a lot different than many of my colleagues and professors. Likewise, my goals as a music educator were different. The majority of my peers longed to teach at well-off schools similar to the ones they went to or even better. I wanted to take the knowledge I learned and take it back to the school system I went to. The same school district didn't have booster parents and relied on government funding for everything, but still lacked up-to-date instruments and music books. The same school district where good teaching was rarely modeled to the students, because discipline was the most important subject in each class and academic studies were forfeited.

My high school, in particular, focused on the arts but only had one jazz band, a string orchestra, a piano class, a guitar class, a percussion class, a couple of harp students, and choir. Many of the schools that my colleagues attended had a concert band, jazz band, track band, marching band, orchestra, and string orchestra as part of their general education electives. I think the most detrimental attribute of my arts education is that, coming to college from a performing arts high school, I could barely read music and had no music theory training, and that was the reason I failed my placement test so many times. My professors and peers could never relate to that because they had been drum major in their marching band from sophomore year, could afford to take private lessons from a young age, took AP music theory, or had that one teacher that inspired them so much that they had to become a music teacher. None of these things applied to me.

Furthermore, I was the only harpist in the music education program, making me more distanced from my peers and professors. Even my experiences as a musician were different than my peers. They were all used to learning music in a large ensemble setting. Most of them had great band directors in high school that they saw at least three times a week. In high school, I was one of the four harpists in the school and because of lack of enrollment in harp, our teacher only came once a week to give semi-private lessons. Before college, I had only played in a large ensemble once in my life. I never knew what it was like to stand in front of or be a part of a music ensemble with 30 or more students.

Also, all of my university methods classes were catered to more mainstream instruments, meaning I was always learning a new instrument where none of the technical skills I knew from the harp applied. At the time, I understood that the likelihood of having a harp program in a public school is very small; therefore, the need for a harp methods course is unnecessary. However, when I didn't automatically relate to the common band and orchestra issues, I felt like less of a musician. I believe my professors thought they were treating me as a hot commodity because I played the harp, but I never felt that way. I felt excluded.

My professors never used my strengths at the harp to help me create my own path or validate me as musician. I find it ironic that the very professors who teach inclusion excluded me because I didn't play a common instrument.

When doing peer teachings, I always had to play a secondary instrument (an instrument that I was learning at the time) because none of my professors even considered the harp as a valid option. I remember, for one peer-teaching project in particular, we were required to bring our instruments (primary instruments for those who played brass or woodwinds, secondary for percussionists and harpists). At the time, I was learning bassoon and could muster up a two-octave scale. My tone was absolutely horrible and I got many looks from my peers and professor because I was messing up the tone quality and balance of the ensemble. For the next peer-teaching assignment, I was placed in the percussion section by my professor to play the bass drum. I believe that as a class we were all taught something that day: If a student doesn't easily conform to personal goals of the director, put them in the percussion section. We often see that done to the "bad kids" in the ensemble, but I never thought it would be me.

I suppose being a music education major would have been easier if I had the dreams of my colleagues and desired to teach in a better school district than the one I was educated in. However, it was never something I considered. Therefore, if I felt the educational practices that were taught to me by my professors would not work for the students I hope to teach, I deemed it irrelevant. I would think, that's all fine and dandy for the students I teach here, but that wouldn't work for the students I will teach at home. They would never sing those songs. Or, how can I make this music relate to their everyday lives where the students are listening for hope from rappers, some of the only black successful people they see, but don't experience success in music class because they can't relate to Jimmy Crack Corn or Sousa's "Nobles of the Mystic Shrine?" Teaching these things would make me irrelevant to my students.

I came to realize that comprehensive musicianship is great for justifying music's academic value, but if music has no aesthetic value for my students, then it is useless. Imagine if the only reason we listened to music is for the purpose of . . . playing music. Why do we play music at all, just to know how to do it? Every skill should have a practical value. It would be like learning math but never using it in real life. Therefore, as we teach music to our students, it should be relevant to their lives.

Student Teaching

As mentioned before, teaching a large ensemble for me was difficult because I had not had much experience being in one, nor was teaching a large ensemble modeled for me before college. As a result, student teaching was very challenging. I often felt like the students were teaching me more than I was teaching them. My main concern in student teaching was the fact that I didn't play the different instruments fluently. This meant that I could not fix technical problems that the students were having. Because of this, I felt like an incompetent teacher.

My cooperating teacher was very understanding of my concerns. She helped me to focus on what I could do instead of what I couldn't do. She introduced me to an orchestra director who also didn't play the typical stringed instruments. One of the most pivotal things she did was affirm me as a musician. She invited me to bring a harp to give a presentation to the students and even play with the high school students. When she did that, she made me realize that I was a good musician and being a harpist does have a purpose in music education. If I wasn't a harpist, I wouldn't be a musician and if I wasn't a musician, I wouldn't be able to become a good music teacher.

Coming Back Home

Coming back home to the City, I was able to witness the state of the students in my neighborhood. It is similar to when I was growing up; however, the children that I grew up with are now the parents. The same people who became prostitutes, drug dealers, addicts, and convicts all now have children and they are worse off than their parents. Because of the parents' lack of education/care, the students are thrown into the world of school where their home lives are completely different than the lives they live at school with no support. In school, they are made to speak with proper English, worry about current events, and play the music of dead white guys. The parents can offer little to no help.

In the midst of it all, I still stand by with the hope that carried me all the way from the slums of the City, to the University, through student teaching, and now back to the City. It is that same hope that convinced me I was able to escape the cycle of things that I have always known and get accepted into college, a foreign world to me and my family. This hope also enabled to persevere though obstacles that I was never prepared for due to poor education. This hope also allowed me to see the bigger picture when I was presented ideals that typically don't exist for children that come from similar backgrounds as me. Finally, hope is what I have for the students that I teach, a hope that I will be able to reach students on a personal level and make music meaningful in their everyday lives.

In Karin's Voice: Boundary Objects

In this final section, I provide a synthesis of Dorothy's narrative and supplement with information from artifacts and our phone conversation, giving particular attention to three boundary objects (i.e., harp, books, and repertoire) that Dorothy carried with her through each stage of boundary crossing. I also discuss how these objects served their expected function in helping her gain legitimacy in a new community of practice, as well as how they failed to do so due to social factors outside of Dorothy's control.

Harp

Dorothy loved playing the harp in middle school, but in the course of her transition to high school she lost interest. Here she attempted the viola but had a teacher who failed her by not providing the education she might have needed for success. This brought her back to the harp, with promise of scholarships because she was told she was "black and good at it" (in other words, this combination was an anomaly)—and Dorothy hoped to get her college tuition paid for through her harp skills. As it turned out, she did not receive any scholarships in music, and was accepted only after two failed attempts taking the theory placement exam.

Rather than being a means to gain legitimacy in this new community of practice, having the harp as Dorothy's primary instrument became one of her greatest sources of difficulty as she navigated the music education program. Dorothy strove to catch up with the rest of the class on secondary instruments in her methods classes, experiencing public embarrassment in front of her peers (accompanied by "looks" from the professor). Most poignant to me, however, was that what she hoped to be her free ticket to college was not considered compatible for any student teaching placements in the area, and, unlike the majority of her peers, Dorothy was required to pay out of her own pocket for extra private lessons on the violin so that she could be considered qualified for a placement.

Perhaps Dorothy could have found a student teaching placement in which she could capitalize upon her harp skills? Not in this area. Dorothy could not afford a car, so she couldn't go far. "You have to have a car if you want to student teach! You just have to have a car!" she was told. There was no public transportation in the area, so she was told that the only option she had was to drop out of school and work until she could afford a vehicle, or to pay for violin lessons and student teach in strings classes at a nearby school.

Consequently, Dorothy paid for private lessons (fortunately with an expert teacher this time) by working while in school. She prepared herself on the violin as best as she could for student teaching, quickly gaining a level of expertise that kept her just ahead of her elementary students. The harp again found a place of legitimacy in this new community of practice, however, when her compassionate and empowering cooperating teacher invited her to bring her harp and play for the children so that they could witness Dorothy's musicianship.

Books

If Dorothy was never required to write a paper in high school, how did she manage to write acceptable entrance essays for college? According to Dorothy, the books she read on her own taught her "how good prose sounded." Her subpar high school education did not prepare her for her general academic courses at the University, however, and she failed her political science class because she was not able to afford the text. Dorothy explained to me that, as a first-generation college student, no one told her about financial aid that might help her afford books. As a result, she failed courses, and was therefore required to stay longer in college (with all related expenses, of course) to complete the program.

Books might have served as a critical boundary object for Dorothy as she transitioned from her home community to college and beyond. Her intrinsic passion for reading might have provided a frame of reference, a way for her to learn and practice the discourse of a new community. Through her love of reading, she might have continued to learn and even thrive at the university level. Ironically, however, her inability to afford university books—coupled with a lack of knowledge about the resources that might have proffered her the texts she needed—led to repeated failure.

Repertoire

Dorothy's love of music was never in question, nor was her general love of learning. She learned music by ear in her home community, similarly to how she learned to write essays by learning what prose should "sound like." She embodied music and utilized it fluently: Her student teaching lesson plans demonstrated that she sat at the piano at the beginning and ending of each class she taught; at the beginning to help tune string instruments, and at the end to play a song that indicated to the students their dismissal from class. Music was a medium that Dorothy utilized to signal transitions for her students as they moved from one classroom—one community of practice—to another. In this particular instance, we finally witness Dorothy having access to social power, acting as a gatekeeper for other children by granting them permission to leave her classroom. Notably, in this unique and isolated exercise of authority, Dorothy relied upon music rather than her own voice to enact the rites of transition.

If not Dorothy's musicality, what does come into question here is the relevance of the musical repertoire that she encountered in her own attempts to cross boundaries. The youth in Dorothy's home community listened to hip-hop. According to Dorothy, they were inspired by rappers, "some of the only black successful people they see." Yet Dorothy gained entrance to the university through the harp, an instrument traditionally associated with European classical music. She realized, as she sat in ensembles and methods courses at the university, that the classical and folk music she was learning had no relation to her life or that of her future students . . . or so she had come to believe. Apparently she hadn't been taught that "Jimmy Crack Corn" tells the story of a black slave, and that it became popular through its performance in blackface minstrel shows. Apparently missing from a discussion of this repertoire—repertoire that she (and her white peers, I am sure) deemed irrelevant to their future students' lives— was a lesson in the history of black oppression. Dorothy was attending a university in an area of the country in which some of the last black lynchings took place, and at a time when police shootings of black youth were epidemic in the country. While her home community was surely up close and personal with the

#BlackLivesMatter movement, she was sitting in classes in a different community, as the only African-American student, learning teaching delivery methods using whitewashed repertoire. I have to wonder if anyone even bothered to mention this irony to her or to her peers. Perhaps her instructors chose simply not to talk about it, because—from their place of privilege—they had the luxury of forgetting.

Conclusion

As I complete this project, I am left with a range of emotions: rage, compassion, puzzlement, and inspiration. It also leaves me with a set of questions regarding why and how this all came to be, and how things might have been different for Dorothy. I also wonder how she might now move forward in her future life, so devoted to making things better for her home community, and I marvel at the possibilities for change that she might now evoke as a result of her experiences and personal insights. As I re-read this narrative in the future—alone and with my teacher-educator colleagues—I hope to continually revisit these issues and consider how those of us who prepare future music teachers might act differently. As Dorothy expressed at the close of her narrative, she has apparently not lost hope for a better future, and she has continually abided by that hope to keep her resilient in every instance of boundary crossing. Dorothy and I share a further hope that, as music teachers and music teacher educators interact with their students, they might be open to taking risks and finding ways to make music learning more relevant to their students, even when it requires them to move more fluidly in peripheral spaces as well.

Discussion Questions

1. In what ways have you personally struggled to gain legitimacy as a member of your current music education community of practice?
2. In what ways have you witnessed issues of race acting as a barrier to legitimacy in any musical community of practice?
3. In what ways have you witnessed issues of class acting as a barrier to legitimacy in any musical community of practice?
4. How does access to information and resources affect a marginalized individual's opportunity to gain legitimacy in any community of practice?
5. When discussing issues of marginalization and oppression, white music educators may feel a mix of emotions as they come to terms with the injustices that a white-dominated society has imposed upon non-white individuals. While honoring those emotions as an important step forward in awareness, what then can be done to effect real change?
6. Considering that students are each members of multiple communities of practice both inside and outside of school, in what ways can music teachers

and music teacher educators foster learning environments that are relevant to their students' lives?

7. How might the identity and practices of current US music education programs transform if previously unaccepted music and skills were welcomed into standard university music education programs?

Note

1 Dorothy has requested that her name and identity remain confidential.

References

Akkerman, S. F., & Bakker, A. (2011). Boundary crossing and boundary objects. *Review of Educational Research, 81*(2), 132–169.

Andersson, I., & Andersson, S. B. (2008). Conditions for boundary crossing: Social practices of newly qualified Swedish teachers. *Scandinavian Journal of Educational Research, 52,* 643–660.

Carlisle, K. (2009). Making school music relevant: Meeting adolescents' need for social justice within a complex and interdependent world. In E. Gould, J. Countryman, C. Morton, & L. Stewart Rose (Eds.), *Exploring social justice: How music education might matter* (pp. 139–151). Toronto, ON, Canada: Canadian Music Educators' Association.

Edwards, R., & Fowler, Z. (2007). Unsettling boundaries in making a space for research. *British Educational Research Journal, 33,* 107–123.

Gallacher, J., Crossan, B., Field, J., & Merrill, B. (2002). Learning careers and the social space: Exploring the fragile identities of adult returners in the new further education. *International Journal of Lifelong Education, 21*(6), 493–509.

Lamont, M., & Molnár, V. (2002). The study of boundaries in the social sciences. *Annual Review of Sociology, 28,* 167–195.

Lather, P. (2003). Issues of validity in openly ideological research: Between a rock and a soft place. In Y. S. Lincoln & N. K. Denzin (Eds.), *Turning points in qualitative research: Tying knots in a handkerchief* (pp. 185–215). Walnut Creek, CA: Alta Mira Press.

Lave, J., & Wenger, E. (1991). *Situated learning: Legitimate peripheral participation.* Cambridge, UK: Cambridge University Press.

Reason, P., & Rowan, J. (1981). Issues of validity in new paradigm research. In P. Reason & J. Rowan (Eds.), *Human inquiry: A sourcebook of new paradigm research* (pp. 239–262). New York: John Wiley.

Star, S. L. (2010). This is not a boundary object: Reflections on the origin of a concept. *Science, Technology, & Human Values, 35,* 601–617.

Star, S. L., & Griesemer, J. R. (1989). Institutional ecology, "translations" and boundary objects: Amateurs and professionals in Berkeley's Museum of Vertebrate Zoology, 1907–39. *Social Studies of Science, 19,* 387–420.

Vygotsky, L. S. (1978). *Mind in society: The development of higher psychological processes.* Cambridge, MA: Harvard University Press.

Wenger, E. (1998). *Communities of practice: Learning, meaning, and identity.* Cambridge, UK: Cambridge University Press.

5

CULTURAL STRADDLING

The Double Life of a Mariachi Music Education Major

Carlos Castañeda Lechuga & Margaret Schmidt

> Race, class, culture, and identity: We can almost guarantee that these four social factors play a role in the academic well-being of all students—complexly so.
>
> (Carter, 2006, p. 304)

Marg's Introduction

The School of Music at ASU has had a mariachi ensemble for more than 25 years, which regularly includes a mix of university students and community members. When the leader of the group, a member of the musicology faculty, retired 4 years ago, a new director was hired. Jeff Nevin had earned a master's degree in music theory from ASU, a Ph.D. in music theory from the University of California-San Diego, and was currently teaching at Southwestern Community College in San Diego. He was also a well-known mariachi trumpeter and teacher. Jeff contacted me (Marg) soon after he was hired, to say that he was planning to bring some of his students from Southwestern to audition at ASU in February and invited me to their auditions. Jeff's goal was to have these students earn teacher certification, so they could return to California and teach mariachi in the schools there. Because of my own audition-day commitments, I only got to hear one of the auditions, that of a tenor who performed a Puccini aria followed by a mariachi tune, accompanied by about seven other students from the Southwestern College mariachi. Both pieces were beautifully sung, and the voice faculty and I were blown away by the heart with which all the mariachis performed.

Carlos was not with them that day. However, the following fall, Carlos transferred to ASU. He came to see me to get help choosing his classes. I learned that he was a trumpet major, had received a scholarship to attend the School of Music, and wanted to get his teaching certificate. I knew we didn't offer a mariachi teaching methods class, so I questioned Carlos about his goals. As a future mariachi educator, he wanted to learn to play violin, so we decided that he would take the string techniques class, as well as our elementary instrumental methods class. I team-taught both classes and was very impressed with Carlos' work ethic—he took all his assignments seriously and made good progress in these fairly traditional methods classes. Toward the end of the semester, Carlos invited me to the ASU Mariachi concert. I went, and was absolutely amazed at the level of musicianship the 40 performers demonstrated: nearly everyone in the ensemble played or sang a solo, and many did both. The mariachi also included community members, ranging in age from 13 to 65, and the concert hall was packed with an extremely enthusiastic audience of friends and family—something that rarely happens for concerts given by the School of Music's major ensembles. Carlos later explained to me that the group was especially large this year, because many in the local mariachi community knew Jeff Nevin's reputation and wanted to learn from him. The next semester, I joined the mariachi myself, and began to learn about the double musical life of Carlos and his friends. I found the story fascinating, and invited Carlos to work with me to write this narrative case study. We met for three formal interviews, many informal discussions, and six working sessions, and collaborated on several revisions of this chapter. In this study, we explore Carlos' experiences in "straddling" the cultures of a traditional music teacher preparation program and his "double life" as a passionate mariachi educator. We also investigate my challenges in helping Carlos prepare for teaching.

Carlos' Story

I was born in San Bernardino, California, but due to my mother's immigration status and my family's financial struggle, we moved to Cuernavaca, Morelos, Mexico, also known as "The City of the Eternal Spring." There I grew up with many different customs and traditions that I no longer observe today, primarily because my family disengaged from several of them. When in Mexico, I clearly remember that every time my mother cleaned the house she would listen to two famous mariachi singers: Juan Gabriel and Rocio Durcal, so as soon as I would hear their music it was an indirect way for me to know that I needed to begin helping with the chores. As a 10-year-old kid, I didn't want to clean and I connected house cleaning with the timbre of the singers' voices, so I couldn't help but hate listening to them. Sometimes the music was so overwhelming that I would go outside, or use earphones and start listening to the pop music which my friends and I liked. Then at the age of 12, we moved to the city of Tijuana, Mexico, to eventually join my father who was working in California.

When I turned 14 years old, my mom finally got her permanent residency so we moved to San Diego, California. Being new to a completely different city, with new people, and not knowing any English made it very hard for me to adjust. I started school in the second half of eighth grade. There were no other English language learners like me, and this middle school did not have an English Language Development (ELD) program. I would sit in class and watch as my teacher made unusual sounds with his mouth and would write words and letters on the board—I had no clue what they meant. Mr. Garcia, my middle school teacher, knew a little bit of Spanish and would help me every time he could, but it was not enough. At the end of the school year, he met with my parents, and told them that he would allow me to matriculate on to high school because he knew I would be integrated in an ELD program that would help me learn English.

During my first year in high school, I joined band, and chose the clarinet because it was an instrument I had seen before on TV shows and in Mexican bands from Sinaloa. When the band performed at the spring concert, my parents learned the school offered a mariachi program, so they offered me 20 dollars to switch from band to mariachi. Even though I hated the music, 20 dollars felt as if I had won the lottery, so I signed up for mariachi. I told the music teacher that I wanted to learn how to play the guitar or violin, but she said there were no more instruments available, so she told me to try the trumpet. The first few weeks, my life felt miserable because I was not learning the instrument I wanted, I did not like the music, and the trumpet would give me strong headaches. It was too late for me to drop the class, and I had already spent the 20 dollar bribe from my parents.

For our final grade in mariachi, we had to perform. We were required to wear a mariachi suit, commonly called a *traje*. I felt extremely embarrassed and stupid. When the teacher called us to come up on stage, I was so nervous, I started shaking and sweating, and my heart felt as if it wanted to come out of my chest. Our first song was "Los Barandales del Puente." I could not look at the audience, fearing my parents and my brothers would be laughing at me. Luckily for me, it was a shared concert with band and choir, and we only had to play three songs. We finished our third song and went back stage. I immediately changed to my regular clothes and swore I would never go through such a miserable experience ever again. After the concert, for the first time in a long time, my parents hugged me and congratulated me for having done such a great job. My friends' parents also came to me, they were all taking pictures and smiling, and seemed to be having a great time. All of a sudden I started smiling and feeling good about the positive attention I received from my parents and the audience. After receiving such attention, my feelings toward mariachi music changed into an intense excitement and powerful desire to undergo the same experience again. It boosted my self-confidence and encouraged me to keep this same type of positive attention for everything else that I did. As time went by, the more I played mariachi, the more I liked the music—perhaps it also helped me feel closer to my old home in Mexico.

Attending College

Typically, the ELD program takes 4 years to complete, however, I was so dedicated and focused that I managed to finish it in 2. This gave me the opportunity to take all AP and honor courses in my senior year. As I succeeded in the high school environment, I felt extremely comfortable to take the next steps toward attending a four-year college. After graduating high school, I went straight to San Diego State University to fulfill my dream of becoming a doctor. My first semester was difficult. I began to feel unsure of my ability to control the English language. I became frustrated because I felt as if I had taken steps back with the language that I had already learned how to speak, read, and write. I found it took much more work to comprehend college-level material assignments. I would read a chapter two or three times before I could really understand what I was reading about, and writing essays took me twice as long to complete as the average student. I was so frustrated with my ability to cope with school work that I became disillusioned with the career I was pursuing. I decided to drop out and enroll in Southwestern Community College, to try to find a new career path.

Once at Southwestern Community College (SWC), I continued taking general education courses and enrolled in basic music classes. I found out that the college offered four levels of mariachi ensembles. I became interested and decided to audition for Jeff Nevin, director of mariachi ensembles at SWC. At the audition, I played the best and most difficult songs I knew. Dr. Nevin told me I played at a good level, but when he asked me to play minor scales and read a mariachi song by sight, I was not very successful, so he placed me in the intermediate level ensemble. He recommended I enroll in Music Theory I—which felt like an insult at the time—and additional musicianship courses to improve on my music skills. This very disappointing experience, however, had a positive impact on my life. I could not stand failing in mariachi music—I was one of the best players in high school! I took Jeff's challenge and enrolled in music theory and became surprised at how much I did not know about music. I thought that knowing most of your key signatures and major scales was all that you needed to know. It was an eye-opening experience that provoked a strong interest and desire to learn more. As a result, I enrolled in more music courses and eventually moved up to the advanced mariachi ensemble. With that group, I had the opportunity to travel and perform around the world. I also had the honor and pleasure of sharing the stage with the world's top mariachi groups and performing on the most iconic stages of Mexico. I recorded trumpet and voice for the ensemble's second album, and once again found mariachi music granting me great opportunities and experiences in my life.

At the recommendation of some music professors at SWC, I joined other ensembles such as Bossa Nova, Jazz Vocal, and Concert Choir. The choir director invited me to perform with the school's orchestra to play first trumpet for the big world premiere of *Misa Azteca* (*Aztec Mass*). I felt special and appreciated, so I challenged myself to play classical trumpet music with an orchestra for the first time in my life. While practicing with the choir and orchestra together, I became thrilled by the sound of the string instruments and the powerful singing of the tenors and sopranos. When we premiered *Misa Azteca* at the Escondido Center of the Arts in Southern California, Dr. Nevin, also a classical trumpet virtuoso, played second trumpet next to me. Playing classical music with the orchestra next to my mariachi professor was a unique and fulfilling experience.

I became inspired by my music professors of SWC. They all demonstrated great passion and love for music, and they constantly commented on my music talents and encouraged me to pursue a career in music. A friend recommended me for a position teaching music at a community center in Mexico. I took the position and began teaching piano, voice, violin, electric bass, and trumpet, all in the same class. Back then, I had no clue how to teach many of these instruments, so I tried to learn a little bit of each on my own. I went through some rough times trying to teach this class. A year later, I was invited to start a mariachi program at a local community center in San Diego. Because I had already taught a music class in Mexico and gained a little bit of experience, and because I was more familiar with the instruments, I accepted the invitation. The program grew from 4 students to 20 within the first few weeks and I was more successful teaching this class than the one in Mexico. I realized I enjoyed teaching so much, and I became more interested in finding new methods to improve my teaching. I knew I had fun in my music courses, so I decided to take my professor's advice and pursue a career in music education.

After five semesters at Southwestern, I earned four associate degrees, but the two I am extremely proud of are the degrees in music and in mariachi specialization. After graduating from SWC, I transferred to California State University-Northridge (CSUN) as a music education major. I felt comfortable studying there, but I was not doing anything but attending classes, ensembles, lessons, and doing homework. I needed to perform mariachi. I needed to teach mariachi!

That same semester, Dr. Nevin was offered a position to teach the mariachi ensemble and a mariachi history class at ASU. He invited two other SWC students and me to transfer there. After talking to Dr. Jeff, I foresaw many of the advantages that transferring to ASU would bring to my career; ASU was a better school of music, I was going to get a scholarship, and there was a mariachi program. Most importantly, I was going to have lots of performing and teaching opportunities with mariachi. On the negative side, I also became aware that it was going to be three times more expensive than CSUN, and I was going to be farther away from my daughter. It was a tough decision to make but at the last minute, I auditioned. Today, I am glad I chose to transfer to ASU.

During my first semester at ASU, I felt disoriented—different weather, different school climate, huge buildings, and different people—and I struggled with money. I was able to share an apartment with one of my friends from SWC, which made the transition and financial crisis less arduous, but even together and with our scholarships and loans, we struggled to make ends meet. We had almost no furniture or dishes, and we slept on the floor. We didn't know any mariachi musicians in the area, so we could not gig or teach to earn some income. We were also too far away from our families to get help from them. Luckily for me, the mariachi program at ASU gave me the opportunity to meet local mariachi musicians and other people I felt comfortable being around. After the first semester at ASU, I started getting called to gig with different mariachi groups in the area. I also started teaching at Rosie's House, a local nonprofit music academy for children, where I was given the opportunity to start a mariachi program with two mariachi friends. Near the end of the second semester, I adapted one side of the house I was renting and turned it into a music studio where I taught private trumpet and violin lessons during the week and coached two local youth mariachi ensembles on the weekends. These teaching and performing opportunities allowed me to cope with my financial struggles—my friend and I were finally able to buy beds.

The ASU trumpet studio also helped alleviate the stress of my transition and finances. There were many remarkably talented trumpet players who shared their knowledge and recommendations with me whenever I had questions about trumpet. They helped me realize how much I needed to learn and were always supportive and accessible. Through the trumpet studio, I started getting called to perform classical music during Easter and Christmas seasons. I also became more active as a mariachi musician, playing at least four hours every weekend during the year.

Since it was a requirement of my degree, I mostly played classical music in trumpet studio and for my juries, but I wanted to show everyone the style I felt most comfortable performing. During the semester before my recital, the trumpet professor allowed me to perform a mariachi arrangement of Vittorio Monti's classic violin solo, *Czardas*, with a small mariachi ensemble on my jury. When I finished playing, the majority of the brass faculty and TAs clapped—a very uncommon occurrence at the end of a jury. This made me feel very nervous, yet extremely excited and special. It was one of the best experiences I had at ASU.

One of my trumpet teachers at ASU was a doctoral student in trumpet performance from Columbia. I played with him in a Latin Jazz band in the community. He also helped me prepare for my senior recital, where I was given the opportunity to play both classical and mariachi music. The classical pieces showcased the technique and style I had learned during my trumpet lessons at ASU, and the mariachi part showcased the music that I highly embraced. The recital was the best part of my undergraduate years. Although Jeff Nevin no longer led the mariachi ensemble after my first year, he drove from San Diego to be present at my recital. This made me feel appreciated and valued by one of the most influential persons in my career.

Student Teaching

I have always loved teaching, but my planning and teaching have not been very efficient. At ASU, I took courses which helped me better understand brass and string instruments and the methods for teaching them to beginning, intermediate, and advanced instrumentalists. During the summer before student teaching, I took Orff and Kodály Level I workshops. The methods used in these workshops were very different from what I had learned in the lab classes, and this triggered a new interest in teaching general music. Although none of the courses I took were specifically designed for teaching mariachi music, they prepared me with the skills I needed to teach any music class, including classroom management, different approaches to teaching rhythm, key signatures, and many other music concepts. We discussed different classroom scenarios and case studies, and analyzed commonly employed strategies. I began to manipulate everything I learned to use it in teaching mariachi music at my house and at the music academy.

Two semesters before my student teaching, as part of my required internships, I worked a few hours a week with an elementary and middle school orchestra teacher. The last semester for my student teaching, I was placed with two different mentors. Half the time I was assigned to be with Valerie, which made me happy because I had already met her in the ASU mariachi class, and I knew she was a great orchestra teacher from whom I could learn many things. For the other half, I was assigned to work with Susan, an elementary general music teacher at one of Valerie's schools. Compared to the internships, student teaching required being at school every day and staying until the end of the teachers' work schedule. It was very demanding not only because of the time commitment, but also because the class dynamics in general music and orchestra were very different. Seeing the kids every day and trying to memorize hundreds of names was an intense experience. Trying to become a good general music and orchestra teacher presented one of my biggest academic challenges due to the limited experiences I had with each.

Both teachers had very high expectations and were very demanding. The most difficult task for me was writing lesson plans for all the classes. The first few weeks, because I was a little more familiar teaching strings, I assumed I did not have to do so much planning as with general music. However, when it was time to present my lessons, I realized how much more planning I needed to do to teach an orchestra class. General music was much more challenging for me. I had not yet developed and experienced falsetto singing to teach songs to the elementary students. Teaching games to kindergarteners and first graders required plenty of structure, scaffolding, and a great amount of patience and energy. By the fourth week of my student teaching, Susan expected me to teach five different lessons each day, from the kindergarten to the fourth grade. It would take me about one and a half hours to write each grade level's lesson plan, and I was also required to memorize all the songs, games, and activities I planned for each lesson. Sleep was not an option until I finished my lesson plans and sent them to Susan; otherwise, I would be in trouble with her, and would be struggling to teach the students. Some days I would just sleep for two or three hours. Toward the end of the first half of the semester, the work load, stress, and lack of sleep started to affect my mood. Valerie was very mindful and extremely helpful because she allowed me to prepare for general music during my assigned time with her, and since she had taught general music before, she shared the strategies she used to memorize songs and games quicker, and gave me several suggestions to improve my general music teaching.

Student teaching was very exhausting, but I improved steadily. After reflecting and dissecting everything I went through, I came to the conclusion that a big part of my frustration and struggle with planning was due to my inability to conceptualize my lessons. In the beginning, I could not imagine how the kids would respond when learning a new song or activity, so it took me a long time to write my lessons. Toward the end, I was able to plan faster and more efficiently. I learned how to present the content in front of the kids, and how to keep the flow and momentum of my lesson based on the students' engagement and response. I learned, applied, and retained many classroom management skills and teaching tools that have been very useful in my current teaching, especially for the younger grades. Even so, undergoing all these experiences in my student teaching incited me to apply to graduate school to refine everything I had learned.

After Graduation

After graduating, I looked for a position where I could teach the music I have always wanted to teach and where I thought I would definitely perform the best, so I looked for a school or a district where I could teach mariachi, but there weren't any available in Arizona. I applied to three school districts and, although I wanted a full-time job, I ended up accepting the first job I was offered, teaching general music to children from kindergarten to fifth grade two days per week. Although I won't ever know for sure, I think that speaking Spanish, being Mexican-American, and knowing mariachi helped me get this particular job. The principal seemed to be interested in having a teacher with a different background and different skills than the typical general music teacher. In the summer following graduation, I attended the Kodály Level II workshop to learn and practice a little more before starting to teach general music at my new job, and it definitely helped me and introduced to me additional techniques to teach young children.

The part-time teaching job allowed plenty of time for my mariachi teaching and my graduate study. I enjoyed that year teaching general music; however, it did not fulfill me as much as my mariachi teaching at the music academy or at my house. Mariachi has always been my main focus and the setting where I feel most comfortable teaching. For the following year, the district added more music teaching positions, so I applied for a half-time position as a middle school orchestra teacher. The position became more attractive after I had the interview with the school's principal; she expressed to me that she loved mariachi music and was open to starting a mariachi program in the future. I received a great recommendation from my elementary principal and, the next day, I received the offer and gladly accepted the position. The school is the district's magnet school for the arts and it is where I currently teach the sixth-, seventh-, and eighth-grade orchestras. Next year I will develop a mariachi program.

I am having a great time teaching middle-school orchestra, and now I'm glad that I didn't find a job just teaching mariachi. I realize that one side of me enjoys stepping away from mariachi life and experiencing orchestral music from time to time. Just like I learned to love mariachi after being provided with great experiences in high school, I have also learned to love classical music after continuously being exposed to it in college. Learning to perform classical technique on my trumpet made me appreciate it more and also improved my mariachi trumpet playing. Now many professional mariachi players are studying classical music, and it makes me proud that the mariachi genre is transitioning into a higher level of performance. Groups are playing more complex music and sound more in tune and well-balanced.

Since Jeff Nevin's departure, I have been helping lead the ASU Mariachi with Valerie, my student teaching mentor. The group is smaller, but still involves a mix of ASU students and community members, including some as young as 12. We prepare for one formal concert each semester, and a few members play together whenever we receive invitations to perform on campus or in the community. I am also leading a mariachi class at a local community college and I continue to teach at Rosie's House, which offers three levels of mariachi instruction. At my house, I teach private guitar, violin, and trumpet lessons, and a beginning mariachi for young kids of ages six through nine. This has allowed me to experiment with introducing mariachi music to children and will eventually contribute to the beginner mariachi method books I plan to write. I discuss teaching ideas often with two other ASU graduates, a classical cellist from Mexico who is teaching orchestra full-time in the same school district, and a classical/mariachi violinist who teaches elementary strings and an after-school mariachi club in another district. The cellist has a mariachi class in his schedule, and I am helping him plan repertoire for his group since he doesn't have much mariachi experience. I have a strong desire to learn more about how children learn. I want to become a good music educator, not just a good mariachi teacher. I want to have a positive impact on my students and inspire them to pursue further education.

Some of the biggest influences in my life have been my high school and college teachers. I have always received a tremendous amount of support and encouragement from non-Latino individuals. Having my peers and professors appreciate me as a Mexican-American and a mariachi musician gave me confidence and motivated me to do my best. I am impressed and disappointed at the same time because the majority of the people who have written about mariachi music or have done big things with mariachi education in the United States have been mainly White American scholars. People like Jeff Nevin who was offered the first mariachi degree in the world, Mark Fogelquist who has been one of the greatest mariachi educators, and Jonathan Clark, a well-known mariachi historian, are some of the big names in the mariachi world, and they are all White. I think it is about time for a Mexican descendant to start doing something with mariachi music education. This has been one of my biggest motivators.

What Marg Learned from Carlos

In writing this chapter, I requested that Carlos help me learn by being as honest as he could about his experiences, and, given the tone of our discussions, I believe that he did that to the best of his ability. Every story offers multiple tellings and interpretations (Barrett & Stauffer, 2009; Chase, 2005; Clandinin & Connelly, 2000). Carlos has presented one telling of his story. Here, I consider Carlos' story from my perspective. First, I will identify some things I have learned from Carlos that I hope to incorporate into my teaching. Then I will discuss the work of other researchers who have helped me better understand Carlos' ability to "straddle" two musical and ethnic cultures. Finally, I will offer some observations about Carlos' success in our university's music teacher education program.

Improving My Teaching

Carlos has reminded me that I could better support all students by learning more about the music that is important to them. Because Carlos was competent in the music valued by the School of Music, I did not consider that our music education course offerings failed to honor, or even acknowledge, the music that Carlos and probably many students care about in their lives beyond school (Abril, 2009; Hartley et al., 2009; Kratus, 2007; Richerme, 2011; Williams, 2011). Without recognizing it, I was promoting a colorblind (Bonilla-Silva, 2014) or "assimilationist [musical] ideology, which presupposes that the proper ends in education will have been achieved when minority groups can no longer be differentiated from the White majority in terms of education, economic status, or access to social institutions and their benefits" (Carter, 2006, p. 307). Although I knew of Carlos' interest in mariachi, had heard him perform, and had attended a few of his classes and concerts at Rosie's House, I failed to fully appreciate the extent of Carlos' "double life," teaching and performing as both a traditional music education major and as a mariachi in the community. I realize now that my semester playing in the ASU mariachi and my attendance at all the group's subsequent concerts should have alerted me to ways that I could have recognized Carlos' musical worlds, simply by taking time to ask questions in informal conversations, and by inviting him to share with the class about his work in the community. As DeLorenzo (2012) warns, "When teacher-educators and preservice teachers have fooled themselves into believing that 'kids are kids' or 'I don't see color [or ethnicity],' they have a huge chasm to traverse to truly understand each child for who he or she is. To ignore color [or musical culture] is to ignore identity. Ignoring identity is tantamount to rendering a child [or preservice teacher] invisible" (p. 45).

In retrospect, I also realized that I failed to provide adequate support for Carlos' transition to student teaching. Due to scheduling complications, Carlos had enrolled in the summer workshops for the Level I Orff and Kodály classes to replace the required elementary methods course, so he never had an extended internship in general music. I assumed that, in the semester before graduation, he was working at least a few hours a week in an elementary music classroom in addition to his orchestra internship, but I failed to confirm that and it somehow slipped through the cracks. In addition, it was only after Carlos' graduation that it occurred to me that he had never experienced anything like a US-style elementary music class in his childhood school in Mexico. This left him ill-prepared for a student teaching mentor with little supervision experience, whose expectations did not fit Carlos' learning style and needs for mentoring. A doctoral student supervised Carlos' student teaching, but he did not learn soon enough about Carlos' struggles in his general music placement and, when he did, it took several weeks for both of us to understand the situation well enough to provide the support that Carlos should have had sooner. This offers an important reminder for me to be more proactive in probing more deeply when a student teacher reports that "everything's ok" or, even more important, to not gloss over a student's report of a small concern.

Cultural Straddling

I have learned that Carlos is both bicultural and multi-musical. Phinney and Devich-Navarro (1997) suggest that biculturalism is "a complex and multi-dimensional phenomenon; there is not just one way of being bicultural" (p. 29). In their study of ethnic identity, they interviewed and surveyed Mexican-American and African-American high school students, and identified at least three ways that students viewed their ethnic and American identities. They found that a few students, the *separated biculturals*, identified strongly with their ethnicity, rejecting most everything they viewed as mainstream American—meaning White —culture. Most students in their study functioned as either *alternating* or *blended biculturals*. The *blended biculturals* described themselves as simultaneously using both sets of cultural codes fairly consistently. The *alternating biculturals* considered themselves as members of two distinct cultural groups, purposefully moving between cultural codes, strategically employing each as needed.

Similar to the alternating biculturals of Phinney and Devich-Navarro (1997), Ogbu's (2004) *accommodation without assimilation* describes a person who easily moves back and forth between cultural and linguistic modes, "more or less liv[ing] in two worlds at the same time" (p. 15). Carter (2006) also studied the complexity of African-American and Latino adolescents' cultural identity. In her study, the students' responses to their in-school academic, cultural, psychological, and social experiences fell into three primary categories. *Cultural mainstreamers* choose to assimilate to the dominant school culture, even in their social peer environments. *Noncompliant believers* adopt markers of their class and race in language, dress, music, and social networks; while they accept the value of education, they often are critical of perceived inequalities in school, avoid aspects of school which they consider too "White," and choose to achieve at levels below their ability. *Cultural straddlers* identify with both school and social peer cultures, developing fluency in the cultural codes needed to move easily between them. Carter suggests that cultural straddlers are in the best position to balance their academic and social lives in school: "Straddlers understand the functions of both dominant and non-dominant cultural capital (Carter, 2003 [in Carter, 2006]) and value and embrace skills to participate in multiple cultural environments, including mainstream society, their school environments, and their respective ethnoracial communities" (Carter, 2006, p. 306). In a later study, Carter (2010) identified this ability to function well in different cultures as *cultural flexibility*.

I explained these research-based terms to Carlos, and asked which categories best fit him. He identifies with Carter's *cultural straddlers* and Phinney and Devich-Navarro's *blended biculturals*, because he feels equally at home in both Mexican and American culture. Carlos self-identifies as Mexican-American. He had never heard the word *Chicano* until he took a Mexican-American studies class at Southwestern College. The teacher said he should only describe himself as *Chicano*, but he resists that term because it was not used in his neighborhood, and he does not like the strident or violent political activism of some who call themselves "Chicano." Carlos reported that one of the doctoral students at ASU had interviewed him about his experiences as a non-White student in the School of Music.

> [Although my high school was predominantly Mexican-American,] I told her I didn't even think about [my ethnicity]. Because all the teachers were very helpful. And plus the musicians here [at ASU], the education people, performance, yeah, although some of them were performance majors, I think they were all, they were all the same, they were all students, they were all learning, and I felt like I got support from everyone here.

Although the above statement may sound like Carlos subscribes to a colorblind view of ethnicity (Bonilla-Silva, 2014), Carter's (2010) study proposes possible explanations for why Carlos feels that he does not think about his ethnicity. Carter found that African-American high school students attending majority-minority schools tended to develop higher self-esteem than peers in majority-White high schools. They were also more successful in honors and AP courses, where they had more same-race/ethnicity peers and were less likely to face a stigma of "acting White." The self-identified "trumpet player ego" Carlos describes may have resulted from similar experiences in his predominantly Mexican-American high school and neighborhood. Carter (2010) also found that students like Carlos who took honors and AP classes tended to demonstrate higher levels of cultural flexibility, feeling at home in both cultures.

Supporting Carlos' Success

Carlos had social, musical, economic, academic, and family supports that combined with his personal drive and work ethic to allow him to succeed at the university. He was actively recruited to the program by his Southwestern College mariachi teacher, Jeff Nevin. He arrived at the university with a ready-made social support system in his two friends from Southwestern who were also beginning degree work at ASU. They lived together and, in this area with a large Latino population, by the end of the first semester, they had located other Spanish-speaking friends in the School of Music who provided connections for housing, food, companionship, and musical identity. This provided Carlos with a comfortable musical and cultural home at the university. Economic support came from the scholarship Dr. Nevin had arranged for Carlos, and the connections to local mariachis Carlos met in the ASU Mariachi, through whom he could find paid gigs and teaching opportunities and form musical friendships.

Academically, in his circuitous educational path as a part-time or full-time student in multiple majors, Carlos had developed sufficient academic skills and background in traditional classical music study to set him on a track for success in the program. As a traditional music major, Carlos brought adequate skills on classical trumpet, and as an experienced mariachi, strong aural skills. In addition, his sincere interest and work ethic allowed him to bring sufficient mastery of music theory, history, and piano skills—places where many transfer students, particularly students with a primary interest outside classical musical tradition, may flounder.

Carlos has an openness to all kinds of music, which has allowed him to integrate the various facets of his musical life. Interestingly, as a child, Carlos initially had an intensely negative reaction to mariachi music. He genuinely loved the music he got to experience by participating in his school band in the ninth grade, in band, choir, and orchestra at Southwestern College, and in concert band at ASU, supporting other researchers who caution teachers to beware of assuming that all students of a particular racial or ethnic background like the same music (Bergonzi, 2006; Delpit, 2006; Kruse, 2013; Lum & Campbell, 2009). Had Carlos' father not bribed him to join the school mariachi, Carlos might have followed a fairly traditional path to becoming a doctor or a clarinet major. Two experiences are particularly illustrative of Carlos' musical "cultural straddling" (Carter, 2006).

One example was his senior recital, a program which included a Vivaldi trumpet concerto, *Besame Mucho*, and five songs with a pick-up mariachi Carlos organized to support his singing of *El Rey* and his trumpet solo on the mariachi arrangement of *Czardas* he had successfully played for his studio jury. Dr. Nevin came from San Diego to hear his recital, and he, the ASU trumpet professor, and the trumpet teaching assistant were all pleased with the performance. A second example is from his general music teaching. Carlos and the two other music teachers at the school decided that the first concert of the year would feature music from different parts of the world. Carlos wrote and taught an arrangement of "De Colores" for his third graders to perform, accompanying themselves with an Orff instrumentarium.

Carlos also credits his family for much of his success: "Because people have always expected a lot from me, it has pushed me to try harder." He remains close to his family, regularly keeping in contact by phone and visiting his daughter in San Diego whenever he can. Shortly after graduation, Carlos was invited to write a short article for *EllaSouthBay*, a San Diego-based journal whose mission is "to elevate the standard of living in the south bay Hispanic community through positive nonpartisan journalism, preserving culturally enriched traditions and promoting hope in future generations" (*www.ourhometownmag.com/esb/*). Carlos chose to write a tribute to his mother and grandmother. Writing about their influence, Carlos credits his *abuela*'s hard work in providing a life for her family in Mexico, and in being an "example of perseverance, persistence, determination, and courage."

> Like my grandmother, and probably inherited from her, my mother has been another example of determination and strength. Crossing the border illegally through the hills and mountains while being pregnant with me, not surrendering to the injustices of being an illegal immigrant for many years in this country plus overcoming the adversity of being a single mother, my mother has been another example of perseverance, and has taught me to fight harder for my goals, and no matter how big or unreachable they are, to never give up on my dreams.
>
> (Ella South Bay, http://ourhometownmag.com/
> esb/issue-archive/, September 15, 2015)

As Machado-Casas (2012) suggests, "While outside identities (those enacted outside the home) ensure physical and social survival, home identities ensure cultural survival" (p. 335; see also Conchas, Oseguera, & Vigil, 2012).

Perhaps the most important contributor to his success was Carlos himself. Carlos had a strong drive to be successful, and he worked hard in his courses at ASU. He himself connected his musical worlds when I did not. In his music teacher education courses, Carlos especially appreciated "getting feedback from other classmates." He valued the final exams for the Art of Teaching classes each semester, where he planned and practiced a lesson with his peers, followed by an opportunity to teach the same lesson with a local school orchestra class. Like many other students (e.g., Schmidt, 2010), he felt that peer teaching was less helpful for his learning, because "of course the lesson plans were successful" with college music education majors. Carlos told me that he was experimenting with applying things he learned in the courses in his mariachi teaching, such as "trying to have everyone engaged," using "simpler vocabulary," "giving the students specific feedback," and "trying to know what the students know before teaching them." From his classes, he also learned to teach mariachi using the score, rather than just relying on his ear and the trumpet part, and to "have a sequence before teaching," such as working on a small part of the piece to help the students master that section, rather than just playing through the piece over and over. Although I only once observed Carlos' mariachi teaching, he applied these ideas on his own because he believed the classes offered "a lot of simple things that you can use for any ensemble, not just strings or band." Taken together, the supports Carlos had mirror those recommended by the participants in Fitzpatrick, Henninger, and Taylor's (2014) study of the experiences of six undergraduate music education majors from traditionally marginalized populations: self-reliance, assistance with the application and audition process, mentorship, and appropriate support and resources. In particular, Carlos' story highlights the value of the support of culturally similar social and musical peers.

A postscript to Carlos' story: Because of his tenacity in persisting to complete his bachelor's degree in four different institutions over 8 years, earning four associate degrees along the way, and graduating from ASU with a 3.83 Grade Point Average, Carlos was selected as the outstanding undergraduate student for the Herberger Institute for Design and the Arts, which includes the School of Music, and received an award at the Institute's commencement convocation. His very proud mother was able to attend. At the time of this writing, Carlos had completed his first year of teaching elementary general music two days per week, and now has assumed a half-time position teaching orchestra in the arts-focused middle school in the same district. He is also taking classes part-time to earn his master's degree in music education, helping lead the ASU Mariachi, teaching a community college mariachi, teaching at Rosie's House, and gigging in the community. Carlos also teaches mariachi classes and private lessons at his home. He said the parents donated chairs and a white board for these classes, which tells me how much they value the opportunity for their children to learn to play mariachi music.

Carlos' story adds to a growing collection of stories about music education majors and teachers with musical interests outside most school of music offerings (e.g., Fitzpatrick, Henninger, & Taylor, 2010; Kruse, 2013; Thibeault, 2009). Kruse (2013) warns us to not assume that all students representing any group will share similar characteristics. As he points out, invitations for students to share their cultures need to be extended with respect to each individual student's situation, because there is a fine line between honoring a student's ethnicity and putting them on display. Kruse cautions that "navigating this line with minority students could mean the difference between embarrassment and empowerment" (p. 38).

My semester playing with the ASU mariachi gave me hints about how many local mariachis there are. They all know each other and ask each other to fill in with their groups when needed. I'm honored to have learned a bit about their musical world. While the ASU mariachi strives to perform with excellent tone and intonation, I have learned that, like Eva's fiddle music in Thibeault's (2009) study, mariachi is above all "people music. . . . It [is] a fun thing, a recreational time, not something to stress about and perfect things. A time of gathering and closeness" (p. 273). I am trying to pay better attention to Kelly-McHale's (2013) advice for teachers to "[seek] assistance from the class as well as [create] a community of learners where each other's strengths and weaknesses are embraced and honored" (p. 207). I intend to do more to incorporate Abril's (2009) suggestion for music teacher educators to "start by acknowledging and celebrating preservice teachers' multi-musical selves," and to "also go one step further by asking [students] to draw upon their diverse musical knowledge, skills and understandings in methods courses, field experiences, and student-teaching" (p. 88). My colleagues and I have made some efforts to create assignments where students include their favorite pop music in classes, but I wonder how many students' double (or triple or quadruple) musical lives and skills remain hidden to me, simply because I don't ask them. Carlos deserves all the credit for integrating his various musical lives in a coherent whole, and he has taught me many important lessons.

Discussion Questions

1. Thibeault's (2009) study demonstrates how one high school student felt about fiddle music—she described it as "a fun thing, a recreational time, not something to stress about and perfect things. A time of gathering and closeness" (p. 273). Do you have music that fills a similar place in your life? How did you discover that music? Try to describe what it means to you and why. Share your music, and some of the reasons it is important to you, with others in your class. Discuss whether and where you might like to be able to include your music in your classes and/or teaching.

2. Discuss the meaning of each of these categories from research studies:

   • separated biculturals, alternating biculturals, and blended biculturals (Phinney & Devich-Navarro, 1997)
   • cultural mainstreamers, noncompliant believers, and cultural straddlers (Carter, 2006)

   What similarities and differences do you find between Phinney and Devich-Navarro's and Carter's categories? Describe real or imagined examples of a person fitting each category that you might find (a) in a music classroom and (b) in a music-making or music-learning situation other than school-based classes. As a music educator, how might you help these people connect their musical worlds?

3. Kruse (2013) points out that there is a fine line between honoring students' ethnicity and putting them on display. What does he mean by this? Give an example of a real or imagined time when a teacher's well-meaning attempt to acknowledge a student's difference might instead embarrass or hurt them?

4. What is one small step you might take to "acknowledge and celebrate" your own or your students' "multi-musical selves" (Abril, 2009, p. 88)?

5. Describe your vision for "a community of learners where each other's strengths and weaknesses are embraced and honored" (Kelly-McHale, 2013, p. 207). How might music be taught, learned, and shared? What would relationships between teachers and learners look like? How might you begin to create such a community in your setting? What would you want to learn or experience to help you enact your vision?

6. This chapter cites several researchers who suggest that for teachers to say, "I don't see color" or "We're all the same inside," might be limiting in their interactions with students. Do you agree? Why or why not? Why might they say that this "colorblind" thinking shortchanges or even hurts students? Is it possible for a person to become truly colorblind? If everyone actually could become colorblind, what would be the benefits and drawbacks?

7. Carter (2010) suggests that some students of color face a stigma of "acting White" if they strive to succeed academically or musically, or if they choose to interact socially with White peers. Read Brewer's (2010) chapter, listed in the references, which describes how four students felt about charges of "acting White" because they enjoyed membership in their high school band.
    Discuss how different students might respond to this accusation, keeping in mind adolescents' sensitivity to their peers. As a music educator, how might you respond if you became aware of students who were targets of this or other taunts?

References

Abril, C. R. (2009). Responding to culture in the instrumental programme: A teacher's journey. *Music Education Research*, *11*(1), 77–91.

Barrett, M. S., & Stauffer, S. L. (2009). Introduction. In M. S. Barrett & S. L. Stauffer (Eds.), *Narrative inquiry in music education: Troubling certainty* (pp. 1–4). Dordrecht, The Netherlands: Springer.

Bergonzi, L. (2006). To see in living color and to hear the sound of silence: Preparing string teachers to teach in diverse classrooms. In J. L. Aten (Ed.), *String teaching in America: Strategies for a diverse society* (pp. 77–100). Fairfax, VA: American String Teachers Association.

Bonilla-Silva, E. (2014). *Racism without racists: Color-blind racism and the persistence of racial inequality in America.* 4th ed. Lanham, MD: Rowman & Littlefield Publishers, Inc.

Brewer, W. (2010). Inside/outside: School music on "The Line." In L. K. Thompson & M. R. Campbell (Eds.), *Issues of identity in music education* (pp. 37–63). Charlotte, NC: Information Age Publishing.

Carter, P. L. (2006). Straddling boundaries: Identity, culture, and school. *Sociology of Education, 79*(4), 304–328.

Carter, P. L. (2010). Race and cultural flexibility among students in different multiracial schools. *Teachers College Record, 112*(6), 1529–1574.

Chase, S. E. (2005). Narrative inquiry: Multiple lenses, approaches, voices. In N. K. Denzin & Y. S. Lincoln (Eds.), *The SAGE handbook of qualitative research* (3rd ed., pp. 651–679). Thousand Oaks, CA: SAGE.

Clandinin, D. J., & Connelly, F. M. (2000). *Narrative inquiry.* San Francisco, CA: Jossey-Bass Publishers.

Conchas, G. Q., Oseguera, L., & Vigil, J. D. (2012). Acculturation and school success: Understanding the variability of Mexican American youth adaptation across urban and suburban contexts. *Urban Review, 44*, 401–422.

DeLorenzo, L. C. (2012). Missing faces from the orchestra: An issue of social justice? *Music Educators Journal, 98*(4), 39–46.

Delpit, L. (2006). *Other people's children: Cultural conflict in the classroom.* New York: The New Press.

Fitzpatrick, K. R., Henninger, J. C., & Taylor, D. M. (2014). Access and retention of marginalized populations within undergraduate music education degree programs. *Journal of Research in Music Education, 62*(2), 105–127.

Hartley, L. A., Heuser, F., Schmidt, M., Weaver, M. A., & Zdzinski, S. F. (2009). Large ensemble music instruction: A phoenix awaiting cremation or reincarnation? Presentation at the Biennial Symposium on Music Teacher Education, Greensboro, NC, September 10–12. http://smte.us/conferences-symposia/2009-detailed-schedule/.

Kelly-McHale, J. (2013). The influence of music teacher beliefs and practices on the expression of musical identity in an elementary general music classroom. *Journal of Research in Music Education, 61*(2), 195–216.

Kratus, J. (2007). Music education at the tipping point. *Music Educators Journal, 94*(2), 42–48.

Kruse, A. J. (2013). "I always had my instrument": The story of Gabriella Ramires. *Bulletin of the Council for Research in Music Education, 195*, 25–40.

Lum, C. H., & Campbell, P. S. (2009). "El Camaleon": The musical secrets of Mirella Valdez. In C. R. Abril & J. L. Kerchner (Eds.), *Musical experiences in our lives: Things we learn and meanings we make* (pp. 113–126). Lanham, MD: Rowman & Littlefield.

Machado-Casas, M. (2012). Pedagogías del camaleón/Pedagogies of the chameleon: Identity and strategies of survival for transnational indigenous Latino immigrants in the US south. *Urban Review, 44*, 534–550.

Ogbu, J. U. (2004). Collective identity and the burden of "Acting White" in Black history, community, and education. *Urban Review, 36*, 1–35.

Phinney, J., & Devich-Navarro, M. (1997). Variations in bicultural identification among African American and Mexican American adolescents. *Journal of Research on Adolescence, 7*, 3–32.

Richerme, L. K. (2011). Apparently we've disappeared. *Music Educators Journal, 98*(35), 35–40.

Schmidt, M. (2010). Learning from teaching experience: Dewey's theory and preservice teachers' learning. *Journal of Research in Music Education, 58*(2), 131–146.

Thibeault, M. D. (2009). The violin and the fiddle: Narratives of music and musician in a high-school setting. In J. L. Kerchner & C. R. Abril (Eds.), *Musical experience in our lives: Things we learn and meanings we make* (pp. 255–274). Lanham, MD: Rowman & Littlefield Education.

Williams, D. A. (2011). The elephant in the room. *Music Educators Journal, 98*(1), 51–57.

6

"PUT YOUR BIG GIRL PANTIES ON!"

A Female High School Band Director's Career in a Culture of Masculinity

Colleen A. Sears

Meet Cathy

Cathy (pseudonym) is entering her 22nd year as a high school band director. She is 52 years old, white, and an alumna of Brownington High School where she now teaches. The school serves approximately 1000 students and is located in a suburban, predominantly white, middle-class community in the Northeast United States where the average household income is $126,000 per year. Music and art are well supported by the district's administration, the community, and parent organizations. Cathy's teaching responsibilities include a 50-piece advanced wind ensemble, a 70-member mixed level concert band, small group instrumental lessons, a 170-member marching band, and pit orchestra. Her advanced wind ensemble generally performs level five and six music and has often been awarded perfect scores at state festivals. The wind ensemble tours nationally and internationally, performs at prestigious venues, and commissions approximately three works per year by renowned composers in the field.

Cathy enjoys her position as a high school band director and believes her job is to give her students the "ability to feel on a very, very deep level." While Cathy now expresses joy and excitement when she talks about her students and her love for teaching, she shared that she was not always so enthusiastic about entering the field of education. "I wouldn't say that there was anything in particular that ignited any passion or inspiration," she said of her mediocre undergraduate experience. After Cathy completed her master's degree in clarinet performance, she was still "dispassionate about teaching," but knew that she would look for a music education position in a school. Cathy taught band, chorus, orchestra, and general music in multiple grade levels for several years in her first place of employment. It was when Cathy was hired for her current position that her love for teaching grew. Of this she said, "It really took all those 7 years of kind of floating around and doing this concert and this event and this sort of thing. Until once I hit the job of my dreams, that's when things really took off."

Cathy is married to Steve, who is also a high school band director. They have three children; the youngest is a high school sophomore. Despite her incredibly demanding schedule, Cathy regularly practices yoga in an effort to "melt away" the stresses of her job. Cathy is keenly aware of gendered currents within the profession and was eager to share her experiences as one of the few female high school band directors of high-performing programs in her area.

Female Band Directors

Female band directors are severely underrepresented in higher education and secondary instrumental music positions (Sheldon & Hartley, 2012). As of 2001, women comprised only 20 percent of the total population of band directors in higher education and less than 25 percent of the high school band director population in the United States ("Gender Trends among MENC Music Educators," 2001). The military history of bands and academic and professional politics in the form of the "old boy" network of male conductors and students have made it difficult for women to enter and thrive in the band-directing profession (Fiske, 1997). Discriminatory hiring practices, lack of role models, isolation within the field, the work/family balance, expectations of traditionally masculine behavior, and the belief that women are incapable of handling a band director job because of discipline problems and classroom management issues that might arise have all been cited as reasons for the lack of female band directors at collegiate and secondary levels (Feather, 1980; Fitzpatrick, 2013; Gould, 1996; Gould, 2005; Grant, 2000; Greaves-Spurgeon, 1998; Jackson, 1996; Sears, 2010).

The presence of female high school band directors conflicts with historically constructed gender roles in secondary instrumental music education (Green, 1997). As a result, women in the field must negotiate the complexities and challenges of working in a male-dominated profession. While much of the existing literature on female band directors has identified the militaristic history of the profession, discrimination (limited opportunity because of gender), isolation (exclusion because of gender), and stereotyping (assumptions about ability based on gender) as barriers that female band directors experience, few studies have examined how women in high school band director positions perceive and engage with these dynamics. By examining how female band directors engage with and navigate the complexities associated with working in the traditionally masculine field of secondary instrumental music education, we may better understand how socially constructed gender roles impact female band director identity both in the classroom and in the larger professional community. Such an understanding may help to name and challenge masculine power structures that continue to serve as barriers to women in music education. According to Savigny, "Feminism as praxis enables women to 'speak out' and have their voices heard, and in so doing question existing structures of power. This in turn provides a mechanism through which change and agency are possible" (2014, p. 806). In the spirit of "speaking out," the purpose of this instrumental case study is to examine how Cathy engages with and perceives issues of isolation, stereotyping, and marginalization in the traditionally masculine profession of secondary instrumental music education and to explore the effect of these perceptions on her personal and professional identities. It is my hope that Cathy's story creates space for "other" women to speak and be heard so that masculine power structures in instrumental music education can be named, challenged, and transformed.

Feminist Poststructuralism

The role of the band director is characterized by the socially constructed, traditionally masculine traits of power, assertiveness, anti-femininity, and toughness (Dodson & Borders, 2006; Green, 1997; Gould, 2005) while expression of emotions and caring for others have been constructed as traditionally feminine behaviors (Gilligan, 1982; Efthim, Kenny, & Mahalik, 2001). Female band directors work in a world where traditional masculinity is expected and rewarded and femininity is regularly criticized, silenced, and rejected.

A feminist, poststructural examination of "the ways in which educational discourses come to be taken as the truth; the construction, prescription and circumscription of individual identities, desires and subjectivities by the state and its educational institutions; ideas concerning curriculum and schooling; and issues of power and control in education" may assist in understanding of how female band directors negotiate the complexities that arise when femininity disrupts the naturalized transparency of the masculine band director (Ninnes & Burnett, 2003, p. 280). As Lamb states, "dominant discourses make available forms of identity which are tightly circumscribed and which exclude many people" (1996, p. 125). The dominant discourses, or institutionalized practices and processes, in instrumental music education have been historically, socially, and culturally constructed by men, leaving little room for women to create their own spaces and identities within the field (Walshaw, 2001). In these small, tightly circumscribed spaces, female conductors often embody and perform the socially constructed behaviors of toughness and assertiveness that signify masculinity while simultaneously performing their own femininity.

Drawing upon the theory of performativity, "gender is in no way a stable identity of locus of agency from which various acts proceed; rather, it is an identity tenuously constituted in time—an identity instituted through a stylized repetition of acts" (Butler, 2003, p. 415). While recent developments such as blind auditions created more equitable opportunities for women in instrumental performance (Green, 1997), these changes have not helped to diversify the population of conductors. Female band directors have been labeled as "other" in a way that perpetuates the notion that women in secondary instrumental positions are unwelcome abnormalities in the profession and are therefore deserving of intense scrutiny, isolation, and stereotyping. Women who conduct in secondary positions are charged with a difficult task. They must assertively interpret the work of a composer, control the performances of the musicians, and ensure that the final product meets expectations of both the public and the conductor. While female conductors fulfill these duties, they also endure criticism about their choice of attire and displays of femininity during performance such as "too graceful" or "too undulating" arm movements (Fuller, 1996, p. 30). Femininity expressed during performance is seen as a point of weakness because it conflicts with the expected stylized repetition of masculine acts.

Females in secondary instrumental music education ultimately shape their identities by negotiating the competing roles and meanings associated with the authoritative conductor and the female body through a careful balancing act of gender performance that allows them to operate within the socially constructed norms of the profession. Female band director identity, or the "categorization of the self as an occupant of a role, and the incorporation, into the self, of the meanings and expectations associated with that role and its performance" (Stets & Burke, 2000, p. 225) can be shaped by the extent to which a female band director accepts, rejects, and negotiates traditional masculine and feminine roles in their positions.

Expectations of Traditional Masculinity

Cathy believes that her teaching position as the head high school band director of a high-performing program is widely seen as a "man's job." While she has noticed a slight increase in the female high school band director population in her area since she began teaching 28 years ago, she notes that the increase has leveled off and women are still widely underrepresented. She attributes this disparity in the population in part to the traditionally masculine character traits that administrators deem necessary to be successful in such a position:

Cathy: I know too many open positions, too many people who were on interview committees, so I know that that is actually the way it is.

Colleen: That the qualities they're looking for are in line with something that's more masculine?

Cathy: Absolutely. They would equate that with classroom management. They would equate that with being able to get out in the community for a parade, on the football field. You have to be very aggressive. You've got to strap your dildo on. I say to myself, put your big girl panties on, and you gotta do it! It's learned behavior. You just have to learn to be like that. It's just the way it is. I don't know a lot about anything else, but I know a lot about teaching high school band and it's just the way it is.

In an effort to thrive in a culture where masculinity is expected and rewarded, Cathy carefully manages and regulates the traditionally masculine and feminine traits that shape her teaching persona.

> Well, you need to have an extraordinary amount of confidence. You have to have a much bigger personality. I'm a very shy person, but my students wouldn't know that because the persona that I've had to learn to become— to be able to manage the group and be successful, and have the kids love the class, and have the directors admire the work, and feel that it's valuable—is one I had to develop. A person who's really not me.

In addition to managing her teaching persona, Cathy also strictly regulates her physical appearance to align with the masculine expectations of the profession.

> You can see how I dress; unisex clothing for me always helped. A man tailored shirt, and a pair of Dockers, and a brown belt and flat shoes. Never heels. It always helped me feel who I needed to be and I had to work to become the picture I had in my head of who I needed to be.

Although Cathy has mastered the masculine persona, she is conscious of the threat that this poses to her feminine identity.

> I honestly feel that we need to be hybrids. I have a certain amount of masculinity in my personality that I have learned to develop to be an effective teacher, all the while nurturing, hanging on to dear life with my femininity because I'm so connected to that.

The work of managing masculine expectations and regulating displays of femininity is a tiring process that wears on Cathy. She sometimes imagines what it would be like to not be conscious of this dynamic.

> I would bet a gazillion dollars that men never worry about any of those issues. My husband is a high school band director and I don't think he's given a second's thought to how much confidence he needs to grow and how much work he needs to do to be able to articulate . . .

Silence

Despite her efforts to perform expected masculine behaviors, Cathy often felt silenced and ignored by males in power. "The old superintendent, it was the type of thing where when I walked in the room, I felt that I could just barely lift my head up because he wouldn't extend me the handshake or there was no talk about the ball—the score of the ball game or you know, anything like that.

We couldn't connect and he wasn't making it any easier for me." In one instance, Cathy was rendered voiceless and powerless when a male administrator verbally berated her.

> We had the old principal who was a very big sports guy. He and I did not get along. We had some problems. I cried in his office a couple of times. Where he hollered at me and I don't know that he would have done that to any teacher. He got angry with me and hollered at me. Because I was brought to tears over a grade. It was a grading incident. I had made what he thought was a judgmental error on something I did with grading. And he saw that I was trying to defend myself and he wasn't going to have it. So he really ripped me apart and I never really much spoke to him again. I used to always keep my head down.

Cathy then explained an interaction that she observed between this principal and her husband.

> My husband, when I was on maternity leave, took my marching band to an event in my place. The district wanted him to do that. And I showed up with the baby in the carriage, and here was the principal and my husband hitting it off. Really hitting it off. Shaking hands, "Hey, how's it going?" Two, tall, 6 foot guys, both bearded and shaking hands and patting each other on the back. And I was really out of my mind angry.

Cathy observed that her husband and the principal shared immediate mutual respect, a type of masculine bond, and a sense of shared power while Cathy felt intimidated, devalued, and small in her interactions with him.

> I was afraid of him. And I was afraid to make appointments to see him. All the while my bands were achieving top scores and we were going on trips and I was getting tons of e-mail from parents and letters. And the band was just getting better and better and all the while I never felt confident enough to handle a simple conversation with him about budget items or something like that.

Cathy speculated on why this difference appears to exist:

> Because women are constantly in our own minds and we're also in everyone else's head. We're always judging—this person is in a rush I have to speak faster. This person is stressed out and I'm feeling that they're stressed out—because women are so perceptive and so intuitive. And I love the fact that I'm that way. I wouldn't want to ever, ever be a guy, ever. I love being a woman. I think women are empowering and it's helped me to be

a sensitive musician and to have very, very musical performances and that sort of a thing.

Cathy went on to speak about some of the adverse effects of this perceptiveness and its relationship to feeling silenced.

It can also really get in our way—when we need to be able to speak up, or go ahead and say it . . . there are times that I wish I didn't have that— just for that one minute. Oh, I just wish I didn't get so choked up when the superintendent looked at me funny—because I didn't finish what I wanted to say.

Cathy's awareness of male administrators' positions of power and the sense of not being taken seriously intimidated her and interfered with her ability to accomplish tasks. Of this she said, "Those were the times when I started to shrink and it interfered with my ability to stay on task and to be very effective as a teacher of a very large program." Cathy was confident in her abilities as a band director, but sometimes wished for an alternative to the awkward dynamic that was present in her interactions with male administrators.

I know what I'm doing, I can see how to work through it, but I'm not getting an understanding from the other side. So it's like a brick wall thing. I do start to crawl under a rock a little bit. Sometimes I wish I could behave more like a guy. In situations like that, guys are just who they are and they just don't . . . it doesn't matter. Sometimes I wish I could just bulldoze through a situation, just being myself, feeling the way I feel, defending my program the way I want or defending a student the way I want to—and not let my integrity be compromised at all.

The male administrators who made Cathy feel voiceless and silenced have now retired. Her new administration is very supportive of her program and she describes her relationship with the current administration as "a love affair." However, she also believes that her long record of dedication to the program and quality performances in combination with highly supportive parental groups (which operate both as formal and informal, social media-based organizations) have created a culture of widespread support and she no longer needs advocate as aggressively for her program as she has in the past.

Sacrifice

In order to fulfill her teaching and professional responsibilities and advocate for her high-performing program, Cathy made many personal and family sacrifices. For a period of time, personal sacrifice meant tolerating sex-based harassment by a vice principal that was in charge of her budget and trip approvals.

He would never really understand how inappropriate his behavior was towards me. He really did love me like a friend or a daughter and I really knew that it wasn't quite his fault. But he would do things in the office in front of the office staff and the other teachers like, give me a hug and kiss me on the cheek. Call me babe and put his arm around me. Very, very, very inappropriate. And do it in front of lots of people and say, "this is my girl" and that sort of thing.

Cathy explained why she was unable to confront this administrator or report his behavior.

I always felt that I could not respond to that because if I did, it could put up a huge wall between us and he was my gravy. He was able to get me the money I needed for my band and gave me permission to take my trips. And it never got to the point where, again—he crossed so far over the line that he could be brought up on charges or anything like that. He would never do that. It was just his way of showing his fondness for me and it was completely and utterly inappropriate.

Cathy knew that when she needed to speak with the vice principal about a professional matter, "there was going to be a lot of 'hey baby, thanks lovey' that stuff." She was deeply affected by the inappropriate nature of these inter- actions. "I really had a sadness. I had a little- I'm generally a happy person, but I had like a mini depression, like I just wasn't happy and that really wore on me for a while."

On several occasions, Cathy made family sacrifices in order to fulfill her professional responsibilities. Cathy has three children and has taken three maternity leaves during the course of her career. "You cannot take a long maternity leave and want to be a high school band director. You cannot. Because you will not get back in where you want to be at." Cathy explained that she maintained close contact with the school while she was out on leave. "I was on the phone and I would take the baby in the stroller and come to the high school. Because it only takes a little bit of time, really, in a matter of days it could fall apart." Finding childcare also proved to be a challenge, even as her children grew older.

Sometimes I've left them when I probably shouldn't have—it was too many hours . . . I cried because I didn't go to my daughter's book reading at school because I forgot and I picked her up at school once and she was a little girl and she started to cry in the car and I said, "why are you crying?" And she said, "you never came." I missed something.

Cathy shared that the extra-curricular responsibilities of a high school position have pushed her limits as a mother. "It's an unbelievable ride but it's insanity all at the same time. But I did start to have a breakdown a couple of years ago. It was very much too much stress. I found myself becoming very unhappy." Cathy found that her family life grew more complicated as her children grew up.

> Their problems get bigger, they get bigger, their needs get more. And then the school was becoming more complicated, I was taking on more. We were going on trips, we were going on festivals. I made more work for myself. It was chaotic at home and school was very chaotic and I started to really break down.

Cathy acknowledges that female band directors with children have to work extra hard at parenting and extra hard at their jobs. Of this she said:

> Can you give everything if you're a woman? You do have a family, you have chores, you have to mother your children. How much of that are you going to give to your program? If your program's going to thrive, you have to give everything and if not, find more. Make more energy, be more, do better. Or else you just cannot have a program that's ever going to matter.

Methods of Coping

Cathy employed a variety of coping strategies that helped and continue to help her navigate the demands of the profession and the pressures of her position as one of the few female band directors in her area. Of her coping strategies, the ones she employed in the face of sex-based harassment were least effective. "I hated going there," she said of her student teaching placement where her cooperating teacher's stares made her very uncomfortable. "I did take a few days off and he (her cooperating teacher) got the impression that I probably wasn't as qualified and that hurt me very much." When tolerating inappropriate behavior from the flirtatious vice principal, Cathy found herself "running and taking some aspirin and just trying to melt it away and say this is not healthy for me." She felt that the sex-based harassment she experienced didn't need to be reported because it didn't "cross the line" and she feared professional retaliation.

To cope with the stress, pressures, and time demands of her regular teaching day and endless extra-curricular responsibilities, Cathy tries to make time for self-care. "The constant rushing is wearing on me," she stated, "so I go to more yoga. I'm trying to really balance it out. I embrace the summers. I miss the kids, but I embrace the summers because I just feel a yearning to live a life where I'm not racing and rushing and feeling like I can't catch my breath. Literally can't catch my breath. And I have to work to slow myself down." Cathy also works to have reasonable expectations of her work-family balance and tries to avoid excessive self-criticism through the realization that "it's never going to be perfect, it's never going to be perfect anyway. If you never have the kids and you're the happiest teacher in the world with the best program in the world—even that's not perfect. Because you never got to have your own . . . having a family is amazing-why would anyone not want to have a family? That's my opinion. So maybe the story is that it's never really that harmonious . . . I just do the best I can do and I just try to forgive myself."

At work, Cathy finds complete refuge from stress, pressure, conflict, and gendered expectations when she is making music with her students. In these moments, she feels that she can truly be herself. "Through the music, everything's free. So once we're playing a pretty ballad, or we're holding a chord, or there's something to be done within the repertoire, or a clarinet lesson, in other words—once you're engaged in the music, none of this exists."

Discussion

Discourses or "social structures and processes that are organized through institutions and practices" shape the way teachers view their own development and the profession as a whole (Weedon, 1997, p. 34). Which discourses then have shaped the development of Cathy's teaching identity? Which discourses have shaped her views on the profession as a whole?

Despite the slight increase in the female band director population since she began her career, Cathy observed that the field of secondary instrumental music education is still male-dominated in population and in behavioral expectations: "Even though we're in 2015 and we've come so far, I still feel like my position is still considered to be a man's position." Valian (1998) stated, "Males tend to be perceived as the norm against which females are measured. When one group—say, in this case, men—is the norm, the other group's behavior—in this case, women's—needs explaining" (p. 26). Secondary instrumental music education is a field where dominant discourses are shaped by practices, processes, and social structures that were created by men, for men. Women are often measured by the extent to which they meet the male standard of effectiveness. In other words, female band directors are expected to perform traditionally masculine behaviors in their positions in order to earn professional credibility and respect. "I feel that being a woman has held me back," Cathy said of this dynamic, "well, I shouldn't say that it's held me back. I feel that it's taken me longer to get to the point where I am today." While Gould (2006) echoed this idea in relation to university band directors, the pervasiveness of expected masculine norms is true for female high school band directors as well. Gould (2006) stated:

> Women must conform to the family of man—which for university band directors is male, white, western European. For the misogynist, women need to be brought (up) to the standard of men, that is, we can include them when they conform to specific (family of man) norms of men; for the paternalist, women are like men—we just have to identify in what

way(s), that is, we can facilitate their inclusion by showing how they already conform to specific (family of man) norms.

This dynamic requires that women complete an extra step in the establishment of their professional reputation, "which does not render it impossible for women to be as visible as their male colleagues . . . but it does make it more difficult" (Savigny, 2014, p. 706). Males, on the other hand, benefit from this dominant discourse and are automatically granted insider status, as was evidenced by the immediate collegial interaction that Cathy witnessed between her husband and the verbally abusive principal.

The lack of female band directors in secondary teaching positions could indicate that the cultural expectation of female band directors to align with dominant male discourses is too great a price to pay if the feminine identity is criticized, silenced, or destroyed in the process. Butler states, ". . . gender is a performance with clearly punitive consequences. Discrete genders are part of what "humanizes" individuals within contemporary culture; indeed, those who fail to do their gender right are regularly punished" (2003, p. 417). Despite her efforts to publicly conform to masculine norms, Cathy's female body and conscious preservation of her feminine identity meant that she would never fully succeed in meeting those masculine expectations and she was subsequently punished by being rendered voiceless in interactions with male administrators, an experience that is shared by many women in male-dominated fields (Lewis, 1986). She also felt that she was not taken seriously by male administrators and, on occasion, her male students. "Every once in a while, I'll see a kid. Again, being perceptive and intuitive when you're a woman, especially when you're a mom, I could always see them looking. It's a certain look that reminds me of the principal. I want to be very clear about this. They played their part. They did their job. But I couldn't kid around with them. Because they were looking at me like, 'Yeah, yeah right.' That sort of thing and it was exactly the same image that I was receiving from the principal." Cathy also endured sex-based harassment by some male administrators, a form of punishment that serves as a type of regulatory mechanism designed to maintain traditional male dominance (Kabat-Farr & Cortina, 2014).

The historically masculine nature of secondary instrumental music education challenges women to find ways to cope with and/or resist male norms in an effort to create space where they can exist and function within the profession. As Abramo (2009) states, "It is the working within and against these discourses that provides an individual with agency, the ability to choose among available discourses, and also resist those which are undesirable" (p. 43). In order to survive in the profession, Cathy initially worked within the confines of masculine-dominant discourses, even when she found them to be undesirable. By intentionally crafting a masculine persona, making personal and family sacrifices, and regulating displays of traditional femininity, Cathy navigated the dominant male discourse system to advocate for her program, function in her position, earn professional respect, and ultimately protect her feminine, maternal identity. Through this navigation, Cathy slowly created space that allowed her to eventually resist discourses that she found undesirable and embrace the more feminine, maternal identity that she valued and protected. The act of having three small children and taking maternity leaves, for example, resists and conflicts with the commonly held notion in secondary instrumental music that having a family and working as a high school band director are inherently incompatible desires (Sears, 2010). In addition, Cathy eventually felt free to perform a more fluid teaching persona in her classroom: "The mastery of this confident persona doesn't come necessarily with a loud voice . . . the idea of anything that I can do to be effective and work with a large group, a large voice, or aggressive behavior . . . sometimes to that end, I'll go down to a whisper or I'll conduct without any verbal communication at all." As she nears the end of her career, Cathy reflects on the length of time it took to for her to feel a sense of freedom from constant expectations of masculinity: "It just took me many years to embrace the fact that I know what I'm doing, I'm okay, and I'm an effective teacher without the big voice and the beard and all that stuff."

Epilogue

Cathy is now 52 years old and will retire in 3 years. Her oldest child is now 24 and her youngest is in high school. In a final email communication, she reflected on the ultimate worth of a career in secondary instrumental music and the silence and sacrifice that went along with it. In Cathy's words, this is "how it all worked out."

> Safely, I'll say that I think my kids are fine, well-adjusted humans that feel loved by their mom, and would not complain that I was any less attentive than the other moms. But here's the point: Not going right back (after maternity leave) would have greatly subtracted my chances of having a "bigger" position, and probably taken those chances away. As for the other side, as much as my guilt follows me into my 50's (and I'm Jewish, which means double the guilt!!), here's the thing: I have maintained such strong relationships with many of my students over the years, and have realized that I have played a part in who they are today. This I can speak of for hours—from the top musicians whom I've helped musically, to those that suffered the loss of parents, conquered illnesses, needed guidance, trusted me with their inner most problems, etc. . . I KNOW for sure that my work as an educator, a music educator made a difference in many, actually in most of my student's lives. From conversations, to letters, to meetings, to emails, through marriages, and children's births, I can write a book. And that for me, puts everything to rest.

Cathy's story illustrates that it is possible yet challenging for women to create spaces for themselves in secondary instrumental music education. For Cathy, it took endurance, sacrifice, and nearly the full length of her career to resist male-dominated discourses. As her career progressed and her confidence grew, Cathy made space for her feminine, maternal identity. Cathy is now at the end of her career and is personally and professionally satisfied with a genuine teaching identity that has positively impacted so many of her students. The length of time that it took Cathy to craft a satisfying teaching identity raises questions about the confines of masculine expectations in the field of secondary instrumental music education. Must women initially adopt and embody dominant masculine discourses in order to gain entry to the profession and earn respect? Are maternal, feminine teaching identities only permitted after a masculine one is firmly established?

According to hooks (2000), "focus on reforms to improve the social status of women within the existing social structure" causes us "to lose sight of the need for total transformation" (p. 160). Progress toward improving the gender disparity among high school band director positions cannot be measured by numbers alone. Progress must also be measured by the extent to which a "total transformation" of oppressive, confining masculine norms is achieved. Research that focuses on models of secondary instrumental music education that adopt maternal, feminine discourses would be helpful. Studies that highlight the benefits of a maternal, feminine teaching persona or innovative programs that address challenges related to the work/life balance could provide the groundwork for a total transformation. A focus on the transformational potential of non-masculine discourses could help female band directors create spaces that allow for fluid, genuine teaching identities at all stages of their careers and ultimately foster a professional climate where resistance, change, agency, and a broader conception of what it means to be a band director is possible.

Discussion Questions and Activities

1. Can you identify specific instances in your personal experiences where institutionalized practices and processes in instrumental music education have excluded, marginalized, or left little room for women to create their own spaces and identities within the field?
2. How might men and women resist and challenge masculine norms in instrumental music education?
3. How does the concept of gender performance apply to Cathy's story? Can you identify situations in your own music experience where gender performance has played a significant role?
4. This case study focused on the experiences of one female high school band director. What kinds of gender roles or expectations might exist for other positions in music education? A high school choir director? An elementary general music teacher? A music technology teacher? Why might this be the case?

5. Examine marketing materials and other media that feature images of male and female conductors. How would you characterize the types of gendered performances that are captured in these images? Do these images align with or challenge traditional gendered stereotypes associated with conductors? What information does this give you about the expectations associated with the role of the conductor?
6. Conduct a mini case study. Interview a female conductor and discover how she perceives and engages with gendered dynamics in the profession.

References

Abramo, M. (2009). *The construction of instrumental music teacher identity.* Unpublished doctoral dissertation. Teachers College: Columbia University, NY.

Butler, J. (2003). Performative acts and gender constitution: An essay in phenomenology and feminist theory. In C. McCann & S. Kim (Eds.), *Feminist theory reader.* New York: Routledge.

Denzin, N. K., & Lincoln, Y. S. (2005). The discipline and practice of qualitative research. In N. K. Denzin & Y. S. Lincoln (Eds.), *Handbook of qualitative research.* Thousand Oaks, CA: Sage Publications.

Dodson, T. A. & Borders, D. L. (2006). Men in traditional and nontraditional careers: Gender role attitudes, gender role conflict, and job satisfaction. *The Career Development Quarterly, 54,* 283–296.

Efthim, P., Kenny, M., & Mahalik, J. (2001). Gender role stress in relation to shame, guilt, and externalization. *Journal of Counseling and Development, 79,* 430–438.

Feather, C. A. (1980). *Women band directors in higher education.* Unpublished doctoral dissertation. University of Mississippi, MS.

Fiske, J. A. (1997). *A profile of women music educators in higher education.* Unpublished doctoral dissertation. Boston University, MA.

Fitzpatrick, K. (2013). Motherhood and the high school band director: A case study. *Bulletin of the Council for Research in Music Education, 196* (Spring), 7–23.

Fuller, S. (1996). Dead white men in wigs: Women and classical music. In S. Cooper (Ed.), *Girls! girls! girls!* New York: New York University Press.

Gender trends among MENC music educators (2001, June). *Teaching Music, 8*(6), 52.

Gilligan, C. (1982). Woman's place in man's life cycle. In *A different voice: Psychological theory and women's development.* Cambridge, MA: Harvard University Press.

Gould, E. (1996). *Initial involvements and continuity of women college band directors: The presence of gender-specific occupational role models.* Unpublished doctoral dissertation. University of Oregon, OR.

Gould, E. (2005). Nomadic turns: Epistemology, experience, and women university band directors. *Philosophy of Music Education Review, 13*(2), 147–164.

Gould, E. (2006, Fall). Monologue(s) of desire: becoming-woman as university band directors. *Gender Education Music & Society, 3.* Retrieved April 19, 2007, from http://queensu.ca/music/links/gems/past/No.%204/gouldarticle.html.

Grant, D. (2000). *The impact of mentoring and gender-specific role models on women college band directors at four different career stages.* Unpublished doctoral dissertation. University of Minnesota, MN.

Greaves-Spurgeon, B. (1998). *Women high school band directors in Georgia*. Unpublished doctoral dissertation. University of Georgia, GA.

Green, L. (1997). *Music, gender, education*. New York: Cambridge University Press.

hooks, b. (2000). *Feminist theory from margin to center*. Cambridge, MA: South End Press.

Jackson, C. (1996). *The relationship between the imbalance of numbers of women and men college band conductors and the various issues that influence the career aspirations of women instrumental musicians*. Unpublished doctoral dissertation. Michigan State University, MI.

Kabat-Farr, D., & Cortina, L. (2014). Sex-based harassment in employment: New insights into gender and contexts. *Law and Human Behavior, 38*(1), 58–72.

Lamb, R. (1996). Discords: Feminist pedagogy in music education. *Theory into Practice, 35*(2), 124–131.

Lewis, M. (1986). A discourse not intended for her: Learning and teaching within patriarchy. *Harvard Educational Review, 56*(4), 457–472.

Ninnes, P., & Burnett, G. (2003). Comparative education research: poststructuralist possibilities. *Comparative Education, 39*(3), 279–297.

Savigny, H. (2014). Women, know your limits: cultural sexism in academia. *Gender and Education, 26*(7), 794–809.

Sears, C. (2010). *Paving their own way: Experiences of female high school band directors*. Unpublished doctoral dissertation. Teachers College: Columbia University, NY.

Sheldon, D., & Hartley, L. (2012). What color's your baton, girl? Gender and ethnicity in band conducting. *Bulletin of the Council for Research in Music Education, 192*(Spring), 39–52.

Stets, J., & Burke, P. (2000). Identity theory and social identity theory. *Social Psychology Quarterly, 63*(3), 224–237.

Valian, V. (1998). Schemas that explain behavior. In *Why so slow? The advancement of women*. Cambridge, MA: MIT Press.

Walshaw, M. (2001). A Foucauldian gaze on gender research: What do you do when confronted with the tunnel at the end of the light. *Journal for Research in Mathematics Education, 32*(5), 471–492.

Weedon, C. (1997). *Feminist practice & poststructuralist theory*. 2nd ed. Maiden, MA: Blackwell Publishing.

7

"CAN'T I SING WITH THE GIRLS?"

A Transgender Music Educator's Journey

Sarah J. Bartolome & Melanie E. Stanford[1]

I'm so sick of being a boy, and though I talk about it all the time, I don't think people truly realize how sad and insecure I really am. I play everything off as a big joke, but deep down, I am terrified of people's true opinions of me and I'm scared. I'm scared of making these changes in my life. I'm scared of becoming a woman . . . and most of all, I'm scared that once I finish with all these changes, I'll look in the mirror and still hate my life. I'm scared that this hatred of myself will never go away. I'm scared that I won't ever be able to live a normal life as a woman. I'm just plain . . . scared.

It's 8:30am on the first day of Spring semester and my sophomores are almost all on time. I go around the room, matching faces with names. I call the next name on my roster, Matthew Stanford, and look expectantly around the room. The student raises a hand and smiles sheepishly, explaining, "Um, I actually go by Mel." I quickly change the name on my roster, greet Mel with the appropriate name, and move down the list. Mel smiles and relaxes back in the chair. As I turn to the next student, I notice a neon green bra strap peeking out from underneath Mel's Mighty Ducks jersey. I feel the question mark on my face but I just smile and continue down my list.

Introduction

The term transgender refers to "people who move away from the gender they were assigned at birth, people who cross over (*trans-*) the boundaries constructed by their culture to define and contain that gender" (Stryker, 2008, p. 1). It has also been described as "an umbrella term for people whose gender identity, expression or behavior is different from those typically associated with their assigned sex at birth" (National Center for Transgender Equality, 2014). In recent years, transgender issues have become increasingly visible in popular culture, leading to a rise in the public's awareness of the lived experiences of the transgender community. TV shows like *Orange is the New Black*, *Transparent*, and *Glee* have featured transgender characters and reality series like *I am Jazz* and *I Am Cait* peer into the daily lives of real transgender individuals. Public figures like Caitlin Jenner, Laverne Cox, and Chaz Bono have also brought transgender issues into the spotlight, raising awareness of the trans community. While the increased presence of transgender individuals in the mainstream media represents a significant and important shift toward transgender visibility, the nearly 1.4 million transgender individuals in the United States still comprise a significantly marginalized community (Flores, Herman, Gates, & Brown, 2016). Transgender individuals experience harassment, physical assault, and sexual violence with alarming frequency and a staggering 41 percent of respondents participating in the National Transgender Discrimination Survey reported attempting suicide (Grant et al., 2011). School contexts have been found to be equally problematic, with trans students reporting high incidences of discrimination, verbal and physical harassment, and assault both in K–12 schools (Greytak, Kosciw, & Diaz, 2009; Kosciw, Greytak, Palmer, & Boesen, 2014; McGuire, Anderson, Toomey, & Russell, 2010) and at the collegiate level (McKinney, 2005; Pusch, 2005; Rankin, 2003). Transgender adults also face significant discrimination in the workplace (Rainey & Imse, 2015); there are still 28 states in the United States that do not have any employment non-discrimination legislation covering gender identity.

The voices of transgender individuals are emerging in the research literature raising awareness among scholars about the experience of being transgender (Bilodeau, 2005; Nordmarken, 2014) and, from an educational perspective, drawing attention to the unique needs of transgender students (Rands, 2009; Seelman, 2016). Case studies in educational leadership have raised questions about the ways policy affects transgender students and their communities (Boske, 2011; Kaiser, Seitz, & Walters, 2014). In education, Rands (2009) has advocated for a "gender complex approach" that accommodates the needs of transgender learners and also draws all students' attention to issues of gender in the classroom.

While recent years have seen a growing body of research on LGBT issues in music education (Bergonzi, 2009; Carter, 2013; Freer, 2013; Garrett, 2012; Paparo & Sweet, 2014; Taylor, 2011), music education research on the experience of transgender individuals remains scant, with a few notable exceptions. Nichols' (2013) narrative study of a gender-variant musician marked the first inclusion of a trans voice in the music education literature. Palkki's (2016) dissertation used narrative strategies to explore three trans students' experiences in secondary choral music programs, examining the ways context, policy, and other factors influenced the participants' negotiation of gender identity. Silveira and Goff (2016) explored music teacher attitudes toward transgender students, finding generally positive attitudes[2] among survey respondents. The authors noted a disconnect between the documented negative experiences of trans students in schools (Kosciw, Greytak, Palmer, & Boesen, 2014) and the positive attitudes of the majority of their participants, raising the question of whether attitudes translate into actions in the classroom. The authors recommended more training for music educators to better support the needs of transgender students in the classroom. Music therapists have also begun to consider the ways their field might serve transgender clients, recognizing the potentially powerful role of music in the lives of gender-diverse individuals (Bain, Grzanka, & Crowe, 2016; Whitehead-Pleaux et al., 2012; 2013).

These initial efforts have drawn the voices of transgender individuals into the scholarly discourse and illustrate a burgeoning conversation about the experiences and needs of transgender musicians. The present investigation aims to contribute to this conversation, exploring the experiences of Melanie, a transgender woman[3] navigating the world of music education from public schools, through college, and ultimately into the field as a music educator. It also incorporates the perspective of Sarah, a music teacher educator grappling with her unpreparedness to support trans students and ultimately finding her way toward becoming a better, more educated trans advocate. We hope that by examining deeply the lived experiences of one transgender music educator we might advocate on behalf of transgender individuals participating in music education at all levels and shine a light on the role of music educators in fostering safe music learning environments for gender-diverse students.

Genesis of the Study

We met during the Spring semester of 2012, when Melanie was a sophomore music education major enrolled in my foundations course. Early on in the semester, Mel (Matthew on my roster) came out to me as transgender in one of her writing reflections. She was worried about how her gender identity might impact her teaching and her relationship with the children in public school classrooms. While I reassured Melanie that I would happily support her throughout her fieldwork, I admit that, at the time, I did not truly consider the implications of her identity as transgender and how it might interact with her development as a music educator. While I proclaimed to be LGBT-friendly in my practice, I was, frankly, oblivious to what it actually meant to support the needs of a transgender student. My ignorance became painfully clear during Melanie's senior year when I misgendered her in one of our elementary methods classes. While she graciously accepted my apology following that incident, I realized that I had much to learn in order to become a true ally and advocate for transgender students. I approached her about the possibility of engaging in some research together and she eagerly agreed. We adopted a narrative framework to tell Melanie's story

(Clandinin, 2013; Clandinin & Connelly, 2000), working collaboratively toward the creation of an "emancipatory-minded story" (Barone, 1995) that would contribute to the discourse on transgender issues in music education.

Over the course of Melanie's senior year of college, we engaged in eight 90-minute oral history interviews focused on her experiences as a transgender student and pre-service music educator. With her permission, I also reviewed the blog that she wrote during her freshmen and sophomore years. During the 2 years following her graduation, we continued data collection, focusing on the ongoing nature of her transition and the continued challenges she faced on the job market and in her first years of teaching. We met annually via Skype for formal "check in" interviews and, in Spring of 2016, I visited Melanie at her school to complete several hours of interviews and two days of observations in her general music classroom. After that visit, I analyzed the full data set and with Melanie's continued input, I drafted a full narrative of Melanie's journey (Bartolome, 2016). During the Fall of 2016, we met three more times via Skype (about one hour each) to complete additional interviews. We also corresponded frequently via email, working toward a collaborative chapter featuring original writing by both of us and exploring more deeply the particular salient themes that emerged from the full data set. We have tried to craft an "artfully persuasive educational story, [. . .] one with the potential for luring readers into [. . .] rethinking their own selves and situations as educators" (Barone, 1995, p. 66).

The first part of this chapter portrays Melanie's experiences growing up and coming to terms with her gender identity, highlighting the particular role of music education during that journey. The second part of the chapter represents our intertwined journeys, incorporating both Sarah's and Melanie's perspectives on critical events during Melanie's pre-service training and her entrance into the field. The final section incorporates Sarah's perspectives on the lessons learned through this research journey and the ways it has changed her practice as a music educator. Throughout the chapter, we have integrated narrative vignettes, affording the reader a window into our lived experiences and an opportunity to bear witness to critical moments in the world of one transgender music educator. While Sarah serves as the primary narrator for this chapter, vignettes are presented in two different fonts to signify the voices of Melanie and Sarah. By sharing our experiences, we hope to raise the visibility of trans issues in music education contexts and inspire the professional community to move toward a more inclusive and welcoming music education culture. We invite the reader to ultimately consider the ways Melanie's story might influence their attitudes toward transgender students and inform their practice as inclusive and socially conscious music educators.

Growing up Trans

During our very first interview, I tentatively asked Melanie, "When did you realize you were transgender?" I quickly followed with a nervous, "Is it ok to ask that question?" She laughed and explained that she gets that question all the time, in a lot of different ways: "People ask me, 'When did you realize you were a girl?' or 'When did you figure out that you were transgender?' Or the more ignorant one: 'When did you decide that you wanted to be transgender?'" She chuckled and threw a little side-eye at me: "I have never really understood that last question, because why would I choose this life? Why would I? [laughing] It sucks." She went on to graciously answer my question:

The truth is there never was one defining moment I could point to in my life and say, "That's it. That's exactly when I knew with absolute certainty I was supposed to be a woman." It took over a decade of uncomfortable moments, a decade of experiences where I recognized that in some way I was different from other boys. The story that I always tell is that I have always known that I was different . . .

> *The bell rings for recess and my class is released to the playground, a noisy and rambunctious pack of second graders bolting towards a few moments of freedom. I hear my name being called by my friends Nicole and Rachel, "Matt! Come play with us!" Though there are other boys in my grade level wanting to play, I run to play with the girls because, well . . . their games are more fun. We decide to play a game, one that results in me being "captured," the first prisoner in our imaginary battle. This can only mean one thing: jail. Nicole and Rachel force me into the girls' bathroom and into my makeshift cell, the very last stall in the row. The stall door locks and I am left trapped. To some boys, this would cause a great deal of discomfort. Being stuck somewhere "just for girls" was not okay. I, however, am quite content, feeling happier and more at ease in the girls' restroom than I ever had in the boys'. "Why aren't you yelling or screaming?" Rachel asks. "It's like you don't even care that you were captured!" Her remark snaps me out of my thoughts, and I quickly begin faking my anger at being trapped in the horrid girls' bathroom. Once my jail sentence is up, I am released from my prison. I exit the bathroom giving little thought as to why it felt so normal to be in a space for girls, while it felt so wrong to use the other restroom daily. Besides, there are more games to play anyway.*

Matthew grew up outside of Dallas, living with his parents and older brother in a small suburban community. He sensed early on that there was something different about him and, more importantly, that whatever it was that was different was something to hide. He preferred playing with the girls in his class, often identified with female characters in stories, and chose female roles when playing games. Melanie recalled, "I had these feelings like I wanted to be with the girls and spend time with the girls and be a girl."

Matthew's formal musical involvement began at a young age. He began singing in the pre-kindergarten choir at his church and, beginning in fifth grade, he joined choir at school where he was quickly recognized for his beautiful soprano voice. Choir emerged as a place where he felt successful, talented, and valued, and singing quickly became his "thing," an activity in which he excelled. When he transitioned into middle school, Matthew was immediately placed in the advanced sixth grade choir, where he continued to shine as a singer.

> *The choral rehearsal was coming to a close and we had just finished polishing up one of the last pieces for our fall concert. I take a deep breath and put my trembling hand in the air, silently cursing at its clear indication of my nerves. My director calls on me, and I squeak out my question, as the rest of the mixed choir looks on, some slightly bemused. "You want to sing with the girls?" my choir director asks. She looks troubled. "Yes!" I manage. "My voice is higher and I just feel more comfortable singing with girls." Something in her strange facial expression tells me that I should prepare for a rejection. But what I get isn't necessarily a rejection, but something . . . else. "You do realize that means you'd be singing the girl songs, right?" I look around at the other guys, the vast majority of them smirking or laughing, and quickly withdraw my question. The way she said "girl songs" was rejection enough for me. I blush and stammer, "Oh. No. Forget it." I slink back down into my seat, humiliated and morose. Choir would be so much better if I could just be one of the girls. But unfortunately, I'm a boy. And there's nothing I can do about that.*

It was during middle school that Matthew's choir participation intensified and he truly found a home in the choir. It was also during this time that he began to experience some conflict between his emerging gender identity and the gendered nature of choir. A request to "sing with the girls" was met with ridicule and he began to hear negative comments from male peers who occasionally bullied him and called him "gay." In seventh grade, the onset of puberty heralded an inevitable voice change and his coveted soprano voice dropped into the low bass range. Matthew was uncomfortable in his rapidly changing male body and struggled to use the alien, masculine voice that came with it. After reading an adolescent novel about a girl being trapped in a boy's body, Matthew had the recurring thought, "Oh my gosh, I wish I would just wake up a girl. I wish this was all just a dream." Toward the end of middle school, an internet search finally gave a name to the feelings Matthew was experiencing: transgender. While having a label for his feelings was a huge relief, it also represented a scary and uncertain road ahead, a journey that was further complicated by his transition to high school.

> *My high school choral director cuts us off, and I intentionally hold onto my low E-flat for just an extra second, so everybody knows who has that*

*low note below the staff. The sopranos and altos are impressed and the
other tenors and basses look slightly jealous. As the director reminds us to
all cut off together (giving me pointed side eye), the bell rings—choir has
finished for the day. My friend Erin rushes over to me, eyes wide. (Erin is
one of the many people who know I identify as transgender, but unlike
most people, she has begun to use female descriptors in everyday
language. It feels amazing.) She says, "Dang girl, that low note was
awesome!" I thank her and explain: "It is still fun to sing so low, even if it
isn't 'girly'." She looks at me, suddenly serious, and says, "Stop worrying
so much about being girly, and just be you. Everything else will fall into
place." After a few minutes of gossiping, I walk away thinking about her
advice. Is it possible to be a girl who sings bass? Surely there are worse
things in the world . . .*

During high school, Matthew continued to find great success as a bass in the
choir. His rich, low voice was valued by his choir teacher, he was singing in
multiple school-based choirs, and he even earned a place in the competitive all-
region choir. He was however tormented by the disconnect between his very
low, masculine-sounding voice and his intensifying internal desire to be more
feminine. Matthew began to confide in close girlfriends who delighted in teaching
him about makeup and other "girly things." He also began to make small, secret
changes, like shaving his legs and wearing a bra under his oversize sweatshirts,
"things that nobody else would notice but things that would secretly make me
feel better."

During that time, Matthew struggled with serious depression: "I was having
a sort of mental overload, just horrible, typical teenage angst, coupled with my
own internal conflict. You know, I didn't really understand what was going on,
but I was just super, super angry about a lot of stuff." His father, recognizing that
something was wrong, confronted him and, after much goading, Matthew finally
revealed his feelings: "I want to be a girl. I am a girl. I feel like I should have
been born a girl. That's what I want to be." While his father was shocked, he
proclaimed, "I love you no matter what." Matthew was immediately enrolled in
weekly therapy, which eventually yielded a diagnosis of gender identity disorder.

Matthew became convinced that he was "a freak" and, like so many other
transgender individuals, he came to the ultimate conclusion that it would be easier
to end his own existence than continue to suffer. Overcome with desperation,
Matthew attempted suicide one night during his sophomore year of high school:

I wrote out a whole letter, like a suicide note. And I thought that you
could OD on anything. Well, the only pills that I had were acne medication.
Which you know, is just stupid . . . but I remember that I took 27 pills
right before bed and I thought, "Oh, I'll just die when I sleep." And I
woke up the next morning feeling awful; my stomach was burning. And

the sad part was that my skin wasn't any better either [laughing] and so I was pissed off about that, too.

Obviously concerned about his mental health, Matthew's parents forced him to continue in therapy throughout high school. Melanie contends that more critical to her ability to begin to come to terms with her transgender identity was her involvement with a local LGBTQ organization: "It was the only place where I could identify as female and be myself publicly. I was actually expected to use the women's bathroom. People used 'she' and 'her' which I had never really encountered before." Through this organization, Matthew met other trans individuals and started to feel safe, accepted, and not alone for the first time.

During this time, choir continued to be a source of pride and satisfaction for Matthew, bolstering his confidence even as he struggled with the masculinity associated with his physical experience of singing and performing in choir:

I kind of had to come to terms with the fact that I had a bass voice and I was singing super low. In voice lessons, I was being taught mostly by men, which I didn't like. I *hated* wearing tuxes. I remember seeing the hideous girl dresses but I still was like, "I want to wear a dress!" even though they were disgusting.

Despite these internal conflicts, Matthew made the decision during the senior year to pursue music education as a career: "I decided that I wanted to go into music education because I loved choir and it was such a huge part of my life. Honestly, I didn't see the point of a performance degree because I knew there wasn't any room for a female bass." Matthew enrolled as a music education major in a large university about four hours from home. When he arrived at college, he was living in an all-male dorm and was terrified to continue the process of transitioning. Despite his fear, he made an important step in the transition during his first year: He decided that his new name would be Melanie, Mel for short. Melanie began introducing herself as Mel and even changed her name on Facebook from Matthew to Melanie. While these steps scared her, they set her further along the path to transitioning fully.

The Lived Experience of Transitioning

The Trouble with Misgendering

It's Wednesday and I sit at the front of the semi-circle, looking out at the faces of 18 senior music education students, all eager to share the trials and tribulations from their very first elementary teaching practicum. It's my favorite part of the semester, hearing their first impressions of the littles, their incredulity at the kids' unexpected musical skills, their overly harsh self-critiques and frustrations at not being perfect the first time. We begin discussing classroom management, as it is the most pressing concern for each and every student in the class. When I ask for some effective strategies that were used during their teaching episode, Mel raises her hand. "Peer recognition was super successful for me. I made an example of this one girl, saying like, 'Wow, I really like how Brianna is sitting tall and ready,' and suddenly the whole class was quiet and sitting tall. It was like magic." I resist saying, "I told you so" and encourage the class to use this strategy: "I saw Mel use peer recognition several times in his class and it was really effective. He chose just the right times to inject those little comments." Mel quietly but confidently reminds me: "She." Internally, I falter. Silently, I think, "Shit." On the inside, my heart explodes. I clench the hand that remains frozen in the air, gesturing towards Mel, as if I could catch those two tiny little words, "his" and "he," pluck them from the air and swallow them back into my throat. On the outside, I make eye contact. I say, "She. Sorry." I smile weakly, take a breath, and continue my lesson. In that moment, I realize that I have no idea what I am doing.

Melanie admits that she chose her name (at least in part) because the nickname, Mel, is not strongly gendered and helped peers come to terms with her gender identity. She explained:

> One of the reasons I liked Melanie was because Mel could be androgynous. My friends just kind of called me Mel for the most part. They still used masculine pronouns though, because I felt bad asking them to use my preferred pronouns. If they called me Mel, I was at least getting there and I figured I could work with that.

Melanie tried to be patient with those who knew her pre-transition, recognizing that they were transitioning alongside of her. As her transition progressed, however, she began requesting female pronouns and reminding and correcting friends when necessary. She explained, "It was kind of a fight, making sure that the correct pronouns were consistently used and that I was consistently treated as female rather than male. There wasn't ever really a space where somebody was always using the correct pronouns for me all the time." One peer in Melanie's music education cohort insisted on using masculine pronouns and her birth name in all their interactions in class, in online course-related discussions, and on social media: "He told me, 'I was brought up to believe that it is respectful to call somebody by their real first name.' He simply refused to use my preferred name and pronouns. It was just mind-blowing. It felt like a constant battle." The experience of being misgendered by friends was troubling, because of the implicit reminders that, despite her best efforts, people were not naturally reading her as female, accepting her as Melanie.

The collegiate classroom was another battleground when it came to pronouns. Despite sending out very thoughtful and professional emails to faculty at the start of each semester, many professors struggled or did not make an effort to utilize the correct pronouns during class time. Misgendering in class added an additional layer of anxiety to the mix, owing to the uneven power relations that characterize the student–professor relationship:

> It was something that I was always very aware of, if a professor said "he." And if the professor said "he" or "his" too much, I felt like I had to put in a verbal reminder. I had to literally correct a professor, which is very intimidating as a student. But I had to kind of learn to deal with that and fight for my identity. Because if people kept seeing the professor consistently use masculine pronouns, they would be more prone to using those pronouns as well.

Melanie also noted the impact of misgendering on her learning experience: "[Misgendering] really takes away from my experience in that class. It makes me kind of just want to ignore the professor, ignore whoever is teaching me, and kind of just not be present."

There were also institutional factors that contributed to the problem of misgendering in the collegiate context. The course management system at the university pulled data from enrollment records and, therefore, Melanie was represented on the roster with her legal name. Every time she commented on a discussion thread, her thumbnail picture was accompanied by her legal name, publicly outing her to everyone in the class. Additionally, for those who were already struggling to make the switch to female pronouns, it implicitly reinforced the identity from which she was trying to distance herself. She explained, "It is especially bad when professors have online forum discussions and you have to post. It automatically shows your legal name. And it sucks."

Throughout the transition, she felt the psychological impact of misgendering, noting, "Being referred to as he or him, it was always kind of a moment of recognition: 'Oh yeah, I'm trans and I have this problem because people are seeing me like this still, even though I am trying for them not to'." Melanie spent a significant amount of energy engaging in daily battles to ensure that those around her respected her gender identity by using preferred names and pronouns.

Finding (A Lack of) Support

I am apprehensive as we enter the restaurant. Since she arrived for this visit, my mom has consistently used my legal name and masculine pronouns and I know that it confuses people. The hostess greets us smiling: "Good morning, ladies. Table for two?" I see the flicker of uncertainty (disbelief?) flicker across my mom's face like a fast-moving cloud. She smiles weakly.

I answer with a broad smile, "Yes. Thank you." After we are settled into a booth, we begin to silently peruse the menu, the tension across the table palpable. The waitress comes over: "Good morning! I'm Brooke and I will be taking care of you ladies today. Can I get you some coffee, ma'am?" While I am grateful for the implicit reinforcement of my gender identity, I almost wish she would stop with the "ladies" and the "ma'ams," if only to keep the peace at our breakfast table. My mom opens her mouth to speak and I hold my breath. She gives her order and then purposefully says, "And then whatever he's having." The waitress is confused. She actually looks around for a man. I snicker internally, vindicated that the restaurant staff reads me as a woman. I am also thoroughly aggravated by my mom's insidious and passive aggressive tactic. Will she ever get over this and accept me as Melanie?

During her transition, Melanie's family was not supportive, refusing to acknowledge her gender identity and insisting on using her legal name and masculine pronouns. She consistently felt pressure from her parents with regard to both her grades and her identity, which were linked in their minds. On her blog, she vented her growing frustration:

My dad has this absurd idea that me being transgender somehow negatively impacts my grades. He tells me that I shouldn't be focused on being Melanie while I am learning. I don't understand how he thinks that because I wear makeup or a bra to class, I am not paying attention or doing my job as a student to learn. It's FRUSTRATING.

Going home for vacations and holidays was always challenging, as it meant "dealing with my obnoxious family who continues to send me swirling into a depression with every mention of my boy name." Melanie's father was outraged about her desire to pursue a name change, insisting that she wait until after college to legally change her name. He furiously contended that "You don't look like a girl and nobody is going to think you are a girl" and expressed his disbelief that any school would hire her. Melanie recalled one heated exchange with her father:

I remember saying, "I still think you think that this is a phase. You've known about this for 5 years now. I have been patient with you and I have tried to help you and I realize that it's hard for you, but I can't keep letting you hold me back at this point."

Aware that she would not find the support she needed at home, Melanie surrounded herself with allies at school, leaning also on the strong support of her voice teacher, who guided her through using her voice and assisted with issues of gender expression. She also sought out the LGBT group on her campus, quickly becoming involved, taking on leadership responsibilities, and embracing her role as what she called, "the token transgender person." She took great pride in helping others find the support they needed to be themselves, serving on panels and educating her community. During her junior year, her confidence continued to grow and she committed more fully to her ongoing transition.

The Challenges of Gender Expression

"Dammit." I swear multiple times as I awkwardly fumble with eyeliner, millimeters away from my twitching eye. This is just not working out for me. I stare at my face in the mirror, trying to look past the few stray whiskers on my chin. I see my awkward attempt at contouring and it makes me feel more like a clown than anything else. Setting the pencil down, I gaze into the sink. How do other girls do this? Why isn't there a school that teaches you how to be a woman? I look at the mirror again, noting my long, unstyled hair. Ugh. I'll have to fix that next, but for now it's back to battle with my unforgiving eyelids. I take a breath and pick up the eyeliner once again.

As Melanie continued her transition, she found that there was a steep learning curve associated with immersing herself fully in "girl culture" for the first time. During our interviews, we often talked about issues of gender expression and other little-known facets of the female experience, including how to braid hair, the phenomenon of "hovering" in the public restroom, and the importance of hair conditioner. She lamented:

> Now not only do I have girl hygiene, but I also have facial hair to deal with. It's really annoying. I have to shave every day now and I usually have to wear foundation just to cover the stubble. And girl pants! The button's on the other side! It's just backwards! I spent 20 years buttoning a button on the left side and now I have to reverse it. There are so many things I am still learning. I'm like, "This is horrible. Why would you go through this if you didn't have to?"

She was also spending a significant amount of time and money shopping for a new wardrobe. She noted, "With my transition, it is already so expensive! I have to make a complete wardrobe change. I have to buy clothes, shoes, makeup, accessories, everything. I have to just throw out everything from before. It's a whole thing."

Another big source of anxiety was related to the use of restrooms on campus:

I was in sort of that awkward place where I felt like I couldn't go into either bathroom, because in either bathroom maybe somebody would say, "Oh you're not supposed to be here." So, I had to learn where all the gender-neutral bathrooms were. And if I needed to go to the bathroom, I had to plan accordingly.

Melanie also began to experiment with her speaking voice, cultivating what she considered a more feminine sound and inflection. She told me, "I talk a lot with a higher larynx. I tend to do that just to be more 'passable', for people not to recognize. It has actually caused some vocal issues for my own singing, but if I bring my voice down back to its natural resonance, people will perceive me as being male." Throughout her junior and senior years, Melanie steadily worked through each of these challenges, successfully aligning her daily gender expression to match her gender identity. As she began to consistently present as Melanie to the world however, she encountered a host of other challenges related to her work as a transgender singer and pre-service music educator.

Life as a Transgender Singer

Choir as a Gendered Environment

I'm not too sure how I feel about this new choir director. I observe him as he walks in, suddenly anxious about what he might say today to make me feel uncomfortable. "Good afternoon, Ladies and Gentleman. Let's split up into sectionals to work on the Bach. Women, stay in here and men, go to Room 114." I'm frozen in my seat as everybody else begins to move. This year, I am finally living full-time as a female, but I still sing Bass II in the choir. Where do I go? A quick look at my outfit would have me remaining in the room. A bright pink shirt with a white bra strap peeking out, paired with black capris and a simple pair of ballet flats declare to the world that I'm a woman. I look up and the majority of the tenors and basses have already left the room. I begrudgingly stand and make my way to the door. Each step away from the other women in the ensemble highlights how different I am. As the door to the main choir room closes, I see the director moving on, completely oblivious as to how he just made me feel. These are the times when I hate choir.

I arrive early to get a good seat by the door. The Candlelight Concert is always packed and while I love attending, when it's over I want to get out and back to the car before the crowds. As the choir begins processing down the aisle of the hall, I see Melanie in her coveted black choir dress (her first, affectionately known as the Garbage Bag Dress). I feel instantly annoyed that the director has placed her on the "Men's Side." Not only does she stick out

like a sore thumb as the only person in a dress, it will also be abundantly clear
to those audience members in her close proximity that she is singing bass.
A bass in a dress. She is instantly publicly outed. The choir processes to
the stage and I breathe a sigh of relief that what must have been an
uncomfortable experience for Melanie has passed. I remember Melanie
saying that the director had mixed them onstage to help her to blend in
between sections, so I am further dismayed when I see her standing on the
edge of the formation, a single woman situated in a sea of tuxedos, while
the rest of the women occupy the other half of the stage. I seethe quietly
in the audience.

The choral context emerged as a significantly challenging context for Melanie
throughout her transition. The consistent use of gendered language during
rehearsals often left her feeling uncomfortable and unwelcome. Despite feeling
this discomfort, Melanie did not feel equipped to confront the director about
this issue, worrying about her place in the university's top ensemble: "I was already
feeling, especially as a first-year, so fortunate to be in the top choir. I didn't want
to do anything to ruin my chances of staying there. So, I just sort of stuck with
being male in that context. I endured it."

During the Fall of her junior year, a new conductor took over the choir
program and Melanie saw it as an opportunity to assert her identity in choir for
the first time. While initially voicing support for Melanie, he only begrudgingly
allowed her to wear a dress for concerts and did not follow through on his
commitment to choose a choral arrangement that would allow Melanie (a female
bass) to blend in between sections. Perhaps the most disturbing interaction
happened just before choir tour, when the conductor made a blatantly transphobic
comment:

> I think one of the worst things that my choir director said to me was,
> "I really just want you to kind of fade into the background and I want you
> to kind of keep quiet because there are some people when we go on tour
> that are going to find this disgusting." With that one statement, I didn't
> feel like I really belonged in the choir and it wasn't a feeling that ever
> changed. That whole experience was very troubling for me. Afterwards I
> was like, I am glad that I am not in his choir anymore and I will not have
> to be under his baton ever again.

While choir had previously felt like a home to her, it suddenly emerged as
an unwelcoming place, fraught with hostile reminders that she did not belong,
that transgender singers had no place in this community. Melanie's experience
in the choir was so challenging that she elected to not participate in an ensemble
in her senior year of college.

Life as Transgender Pre-service Music Educator

Transitioning While Transitioning: Negotiating Gender and Teacher Identity

The autumn wind blows relentlessly through me and I fervently hold my skirt down so as to avoid a humiliating wardrobe malfunction. I shiver as I stop in front of the doors of the high school. It's time for my first choral practicum in front of real high school students—my first time presenting as female in the classroom. My mind is a mess and I can't help picturing all of the ways this could go wrong. The first thoughts are the obvious ones: "What if they can tell that I'm not a cisgender woman? What if they see through this skirt like the façade that it is and read me as male? What do I do?" Then I remember I also have to worry about actually teaching them . . . The click of my heels reverberates down the empty hallways. Each step seems to bring me closer to certain peril. As I walk into the choir room, I am met with thirty sets of high school eyes. It takes every ounce of strength that I have to go and sit down with the other members of my collegiate class. When it's my turn to lead the warmup, I freeze. Can I really do this? Somehow, I muster the courage to step onto the podium. Nervously, I direct the students to stand up. They obediently stand. No one snickers or mentions my physical appearance. They gaze at me expectantly. I sigh internally with relief, bring my voice into a comfortable falsetto, and begin my rehearsal.

Melanie stands nervously at the front of the room dressed in brand new "teacher clothes." She looks back at me, seated in the corner of the room in a little person chair, computer on my lap, waiting for her lesson to begin. I smile and nod encouragingly. We hear the buzz of second-grade voices coming down the hall and Melanie takes a deep breath as 22 curious second graders file into the room, find their seats, and look at her expectantly. The classroom teacher announces, "OK, friends, it's time for music. Would you say good afternoon to Miss Stanford?" The children dutifully reply in chorus, "Good afternoon, Miss Stanford." I watch with bated breath, monitoring the students' reactions to Miss S., ready to jump in should the need arise. One child looks up at Melanie, his head tilted back, eyes wide. He leans over and whispers to his neighbor, "Wow, she's tall!" I look around at the classroom full of smiling second graders and realize that it's fine. They are singing beautifully already. Melanie looks comfortable and confident. I sneak out of the room, relieved, and let Melanie teach her lesson.

From the beginning, Melanie had significant fears about how her gender identity might affect her training as a music educator. For her entire first year and most of her second year of college, she resigned herself to presenting as male any time she was working with students in public school classrooms. Afraid of the kinds of issues that might arise, she explained, "I sort of had the normal fears along with, 'Ok, well, what if this kid isn't sure of my gender or isn't sure of how I am presenting? What if they tell their parents? What if they tell their teacher?' And then it could be a whole thing." In her junior year, Melanie committed fully to presenting as female every day and she was suddenly confronted with the realities of negotiating both her gender identity and her teacher identity simultaneously in a new way:

> My cisgender peers don't recognize all the extra things I have to think about while I am teaching. Like when I am speaking, I am constantly thinking, "Oh, is it too high of a pitch? Is it too low of a pitch? How am I sounding inflection-wise? Is my fundamental frequency too low? How's my voice? Are my mannerisms feminine enough?" Meanwhile they can just say, "OK, here we go!" and teach. They were worried more about teaching. And I had those same fears, but I also had that extra fear of "Oh my gosh, they could recognize that I am not female."

Issues of voice cropped up repeatedly, as she worked toward a stronger, healthy falsetto singing voice that would be convincingly female. Her attention to issues of voice and consistent work in the voice studio allowed her to successfully find a teacher voice and singing model that was healthy and sustainable and also supported her gender identity in the classroom. As she prepared to graduate from college, she happily noted, "In terms of my identity during fieldwork, I think it was fine. There wasn't any kind of gender confusion with the students." Through careful preparation and attention to issues of gender expression, Melanie successfully negotiated her dual emerging identities, simultaneously cultivating her teacher identity while continuing to solidify her identity as Melanie.

Life as a Transgender Music Educator

Finding a Job

It has only been a few weeks as a long-term substitute choral/band director in an inner-city school, but I am exhausted. I check my phone for the time. 6:45 a.m. Great, I still had a few minutes to sign in before having my first class ready to go. The school secretary stops me mid-sign in and reminds me to turn in my Praxis scores so that I can get slightly better substitute pay. Reassuringly, I tell her she would have them soon and hurry away to my classroom. Actually, I have no intention of turning in my Praxis scores to her. What she doesn't know is I have already called the Educational Testing Service (ETS) 4 times to try and have my birth name changed to my legal name on my score report. On the phone with ETS, I have explained how the Texas court order directed any agency to formally change my name in the system. I have offered to fax over copies of my now-correct driver's license and Social Security Card. Every time, the ETS representative politely declined, saying it wasn't their policy. Each time, I hung up in anger. I think about what would happen if I turned in my Praxis scores. The secretary could refuse them, saying that the scores aren't mine. I would be forced to out myself and I could possibly face discrimination or termination because of it. I even printed out the reports and whited out all but the first initial of my name. Maybe that would work? Staring at the paper, I realize it would be easier to just accept the lower pay, just deal with it for these last months before summer. I ball up the score reports and throw them away as my first student enters the room.

As Melanie mounted a job search in her home state of Texas, she began to suspect that her gender identity might be influencing her ability to get a job. All applications required a background check, which meant disclosing her legal sex[4] (male) and would also pull up record of her name change. She was repeatedly turned down for jobs after very positive on-site interviews and on one occasion a verbal offer fell through at the last moment. A colleague she ran into at a conference went so far as to advise her to seek employment out of state, implying that it would be nearly impossible for her to find a job as a transgender individual in a conservative state where "everyone knows everyone in choral music." Despite this disheartening advice and repeated rejection, Melanie persisted. While she was offered one high school choral position, the conservative nature of the community and the fact the district Equal Employment Opportunity (EEO) policy did not include gender identity led her to decline the offer. She ultimately accepted a position at an elementary school outside of Houston, beginning her career as a K–5 general music specialist.

Finding Her Way

About 10 minutes before the start of my first class, my principal enters my room. A veteran himself, he tells me just how much he enjoyed yesterday's Veterans Day performance, noting, "I was just at the administration building bragging about you!" My smile gets bigger. As he turns to leave my room, he throws back over his shoulder, "By the way, the HR Director wanted to meet you, so she's going to come to your room right after school. I'm sure it's nothing bad! Have a good day!" My face falls. Just like that, my jubilation is replaced with anxiety. Throughout the day, I fret. This was somebody who could easily fire me, if she had cause. My district is one of the many that doesn't list gender identity and gender expression as protected in their Equal Employment Opportunity statement.

When the last bell rings, the HR Director walks into the room. My heart is pounding. Once we settle in chairs, she begins her spiel. I can't help but notice how cautiously she chooses her next words. "So. . . . you told a couple of teachers something about you, and a couple of parents found out." I nod, dreading whatever would come next. "Right now, the only concern is . . . are you using student bathrooms?" Immediately, I'm annoyed, embarrassed, and confused. Why is everybody in this country so concerned with my bathroom habits as a transgender person? I calmly assure her that I only use faculty bathrooms. She is visibly relieved and a cloud lifts. "Okay, great! That was the only question I had to ask. Now I just want to get to know you." I exhale a shaky breath. It appears I will teach another day. . .

While Melanie quickly developed positive relationships with her colleagues, administration, and students, a small administrative irregularity left her feeling a bit uneasy. On the school website, she was listed as Mr. Melanie Stanford. Since the server pulled teacher profiles and contact information directly from HR, and Melanie was required to include her legal gender on her application, the webmaster was unable to change her title on the website. She was initially concerned this small disclosure might provoke curiosity or incite doubt regarding her gender identity, but she was able to chalk the mistake up to clerical error. While her interaction with HR regarding her identity was nerve-wracking, the representative was ultimately supportive and even managed to change the troubling "Mr." on the school website. When pressed, Melanie couldn't recall a single incident related to her gender identity in the elementary classroom: "You know, throughout that whole first year, there was never any comment about my appearance, never any comment about gender or anything like that. I think kid-wise, everything was great."

At the end of her first year of teaching, Melanie was offered a position teaching middle school choir in a nearby district. Thrilled to be back in the choral classroom, Melanie confidently embraced a new adventure with middle school singers. Now that she is in her second year of teaching, Melanie has begun to recognize the more subtle ways her gender identity interacts with her social and professional environments, especially given the single-gender nature of her choirs. She explained, "I am running into issues that I think cisgender female directors encounter. So like, bonding with the guys . . . Sometimes I have more trouble relating to the guys than the girls which shouldn't be abnormal but it still feels a little abnormal." She also described her relationship with her middle school girls:

I am around middle school girls so much now and their femininity is starting to blossom. It has really just completely thrust me into "girl world." Today my treble choir talked about me being the "Queen" of the choir and then instantly assumed I had a boyfriend (and not a girlfriend because hetero-normativity is a thing. . .). Now I'm just "one of the girls" with my treble choir.

She also noted more vocal challenges, balancing her desire to model for the boys and also present a female singing voice:

> I had to struggle, adapt, and kind of figure out little ways and tricks to get them where I needed them to be without "ruining" my passing, or switch-ing into a "male" voice. For the basses, when I model singing for them, if it's low, I fake "bottoming out," so there's no suspicion. Even though I can sing lower than every single one of those boys there. I will kind of drop down to where it's in that ambiguous, androgynous space and so far that has worked. I haven't had any "Wow, she sings really low" comments. And so it's been kind of an interesting little adventure.

When I ask her about any gender identity issues with colleagues or admin-istration, she shrugs and offers, "I think it has been kind of smooth sailing, all things considered. Which is good!" We spend the rest of our last interview talking about repertoire, the upcoming district competitions, and *The Walking Dead*—just a couple of girls catching up. She excitedly regales a few stories in her Melanie way: "Oh my gosh, last week, my dad answered the phone, 'What's up, daughter of mine?' It was amazing!" Then, "So, I am chaperoning this laser tag field trip for my boys' choir and they were like, 'Miss Stanford, you are going to be the only girl there. You are going to feel so weird!'" Then, "Yeah, I have to be at school at like 7:45 tomorrow morning for a festival . . . I'd better get to bed." As we say our goodbyes, marking the end of our last "official" interview, I think about how long and arduous her journey has been and marvel at the independent, confident young professional that she has become. As I shut down my computer, I pause for a moment, grateful for my own small part in her journey and confident that her remarkable story will light the way for others behind her.

Lessons Learned

My experiences learning from and alongside Melanie have changed my practice as a music educator in multiple ways. I am aware of the fundamental importance of utilizing preferred names and pronouns and the impact these small affirmations have on the psychological well-being of transgender students. In an effort to be a better trans advocate, I know the locations of gender-neutral restrooms and the availability of LGBTQ organizations on my campus and in my community. I also actively strive to cultivate safe spaces for gender-diverse students in my office and my classroom. Armed with a deeper understanding of the experience of trans students, I am able to serve as a role model for students and other faculty, advocating on behalf of the trans community and speaking out when I observe or overhear anti-trans comments or rhetoric. I have also worked away from the gender binary in all my teaching, excising "ladies and gentlemen" and "boys and girls" from my teacher lexicon.

After learning Melanie's story, I recognize that the choral classroom in particular can be fraught with challenges for trans students. Given their strongly gendered nature, the issues of voicing, formation, and uniforms represent particularly powerful choices and must therefore be handled thoughtfully and in collaboration with trans singers. I work hard to avoid gendered language when referring to sections and I consider the possibility of flexible voicing to accommodate trans singers. I also acknowledge the gendered nature of repertoire and consider the ways strongly gendered repertoire might both alienate trans singers and also perpetuate gender stereotypes and heteronormativity. I have taken Melanie's experiences as a cautionary tale of the ways choirs can drive away transgender singers and instead seek ways to make small but critical adjustments to ensure a safe, welcoming, and inclusive space for all singers.

Finally, as a music teacher educator, I recognize the particular challenges (psychological, emotional, physical, and financial) associated with negotiating emergent teacher and gender identities simultaneously. I am aware of the issues of voice in the classroom, the challenges of gender expression, and the enormous stress associated with simultaneously worrying about gender identity and the complex art of teaching. I have educated myself about local and national EEO and other non-discrimination policies so that I can assist trans (and LGBQ) students in making informed choices about where to live and work. I now directly address issues of gender identity within my music education courses, drawing attention to the ways gender identity intersects with teaching and learning and raising awareness of the role of music educators in embracing students of diverse gender identities.

I believe that through this process I have emerged a more empathetic advocate, better informed and better equipped to support the gender-diverse students that enroll in my courses. I hope that Melanie's story may serve to raise awareness of the needs of transgender students in music education contexts and the multiple roles and responsibilities music educators have in fostering equitable learning environments for students of diverse gender identities.

Given the recent rise of transgender visibility in our society, I believe more and more transgender students will be free to be open about their identities. I think what's most important is that at the end of the day, transgender students are people and they deserve a place to belong. Music educators especially have the power to have a positive impact on the lives of trans students. Cultivating a safe space in the music classroom and enacting accommodations that will help trans students to feel comfortable and welcome will allow them to succeed not only in music class, but in their everyday lives.

Discussion Questions and Activities

1. How are music educators uniquely positioned to support the needs of transgender students?
2. Is music education inherently gendered?
3. How has gender influenced your own life and education? Have you ever felt discriminated against because of your gender?
4. How does the gendered nature of repertoire influence student experiences in choral or other music education contexts?
5. What are some concrete ways that you could change your own practice to be more inclusive of students with diverse gender identities?
6. Spend 24 hours avoiding use of all gendered pronouns. Write a reflection about this experience.
7. Spend one hour consciously noting all of the contexts where you encounter gendered language. Keep a log of each instance and the context where it occurred. Compare totals with classmates and discuss the pervasiveness of gendered language across contexts.
8. How have transgender individuals historically been portrayed in the mainstream media? How have movies and television portrayed transgender individuals more recently? How does this affect our society's perception of the transgender community?

Notes

1   Melanie chose to use a pseudonym to protect her from discrimination in the workplace, as gender identity and gender expression are not protected under the Equal Employment policy in almost all Texas school districts.
2   From a statistical perspective, the majority of participants in the Silveira & Goff study (n=657) expressed positive attitudes toward transgender individuals and students. For example, most participants agreed (45.2 percent) or strongly agreed (38.6 percent) with the statement, "Transgender individuals should be accepted completely into our schools." It should be noted, however, that anti-transgender bias was also revealed in some responses. For example, more than 20 percent of participants disagreed or strongly disagreed that "Transgender people are an expression of the natural continuum of gender," and more than 10 percent of participants agreed or strongly agreed that transgender is "immoral" or "a sin."
3   Melanie self-identifies as a MtF (male to female) transsexual. The term transsexual refers to individuals who intend to physically alter their body as part of their transition. This might entail hormone therapy, breast removal or augmentation, or gender-affirming surgery. The term transgender includes a wide spectrum of gender-diverse identities including gender fluid, gender non-conforming, bi-gender, two-spirit, and genderqueer, to name a few. It should be noted that not all transgender individuals identify as transsexual or elect to transition (National Center for Transgender Equality, 2009).
4   Texas is one of the several states that has ambiguous laws regarding gender marker changes, so Melanie was not able to change her gender marker when she completed her name change.

References

Bain, C. L., Grzanka, P. R., & Crowe, B. J. (2016). Toward a queer music therapy: The implications of queer theory for radically inclusive music therapy. *The Arts in Psychotherapy, 50,* 22–33.

Barone, T. (1995). Persuasive writings, vigilant readings, and reconstructed characters: The paradox of trust in educational storysharing. *International Journal of Qualitative Studies in Education, 8*(1), 63–74.

Bartolome, S. J. (2016). Melanie's story: A narrative account of a transgender music educator's journey. *Bulletin of the Council for Research in Music Education, 207,* 25–47.

Bergonzi, L. (2009). Sexual orientation and music education: Continuing a tradition. *Music Educators Journal, 96,* 21–25.

Bilodeau, B. (2005). Beyond the gender binary: A case study of two transgender students at a midwestern research university. *Journal of Gay & Lesbian Issues in Education, 3*(1), 29–44.

Boske, C. (2011). My name is Michelle: A real-life case to raise consciousness. *Journal of Cases in Educational Leadership, 14,* 49–60.

Carter, B. (2013). "Nothing better or worse than being black, gay, and in the band": A qualitative examination of gay undergraduates participating in Historically Black Colleges or University marching bands. *Journal of Research in Music Education, 61,* 26–43.

Clandinin, D. J. (2013). *Engaging in narrative inquiry.* Walnut Creek, CA: Left Coast Press.

Clandinin, D. J., & Connelly, F. M. (2000). *Narrative inquiry: Experience and story in qualitative research.* San Francisco, CA: Jossey-Bass.

Flores, A. R., Herman, J. L., Gates, G. J., & Brown, T. N. T. (2016). *How many adults identify as transgender in the United States?* Los Angeles, CA: The Williams Institute. Retrieved from, http://williamsinstitute.law.ucla.edu/wp-content/uploads/How-Many-Adults-Identify-as-Transgender-in-the-United-States.pdf.

Freer, P. (2013). Challenging the canon: LGBT content in arts education journals. *Bulletin of the Council for Research in Music Education, 196,* 45–63.

Garrett, M. L. (2012). The LGBTQ component of twenty first century music teacher training: Strategies for inclusion from the research literature. *Update: Applications of Research in Music Education, 31,* 55–62.

Grant, J. M., Mottet, L. A., Tanis, J., Harrison, J., Herman, J. L., & Keisling, M. (2011). *Injustice at every turn: A report of the national transgender discrimination survey.* Washington, DC: National Center for Transgender Equality and National Gay and Lesbian Task Force.

Greytak, E. A., Kosciw, J. G., & Diaz, E. M. (2009). *Harsh realities: The experiences of transgender youth in our nation's schools.* New York: GLSEN.

Kaiser, M. M., Seitz, K. M., & Walters, E. A. (2014). Transgender policy: What is fair for all students? *Journal of Cases in Educational Leadership, 17,* 3–16.

Kosciw, J. G., Greytak, E. A., Palmer, N. A., & Boesen, M. J. (2014). *The 2013 National School Climate Survey.* New York: GLSEN.

McGuire, J. K., Anderson, C. R., Toomey, R. B., & Russell, S. T. (2010). School climate for transgender youth: A mixed method investigation of student experiences and school responses. *Journal of Youth and Adolescence, 39,* 1175–1188.

McKinney, J. S. (2005). On the margins: A study of the experiences of transgender college students. *Journal of Gay & Lesbian Issues in Education, 3*(1), 63–75.

National Center for Transgender Equality (2014). Transgender Terminology. Retrieved from http://transequality.org/issues/resources/transgender-terminology.

Nichols, J. (2013). Rie's story, Ryan's journey: Music in the life of a transgender student. *Journal of Research in Music Education, 61*, 262–279.

Nordmarken, S. (2014). Becoming ever more monstrous: Feeling transgender in-between-ness. *Qualitative Inquiry, 20*, 37–50.

Palkki, J. (2016). "My voice speaks for itself": The experiences of three transgender students in secondary school choral programs. Unpublished doctoral dissertation, Michigan State University, East Lansing, MI.

Paparo, S., & Sweet, B. (2014). Negotiating sexual identity: Experiences of two gay and lesbian preservice music teachers. *Bulletin of the Council for Research in Music Education, 199*, 19–37.

Pusch, R. S. (2005). Objects of curiosity: Transgender college students' perceptions of the reactions of others. *Journal of Gay & Lesbian Issues in Education, 3*(1), 45–61.

Rainey, T., & Imse, E. E. (2015). *Qualified and transgender.* Washington, DC: Office of Human Rights.

Rands, K. E. (2009). Considering transgender people in education. A gender-complex approach. *Journal of Teacher Education, 60*, 419–431.

Rankin, S. R. (2003). *Campus climate for gay, lesbian, bisexual, and transgender people: A national perspective.* New York: The National Gay and Lesbian Task Force Institute.

Seelman, K. L. (2016). Transgender adults' access to college bathrooms and housing and the relationship to suicidality. *Journal of Homosexuality, 63*, 1378–1399.

Silveira, J. M., & Goff, S. C. (2016). Music teachers' attitudes towards transgender students and supportive school practices. *Journal of Research in Music Education, 24*, 138–158.

Stryker, S. (2008). *Transgender history.* Berkley, CA: Seal Press.

Taylor, D. M. (2011). Identity negotiation: An intergenerational examination of lesbian and gay band directors. *Research and Issues in Music Education, 9*(1).

Whitehead-Pleaux, A., Donnenwerth, A., Robinson, B., Hardy, S., Oswanski, L., Forinash, M., Hearns, M., Anderson, N., & York, E. (2012). Lesbian, gay, bisexual, transgender, and questioning: Best practices in music therapy. *Music Therapy Perspectives, 30*, 158–166.

Whitehead-Pleaux, A., Donnenwerth, A., Robinson, B., Hardy, S., Oswanski, L., Forinash, M., Hearns, M. C., Anderson, N., & Tan, X. (2013). Music therapists' attitudes and actions regarding the LGBTQ community: a preliminary report. *The Arts in Psychotherapy, 40*, 409–414.

8

LIKE PUTTING A CIRCLE WITH A SQUARE

A Male Alto's Choral Journey

Vanessa L. Bond

> It must be stressed, again, that vocal production being recommended for the pure upper register, (CT-dominant) register of the male changing voice is not falsetto. The falsetto voice is a "false" voice, a product of strained vocal technique—the larynx rises and cuts out the laryngeal resonator, resulting in a weak, unsupported sound. A male singer is incapable of making a crescendo when singing in falsetto. Every effort must be made to avoid a falsetto sound.
>
> (Phillips, 2013, p. 126)

My stomach dropped as I read this passage in preparation for Thursday's class. When creating my syllabus at the beginning of the semester, I relied mostly on readings from our central text and added this one last minute as an examination copy of the new edition of *Teaching Kids to Sing* had arrived in my campus mailbox a few days before the term began. I did so by relying on my knowledge of the previous edition, thereby missing this and other sections, and without knowing the students who would be present in the course. Now having spent several weeks getting to know them, I read this paragraph in horror. "Oh gosh," I thought, "I wonder how Jamey feels when reading this? When someone is telling him his voice is not legitimate?"

I first met the sassy and sarcastic Jamey Petrus in a K–12 vocal development class during his junior year in the music education program at our university. Seemingly sure of his opinions and obviously skilled musically, Jamey was an enthusiastic student who did not shy away from attention. In high school, he was "always in the front row," and the "choral superstar" of his high school program, most assuredly found in the chorus room on any given day. As he stated reflectively in one of our interviews, "I was always the first person in the chorus room. The LAST (laughs) person in the chorus room. I loved it. I absolutely loved it." As one who would rather "risk it on the telephone pole" (i.e., take a class called project adventure in which you climb a telephone pole and walk across a tightrope), than do sports, his public school associations were primarily musical in nature. This description might match any number of undergraduate students enrolled in a choral methods sequence; what makes Jamey's story unique is that he classified his voice as a countertenor for solo work and an alto in choir.

Vocal development and classification are typical topics of consideration for any choral director. As a result, these topics are habitually addressed in choral methods and vocal pedagogy courses. For the majority of choral music education students, their vocal development and classification experiences are legitimized in the resources they read and discussions they have in class. This was not the case for Jamey. Throughout the semester of his K–12 vocal development course I would attempt to describe the anatomy and physiology of the voice, inclusive of physiological changes that occur with maturation. All students responded with curiosity and questions, but the most jarring came from Jamey. "What about me?," he would ask. "How do I fit into this?" Ultimately, he was asking, "where do I belong?"

These questions alerted me to experiences I had never thought to question, to strategies unexplored, and to resources that required critique and thoughtful framing. In those moments, I realized I was unprepared for Jamey's presence— I wondered if I would be alone in my response. As so often happens in the work of a researcher-practitioner, I used this wonderment to embark on a new inquiry. The purpose of this narrative inquiry was to explore the detailed experiences of a choral singer and undergraduate music education student whose voice did not fit traditional choral classification.

Writing a Story of Jamey

From the initial research light bulb moment it appeared obvious that narrative inquiry would best fit the search to articulate Jamey's experiences. The nuance, the ambiguity, and the many possible interpretations of his experiences all pointed to story. As Brewer wrote, "It is the multiplicity of perspectives, the plurality of possible interpretations, and the invitation to each reader to share in the construction of meaning, that make narrative inquiry so powerful" (2014, p. 25). In looking deeper into the potential approaches to narrative, of the three primary approaches (Stauffer, 2014), critical storytelling (Barone, 1992), which aims to bring forward voices not typically heard, provided the most appropriate lens through which to share this tale. Critical, honest stories (Barone, 1992) require "heightened empiricism" (p. 142), an acute sensitivity to lived experience observed in detail, to construct a story with "a clearsightedness that avoids sentimental distortions . . . and cruel prejudices . . ." (p. 143) while "inviting a reexamination of the values and interests undergirding certain discourses, practices, and institutional arrangements found in today's schools" (p. 143). Surfacing in recent years in music education, scholars Nichols (2013) and Brewer (2014) used critical storytelling to shed light on the experiences of a transgender student and a dually nontraditional (i.e., age and informal music background) music education student, respectively. Their narrative accounts alerted the field to voices not heard in the research literature, calling on music teachers and music teacher educators to critically reflect on the underlying values and expections of our educational institutions and who they serve. In presenting Jamey's story, I hope to invite critique of several normative practices within choral music education, such as gender-voice part associations and the rehearsal/performance practices that reinforce these associations; his seemed a "stor[y] that explore[d] the connections between the pain of isolation, its attendant injustices, and the school as a socio-political institution" (Barone, 1992, p. 143).

I heard Jamey's stories through a series of four face-to-face, semi-structured interviews over the course of a year. We completed the first interview at the end of his junior year using open-ended questioning about Jamey's experiences participating in choirs, preparing to become a choral music educator, and directing choirs. Although open-ended questioning continued in the remaining three interviews, I attempted to elicit new discussion through prompts. In the second interview, I used excerpts from published works about voice classification and development to guide our dialogue. The prompt excerpts were chosen from readings Jamey had experienced in his coursework and those commonly used in choral methods classes. The third interview was a sharing of Jamey's "memory box," a collection of materials that Jamey chose to reflect his choral experiences. These materials included a "golden ticket" award from middle school, photographs of concerts, festivals, All-State/All-Eastern experiences, his high school choral director, and choir trips to Disney, as well as YouTube videos of the All-State and All-Eastern performances. Jamey explained the significance of the items and stated why he chose to include them in his collection (a combination of accessibility, convenience, and saliency). The fourth and final interview took place after his student-teaching semester in which my questions were focused on this capstone experience of the program. I was purposeful in varying the interview formats in order to prompt discussion in different ways, eager to bring forth the depth and breadth of Jamey's experiences.

Hoping to avoid any perceived power imbalances, I asked Jamey to meet with me in a place of his choosing for our interview series. For the sake of finding a quiet atmosphere and sheer convenience, he chose for us to be in my office on campus, sometimes after a brief walk to the student center to grab a coffee. My initial concerns about Jamey feeling apprehensive to share his choral experiences and views about teacher preparation were quickly put to rest by his outspoken and gregarious manner. Our talks averaged an hour and 20 minutes each and were audio-recorded for transcription purposes. After transcription, I read and re-read the transcripts, making analytic memos (Emerson, Fretz, & Shaw, 2011;

Miles, Huberman, & Saldaña, 2014) to capture my thoughts, respond to powerful statements that Jamey made, and to articulate questions that arose from our conversations.

Through narrative analysis (Polkinghorne, 1995), I wrote and re-wrote narrative texts, eventually arriving at a potential representation of Jamey's restorying that I hoped attended to the qualities of what Barrett and Stauffer (2012) deemed resonant work, meaning respect, responsibility, rigor, and resiliency. Once I prepared the initial research text, I sent the representation of his story to Jamey for his feedback. Having already built a strong mentor–mentee/teacher–student rapport, time was needed to make a slight shift to develop the collaborative trusting relationship (Connelly & Clandinin, 1990; Stauffer, 2014) desired in narrative work; this switch also corresponded with the shift to a colleagial relationship as Jamey graduated and found employement close to the university. Jamey's feedback was minimal, but still incorporated into the text in an iterative process until he was comfortable and confident with the representation of his restorying. The resulting narrative account, therefore, is a co-constructed work. This is *a* story of Jamey, but not *the* story of Jamey as one definitive version does not exist; the promotion of one truth goes against the postmodern underpinnings of narrative work in general and critical storytelling in particular. Rather, it is the result of storying that occurred "within a speaker-listener relationship located in time and place contexts" (Stauffer, 2014, p. 177). I will share Jamey's story in its entirety prior to offering commentary on his tale. Following Nichols' (2013) model, I have prioritized Jamey's experiences and interpretation of those experiences as a separate, intact text in order to honor his meaning-making process; the Commentary section will contain my interpretations as a music teacher and resesarcher, and the ways in which my perspective of singer's choral experiences have been transformed.

A Story of Jamey

Jamey's choral history began in his church, not as a formal experience, but as he stated, "it was just like, 'aw, you're a little cute little kid. Go up and sing with the old church ladies.'" Choir started in earnest in fourth grade as an initial entrée into "what choir is," and fifth and sixth grades marked Jamey's first part-singing and select choir experience. After singing as an alto in the standard and select chorus in fifth grade, "in sixth grade I was in the same two groups as a soprano, which was interesting (pause), odd. When you think, 'oh, you're getting older, your voice is going to drop,' no, [mine's] going to get higher." Fifth and sixth grade were also significant because they provided Jamey with his first "all-whatever" experience (i.e., district, region, and state) in which he was able to meet others with a similar zeal for choral singing.

With a new teacher, a new schedule, and a new voice assignment, the transition to middle school was abrupt. Although thrilled to move to an every-other-day 42-minute choral rehearsal, Jamey was distraught with being forced to sing baritone simply because he was male. "Since I was [a] guy, 'oh, you're automatically a baritone.' Not that I had just been singing soprano for a year. Cause my voice is really going to mature that much from June to September," he stated sarcastically with a laugh. The middle school repertoire was exclusively soprano, alto, bass (SAB) voicing in both his school and All-County experience, and this proved frustrating for Jamey:

> Middle school (pause), I was a frustrated singer because I was pretty pissed that I was a soprano and then I would have to sing this low [baritone part]. And it was very uncomfortable. So, and I'm SURE that's, you know, you're going to have young boys who go into middle school choral programs and that's where you're going to lose them because they all of the sudden don't feel comfortable and they're also in middle school and they're (pause) AWKWARD as all hell. And you're going to lose them. And that's why, "uh, I don't want to do this anymore"—I would often not sing. I would sit there in choir (gestures sulking). "Why aren't you singing" (pretending to be the teacher)? I can't sing this (gesturing toward fake music). (pause) "You have to sing this" (again, being the teacher). "I CAN'T sing this. It's too low."

Jamey feels that his voice is still changing, but remembers the start of the change beginning in seventh or eighth grade. The lack of clarity about this experience seems to indicate that his voice change was not as dramatic an event as it can be for some young men (Killian, 1997). Still, he continued to struggle with the baritone designation and was labeled a tenor in his freshman year of high school. For the first time since fifth grade, Jamey was not selected for the auditioned choir that year and was "HUGELY disappointed." However, nothing but public success and varied choral experiences characterized the rest of his high school years.

Jamey's middle school teacher took the high school position starting with his sophomore year. Naming her one of his "best friends," their relationship was quite significant in his musical development, as she also became his voice and piano teacher. In this supportive environment, Jamey went to All-County chorus in 10th grade, All-State in 11th and 12th grades, and All-Eastern in 11th grade all as a Tenor II. The All-Eastern experience was "mindblowing" and the greatest highlight of his choral experience. In addition to adding to his confidence as a musician ("And that's when I thought, I was like, I'm it. OOOOH, yeah. This is the face of the choral program here," he stated laughing), All-Eastern was enlightening about career aspirations—Jamey credits this moment in time as his occupational light bulb, "I LOVE this. This is what I'm going to do." All-Eastern also foreshadowed the vocal struggles to come:

> It was also one of the first experiences where I was like, "Wow, it's really hard to sing some of these notes." I remember I was a high school junior and some of them were up there and I'm surrounded by guys and they're like, "Yeah!" and I'm like, "Why am I singing in my falsetto for this? Why can't I sing this? It's so difficult." It sat really high and I was like, "What is going on?"

Despite being uncomfortable, Jamey did not share his concerns with others and was unmotivated to explore his voice because ultimately he was successful as a singer. Much of his emerging identity was tied to this success and his general comfort in the musical and theatrical happenings in his school. This comfort may have, in part, attributed to Jamey's coming out in high school. He described this experience as happening in phases:

> Each of the 4 years in high school was kind of like a new phase for me. My first year was just kind of like, "Oh, well I'm in high school now. Cool." And then, sophomore year it was just kind of like, "What is this?" And then junior year was like, "Oh, sweet god. Oh god. What am I going to do?" And senior year was like, "Eh, so what? Whatever. I'm cool." And of course, all of my friends were like, "Oh, you're kidding me. We knew from day one." I was like, "Well, you could have spared me quite some time!"

This is not to say that Jamey did not encounter or witness any harassment, but he chose to focus on the positive aspects when sharing his experiences and only mentioned negative interactions in response to some of the reading prompts I shared with him about bullying (see Phillips, 2013, Chapter 5). He agreed with some of the stories shared in the chosen excerpt that if you are a male in choir "you're going to get some heat from some of the other guys." Again, he did not dwell on negative comments in our conversations or in real time as they were rarely directed at him personally. When overhearing disparaging remarks aimed at his classmates who were gay, he thought to himself, "you've got to be kidding me. Grow up." He confided that he never chose to respond because of an incident that occurred during a choir rehearsal in which his safety and comfort in the high school music wing were threatened.

The symphonic choir was in concert mode, rehearsing on the risers in the school's auditorium. Someone in the choir sang a wrong note and Jamey, as the senior, All-Eastern participant, and "choral god" there, "of course, I made a face and my teacher stopped the piece" to tell Jamey she would handle it without his facial expressions. The student singing incorrectly was behind Jamey and his teacher called this student out individually to make a corrective comment.

> We were getting off the risers and he was like, "Oh, you fucking faggot. What is wrong with you? What, you think you're so perfect you fucking

faggot? Come here, I'm going to beat the shit out of you." That was the first time ever, in my life, I'd ever been attacked. He never touched me; he never physically attacked me. But, verbally, emotionally, mentally.

Jamey's best friend at the time pushed him out of the way to help protect him physically as she saw that he was unable to respond. "I couldn't talk. I couldn't move," Jamey recalled. The choral director removed both Jamey and the other students from the classroom and sent them to the assistant principal where the other student received a "slap on the wrist. He was just like, 'don't use that word again' and he was back in class." As a student who "never ventured out" of the music wing, this incident altered a significant space for Jamey and made its mark on his intentions for his future classroom:

> The chorus room was where I was safe. The minute I walked down to the music department it was like (he sighs in relief and lets the tension fall from his body) because all the music kids, we were the overachievers. It's just like here at school. All the music kids are the high overachievers; we're the more mature kids. We have the profound art forms (sarcastically). We're gifted. So, we didn't do that. We didn't talk like that to each other. We didn't do things like that to each other. And, for a few days it was just like, my safe zone is really not safe right now. And that's when I was like, I really need to do something about this because this can't happen again. I can never let that happen to a student when I'm a teacher. Absolutely not.

In pursuit of his career goal as a choral music teacher, Jamey applied to the music education program, auditioning as a tenor for admittance into music school. He studied as a tenor for a year and a half, but began to notice differences between his singing experience and those of his peers.

> I was just having so much discomfort as a tenor and I was getting so frustrated because I said if I'm a tenor, I'm listening to all these other tenors sing and they're singing in the stratosphere and [my teacher] told me, he's like, "well, you're not going to be a high flying tenor." And I was FINE with that. But, if you're going to call me a tenor, if I'm going to study as a tenor, I have to be comfortable singing in that range and I wasn't. And he was like, "you know, for a tenor you should have no problem singing a G." And I would be lucky if I could sing, comfortably, an E or an F, you know, in that range. And that was a workout for me. But I didn't have (pause) on the opposite end of the spectrum, I didn't really have a low baritone range. I was lucky if I could sing a Bb. Anything lower than that was just "bleh" (making a sound). So, I had a really constricted range. (pause) And then, finally one day, I said, look, this really is not working out. I know I have

this really crazy falsetto. Let's see if we can do something with it. And (pause) I had a two and half octave falsetto that just magically appeared. And I was like (pause) oh. And he said we should do something about that. I said, I know. So finally we made that switch. And it was, it was SO much more of just like, "ok, THIS is what singing is supposed to feel like."

Although he still had some discomfort at times due to the need to create a solid technique, Jamey was relieved at finding his voice. Whereas most faculty were supportive of his transition, Jamey still credits his lack of moving into the more advanced choirs as a result of his voice-variant classification. He remained in the same ensemble for all 4 years of his undergraduate studies. "I STILL face a lot of opposition," he noted. "I don't think people take it as a serious (pause) voice type." For example, it was difficult to be declared a countertenor on official university paperwork and Jamey needed to meet with the vocal department chair several times in order to work out logistics. The semester after Jamey made the switch, a new voice teacher forced him to return to tenor repertoire despite Jamey declaring that he was a countertenor in every lesson. Although he reverted back to countertenor study with a new teacher that next spring, the back and forth was a challenge vocally as well as mentally.

You have to do this, and you know EVERY voice teacher is going to tell you something different. And, no, yes, no, yes. This is what you're doing wrong, this [is] what you're doing wrong. It was the BIGGEST, just (pause) for ME, mind game and it was so frustrating.

Negotiating this change in regard to his identity as a musician was also a struggle at times. Despite being forthcoming about his sexual orientation, Jamey was concerned about being boxed into a stereotype:

I realized, and this goes into a lot of self-identity as a countertenor, I feel like it's your stereotypical gay male. It's like that's the countertenor. You know what I mean? And I think a lot of people are like, well, oh, OBVIOUSLY. OBVIOUSLY you're a gay male so you want to sing like a FABULOUS woman. (laughs) I think that's ridiculous. And I've had people say that to me—that's where I feel most uncomfortable. That I feel like I'm kind of being (pause) squashed into this stereotype of what the countertenor looks like and how the countertenor acts. Not necessarily in a rehearsal or in a musical setting at all. Just in LIFE.

In trying to establish himself as a countertenor, Jamey relayed that voice pedagogues suggested to him that, if identified himself as a countertenor, that he should be using that voice consistently regardless of context (i.e., private study, choral rehearsals, and coursework). Following this advice, he sang alto in his lab choir for conducting class. His professor, apparently annoyed with his consistent use of this timbre, remarked to him, "you're not going to use that voice all of the time, are you?"

Jamey also communicated that he faced opposition from the repertoire as well. "For Moses Hogan, the alto lines[1], you've got to be quite the woman. Quite the, you know, givin' it all you got. Let alone a countertenor. Forget it." The soulful, husky tone, which is not the ideal countertenor timbre, proved challenging, a challenge he felt most choral educators will face. "Finding repertoire to accommodate this voice type is not easy and I don't think, because it's not a common voice and it's not really a common voice type to sing in choirs, I don't think conductors and choral people really know how to do that." But he warns that it is imperative to choose repertoire wisely if you hope to provide a relevant experience for all students. Otherwise, "they're going to feel bored and just useless because that's exactly how I felt."

Jamey's student-teaching semester provided opportunities to explore and uncover his philosophical beliefs, and put his educational theories into practice. He developed many ideas about how he plans to address challenges related to gender and voicing in his future classroom, some with clarity, others with questions. For example, Jamey declared "never being a fan of" using gender as a separating tool:

> Even in elementary methods when we are doing folk dances, "this is the gents line, this is the ladies line. All the gents find a lady partner." No, you don't have to do that. Line one, line two; find a friend. Boom. There you go. I'm sorry I'm not being as authentic as possible. But guess what? Things have to adapt because that's not how things are going to be. Also, for some reason, everyone always says, "Good morning boys and girls. Welcome. Come sit in a circle." And at some point I adopted, "girls and boys." Our professor was like, "Why do you always say 'girls and boys?'" and I said, "I don't understand why everyone says boys and girls." Why are the boys first?

Other ideas, such as voice classification, proved more challenging to reason out. Jamey felt that a label-free approach for younger children made sense: "I'm glad I found that educational tool because that's really going to help me as an educator." However, he saw value in classifying voices as students matured, even though the path to voice classifications that worked was unclear. He found classification "confusing" and "difficult to grasp" with too many categories for men. He offered that it might be easier with just one or two designations, but that these would be too broad and ambiguous as well. "Just everyone get in a room. You have an hour. Just pick four voices, however many you think we have or whatever," he stated with exasperation. "I know not everyone is going to fit into that categorization, [but] I think if there was less gray area and more clearly defined [categories], it would help people figure out where their voice really lies because, for me, it was such a frustrating thing." Categorization continued to be an area of ambiguity in relation to Jamey's vocal modeling in the classroom.

Jamey modeled primarily in his baritone range for both his secondary choral and elementary general placements. "Sometimes [in treble choir], if it was a part that was accessible to me, I could flip up if I really want to say, 'okay, this what I'm hearing. This is how I would sing it. There's my idea.'" However, Jamey believed that his mezzo-soprano differed so much from a high school alto that it was not the "best option" for modeling. He depended primarily on spoken teaching strategies, such as descriptions of how to make physical adjustments. "That was fine," he recalled, "but the modeling kind of became like, 'oh well.'" Jamey's confined baritone range made modeling for basses a particular problem. When his cooperating teacher suggested modeling in his "other voice," Jamey did not see the value: "I felt like, well, if I'm modeling for the basses, it defeats the purpose to sing as a woman, as a countertenor." Jamey modeled exclusively in his baritone range at the elementary level as his cooperating teacher was male and the students were "used to that. The only thing that was different was the timbre of our voices."

Ultimately, Jamey stressed that music should be available for every student and that decisions about voicing, repertoire, and the classroom environment are best made on a case-by-case basis. Strategies such as seating certain kids on the edge of a section might be confusing for some, causing them to sing with a range that is not healthy; for other kids, it could be their preferred physical arrangement. Keeping clear lines of communication open to make room for individuals, rather than broad labels or stereotyped experiences, seemed to be a clear take-away for Jamey from his experiences. By encouraging students to be self-aware of and articulate their singing experiences, one might avoid the vocal strain or mental stress that can accompany being forced into a box.

> Those kids [that have atypical experiences] have to go somewhere and you can't just throw them and sort of, you know, put them into a voice part they don't fit. And that's exactly how I felt growing up through the program. It was kind of like when, you know, when you're a kid and play with the shapes and put the square with the square. Well, this is like putting a circle with a square: it's not going to fit.

Commentary

Jamey's story is complex. In his words is a mixture of pride, doubt, frustration, and excitement. Above all, a yearning to belong appears to permeate Jamey's past; alongside this thread comes many contradictions. Although pleased to stand out for his musical accomplishments in grade school and not afraid to challenge the status quo of the collegiate voice department, there was a strong desire to classify himself and associate with a group throughout his remembrances. Jamey advocated for recognizing and embracing difference, but also strived to find a categorization system that would fit everyone. He hoped to see his story in others' experiences shared in textbooks and addressed in music teacher education, but he worried about being boxed into a stereotype if associated with a countertenor identity. Contradictions in regard to gender and musical identity also surfaced.

Whether referencing choral classifications or folk dances in an elementary general music class, Jamey balked at using gender to define groupings or range. Still, in referring to his own voice, he spoke in conflicting, gendered ways. At times, he was annoyed by feminized references to his voice, "People always say, 'What do you want to call this? Is this your lady voice?' No, (exasperated) it's not my lady voice." Yet, when referencing his chest voice, he often spoke of his "man voice" and, similarly, connected his countertenor range to singing "as a woman" as seen in his recollection of vocal modeling during student teaching and memory of singing the works of Moses Hogan. Perhaps subconscious, his inconsistent range-gender associations may be a reflection of Jamey's search to rediscover or redefine his musician identity.

In high school, Jamey's musical success reinforced an identity as a performer, as a tenor, and as "the choral superstar." Upon being less successful as a soloist in college due to vocal discomfort and frustration, and in connection with his progression through the music education program, Jamey's musician identity shifted from performer to conductor:

> Because of so many frustrations going on with my own instrument, I just don't want to do this [be a singer]. It was so frustrating. And I just loved being the teacher more than being the performer. "You don't want to perform anymore?" No! I saw a friend over the weekend. He's directing a show this summer. "You'd be perfect." I don't perform anymore. I haven't performed in years. I don't want to do that anymore. You need a music director? You need a conductor? Call me because that's what I love to do. Don't ask me to perform. I just don't like it anymore because of so many frustrations, so many things, and their [teachers'] lack of knowledge about my particular situation. It's hard to, how can I learn about my own situation if I don't have too many people telling me what's going on because they don't really know. You know? No one in the voice faculty here is overly equipped for the countertenor voice.

Jamey also discussed a lack of desire to sing as a solo countertenor, noting that for public performances, such as being a cantor in church, he used his baritone voice; these feelings contrasted with his attempts to take on a countertenor identity seen in his recollections of conducting class. Despite declaring his classification as a "countertenor and I sing alto in choir," Jamey's vocal identity seemed tenuous in conversations about his voice. Perhaps best exemplified in response to my question about vocal modeling, Jamey's vocal designation seemed unsettled:

Vanessa: Do you ever model in your voice?
Jamey: Which one?
Vanessa: Well, right. Exactly.

I point out these contradictions not to be critical of Jamey, but to highlight the ambiguity and uncertainty of his lived experience, traits found in all lived experience. Such ambiguity is at odds with the human affinity to create order, a need that is perhaps the impetus for the profession's comfort in continuing to classify developing voices into discrete categories that may or may not be appropriate. "Putting a circle with a square," as Jamey stated, is the clean, easy "fix," but not a real response to the nuanced reality and development of individual singers.

Despite the uncertainty about his voice expressed explicitly and implicitly in Jamey's words, his views on the responsibilities of music educators were well-defined. In reaction to his experiences as a student and a teacher, Jamey remarked on the unique psychological role that music teachers serve. When choosing a confidant in his coming out process, "it wasn't going to be my history teacher, my English teacher, my guidance counselor. . ." or any other school or community resource. It was his music teacher that "helped me through that," who reassured him and provided the space he needed to be vulnerable. The music itself also had an emotive effect; "Music has always, always been there whenever I'm the happiest person, I am the most miserable human being, every single moment." Jamey's reference to the healing nature of music and to the music wing as his "safe zone" echoes other accounts of the school ensemble as a team (Parker, 2014), a culture of its own (Morrison, 2001), a "home away from home" (Adderley, Kennedy, & Berz, 2003), or a "safe space" (Palkki & Caldwell, 2015). Anticipating that music students generally feel a greater sense of community in music ensembles than in non-music courses (Morrison, 2001), Jamey's suggestion that all pre-service educators should prepare to handle a variety of psychological and sociological concerns seems warranted.

Jamey's story serves as a reminder that one size does not fit all in education. Critical storytelling provided the desired tool to grapple with the nuance (Stauffer, 2014) and paradox of his experiences, and although a concrete list of implications is not the goal or an appropriate outcome of narrative work, his story does raise questions about current practices. For example, in what ways do the musical traditions in schools require students to categorize themselves and, in doing so, force them to fit into a box? Without a student like Jamey, who pushes against established groupings, how might music educators make it known that they are open to different possibilities? As Jamey noted in our conversations, countertenors specifically, and voice-variant singers in general, are relatively rare. While he believed that this, at the very least, necessitates a discussion among music teacher educators and students about the possibility, I argue that a more holistic, cultur- ally responsive (Gay, 2010; Ladson-Billings, 2009), or sustainable (Paris, 2012) approach to choral music education/teacher education is required.

For example, students could develop a critical consciousness in methods classes by being asked to read analytically and consider the counter-example to the majority experience. Music teacher educators must problematize heteronormative practices, and "misogynistic and homophobic" discourses (Koza, 1993, p. 48) that are reinforced in many methods texts. Collegiate faculty can also engage students in conversations about attire, formation, travel logistics, non-gendered language, and repertoire selection with a critical view in order to broaden their perspective to better prepare for the individuals present in their future classrooms. In doing so, one might address differences of all kinds in a holistic manner, much in the same way that Universal Design for Learning (Meyer, Rose, & Gordon, 2014) encourages educators to plan pre-emptively with an environment and strategies that will address all learners, rather than planning for the majority and making accomodations on an individual basis. Such strategies might include consistent vocal exploration (Palkki, 2015), using falsetto as a pedagogical tool for all, and non-gendered and/or rotating part assignments. In doing so, a choral educator might influence the socioemotional well-being of students and create a space where the ambiguity in life is reflected in the school music program.

Considerations of a Narrative Approach

The strengths of a narrative approach lie in the preservation of nuanced data, encouragement of verisimilitude, and engagement of the reader in the meaning- making process. A well-crafted critical story stems from rigorous scholarship, artful writing, and an ability to draw the reader into "the tensions and ambiguities of the text" (Stauffer, 2014, p. 175). Within this process, the author is required to make choices—what experiences will be included, when, and how? In re- presenting Jamey's story I strived not to focus on his negative encounters, however jarring, in order to avoid presenting a story of victimization often found in the meta-narrative of student difference in school. To retell his story in a manner that prioritized upsetting occurrences would have conflicted with the generally enthusiastic and joy-filled manner in which Jamey recounted his tales. The critical bullying incident, however, seemed too important, too aligned to the "central metaphor" (Barone, 1992), to leave out as it illustrated the strong sense of safety and identity association Jamey felt to the music wing up until that moment. Yet, this confrontation was a rare dark moment in an otherwise bright high school choral experience.

Jamey's story has the façade of cleanliness, of being linear, neatly segmented, and contained within defined time periods—this appearance of tidiness and resolution can be considered a problematic aspect of narrative framing (Nichols,

2013). As Nichols stated, "Narrative packaging fosters intelligibility by stratifying the research text into a bounded form, but it also can erase the potent ambiguity of lived experience" (p. 275). Contradictions between theory and practice, and feeling and action, will continue to emerge, one might expect, as Jamey navigates the intersections of his personal, musical, and occupational identities. Regardless of the success with which I was able to present the lack of resolution in this particular telling, there is no single story that can encompass Jamey's choral journey. This is but one possible chronicle, nor is it meant to be a representative case of a choral student with a variant voice type. As Jamey put it, "Obviously, everyone is going to have a different path where they ultimately end up and this just happens to be mine."

Narrative inquiry is less about finding answers and more about raising questions, persuading the reader to ponder that which one might take for granted. "The power of narrative inquiry lies in the possibility of troubling certainty, and once troubled, in the possibility of change" (Stauffer, 2014, p. 181). What questions emerged from this tale? How might the practices of music teachers and teacher educators change in light of this narrative account? Have Jamey's experiences caused you to trouble certainty?

Discussion Questions and Activities

1. Create a list of the many ways students are categorized in the music classroom. What is the impetus for such classifications? For whom are they helpful? For whom are they detrimental?
2. Build a timeline of your own musical journey throughout your PK–12 schooling. How do your experiences align or differ from Jamey's? From others in your class? From those who did not continue in school music programs?
3. In what ways is gender highlighted in the choral classroom? The instrumental classroom? The general music classroom? Who benefits when gender is highlighted? Who is harmed?
4. Select at least two of the following choral music methods texts and investigate how voice classification is described. What similarities and differences are found between texts? What terms are used? Do classifications have explicit or implicit connections to gender? Are there references to the possibility of singers who do not fit within the categories the author has established?

   - Brinson, B. A., & Demorest, S. M. (2013). *Choral music: Methods and materials* (2nd ed.). Boston, MA: Schirmer.
   - Holt, M., & Jordan, J. (2008). *The school choral program: Philosophy, planning, organizing, and teaching.* Chicago: GIA.
   - Phillips, K. H. (2013). *Teaching kids to sing* (2nd ed.). Boston, MA: Schirmer.

5.   Describe your vision for creating a classroom space in which "the ambiguity in life is reflected in the school music program." How might this vision influence your program policies? Your day-to-day teaching behaviors?

Note

1.   Alto lines in the spirituals arranged by Moses Hogan tend to have a wide range and are sung often with a rich, robust tone, making them a potentially greater challenge for countertenors.

References

Adderley, C., Kennedy, M., & Berz, W. (2003). "A home away from home": The world of the high school music classroom. *Journal of Research in Music Education, 51*(3), 190–205.

Barone, T. E. (1992). Beyond theory and method: A case of critical storytelling. *Theory into Practice, 31*(2), 142–146.

Barrett, M. S., & Stauffer, S. L. (2012). Resonant work: Toward an ethic of narrative research. In M. S. Barrett & S. L. Stauffer's (Eds.), *Narrative soundings: An anthology of narrative inquiry in music education* (pp. 1–17). Dordrecht, The Netherlands: Springer.

Brewer, W. D. (2014). Searching for community: The role-identity development of a dually nontraditional music education student enrolled in a traditional degree program. *Bulletin of the Council for Research in Music Education*, (200), 23–40.

Connelly, F. M., & Clandinin, D. J. (1990). Stories of experience and narrative inquiry. *Educational Researcher, 19*(5), 2–14.

Emerson, R. M., Fretz, R. I., & Shaw, L. L. (2011). *Writing ethnographic fieldnotes.* 2nd ed. Chicago, IL: The University of Chicago Press.

Gay, G. (2010). *Culturally responsive teaching: Theory, research, and practice.* 2nd ed. New York: Teachers College Press.

Killian, J. N. (1997). Perceptions of the voice-change process: Male adult versus adolescent musicians and nonmusicians. *Journal of Research in Music Education, 45*(4), 521–535.

Koza, J. E. (1993). Big boys don't cry (or sing): Gender, misogyny, and homophobia in college choral methods texts. *The Quarterly Journal of Music Teaching and Learning, 4*(4), 48–64.

Ladson-Billings, G. (2009). *The dreamkeepers: Successful teaching for African-American Students.* 2nd ed. San Francisco, CA: Jossey-Bass.

Meyer, A., Rose, D. H., & Gordon, D. (2014). *Universal design for learning: Theory and practice.* Wakefield, MA: CAST.

Miles, M. B., Huberman, A. M., & Saldaña, J. (2014). *Qualitative data analysis: A methods sourcebook.* 3rd ed. Thousand Oaks, CA: Sage Publications.

Morrison, S. J. (2001). The school ensemble: A culture of our own. *Music Educators Journal, 88*(2), 24–28.

Nichols, J. (2013). Rie's story, Ryan's journey: Music in the life of a transgender student. *Journal of Research in Music Education, 61*(3), 262–279.

Palkki, J. (2015). Gender trouble: Males, adolescence, and masculinity in the choral context. *Choral Journal, 56*(4), 24–35.

Palkki, J., & Caldwell, P. (2015). The role of secondary school choral programs in creating safe space for LGBTQ students. Paper presented at the ACDA National Conference, Salt Lake City, UT.

Paris, D. (2012). Culturally sustaining pedagogy: A needed change in stance, terminology, and practice. *Educational Researcher, 41*(3), 93–97.

Parker, E. C. (2014). The process of social identity development in adolescent high school choral singers: A grounded theory. *Journal of Research in Music Education, 62*(1), 18–32.

Phillips, K. H. (2013). *Teaching kids to sing.* 2nd ed. New York: Schirmer.

Polkinghorne, D. E. (1995). Narrative configuration in qualitative analysis. *International Journal of Qualitative Studies, 8,* 5–23.

Stauffer, S. L. (2014). Narrative inquiry and the uses of narrative in music education research. In C. Conway (Ed.), *The Oxford handbook of qualitative research in American music education* (pp. 163–185). New York: Oxford University Press.

9

ZEKE'S STORY

Intersections of Faith, Vocation, and LGBTQ Identity in the South

Don Taylor & Zeke

> *I have a story that may make your mind just blow. This is one of those things you don't talk about in our family that much. My great-uncle passed away this past year. He was 96. And back in the day when he was in the military, he was gay, and they actually did a lobotomy on him. My grandmother told me when I was about 12 years old. She's like, "Well you know, your great-uncle one time was gay, and he had surgery. He acted very effeminate, but he got married, and he had three kids." I was like, "Well, I'm not going to question it because they may get suspicious."*

Zeke's story of his great-uncle serves as a stark reminder of how gay men were treated in this country not so long ago. Had either of us been born at an earlier time, we might have endured the same fate. Although Zeke is 24 and I am 54, we share the common experience of growing up in rural southern regions where any deviations from hegemonic masculinity were socially and morally suspect. As boys who valued music over sports, we understood what it meant to be an outsider. The church was our saving grace. Within congregations, our talents were nurtured and celebrated, validating both social and spiritual identities. This is where we belonged and where we found purpose for our lives. Yet as we grew older and began to acknowledge an orientation toward men, we began to question that purpose. The very institution that celebrated our musicianship also condemned a core part of our identity that could not be changed. Where did we belong now?

Through the course of this study, Zeke shared many stories with me, but the story about his great-uncle continued to haunt my mind. I wondered what kind of effect hearing that story had on his young psyche, and to what extent did this information intersect with other messages he received from home, school, and church? My own path was difficult enough, but I learned that his was even more traumatic, leading him to leave his family and his home state, and to abandon his musical aspirations as a choral educator. Over the past 12 years as a teacher educator, I have met several young pre-service choral educators enduring similar struggles with their sexual orientation. Some have come out as gay but have engaged in self-destructive behaviors that make finishing a university degree almost impossible. Others have married young women who either had no idea, or were willing to deny, that their new husbands might be attracted to men. Others have found a way to integrate sexual and faith identities in healthy ways that support their professional goals as emerging music educators. Fortunately, Zeke's story falls into the latter category. He is one of the most talented emerging choral directors I have ever met, and yet his path has been rocky as he has struggled to reconnect with family and regain personal confidence in his potential as a music educator.

For years, stories like Zeke's have been silenced, but I wondered what we as educators might learn from examining his experiences. What messages did he receive growing up that validated his potential, and what other messages made him question his self-worth? How might his story inform our teaching philosophies to be more inclusive of all children? And what might teacher educators learn about working with students like Zeke whose home environments might be radically different from the oftentimes liberal atmospheres of the university campuses where we teach?

In 2009, Louis Bergonzi published an article in *Music Educators Journal* that implored music educators to consider the lives of LGBTQ students. Hailed by allies and vilified by critics, his voice paved a path for continued inquiry into intersections of race, culture, and hegemony in music settings (e.g., Carter, 2013; Nichols, 2013; Paparo & Sweet, 2014). Many young aspiring musicians may find primary support within school programs that may be supplemented in other local forums, such as community bands and orchestras, chamber music groups, or church choirs. For choral musicians, churches often provide particularly fertile ground to support ongoing music education. Yet, for gay choral musicians, the intersection of music and religion can sometimes be complicated. Churches may affirm musical identities and provide a sense of community belonging (Rohwer, 2010; Seago, 1993), yet condemn those whose sexual orientation does not adhere to heteronormative ideals (Chaparro, 2012; Harrison, 2009). Zeke's story of becoming a music educator displays this complexity.

I utilized concepts from narrative inquiry to tell Zeke's story. Pseudonyms were used for all individuals and locations. In many ways a broad umbrella term, researchers have embarked upon narrative inquiry in varied ways. Squire, Andrews, and Tamboukou (2008) described, "Narrative research is a multilevel, interdisciplinary field and any attempt to simplify its complexity would not do justice to the richness of approaches, theoretical understandings and unexpected findings that it has offered" (p. 12). Chase (2011) described that narrative inquiry may illuminate participants' quality of life, serve as social action, and/or identify oppressive discourses and the ways in which narrators disrupt them. Within the contexts of LGBTQ narratives, Valentine (2008) described storytelling as an emancipatory act that illuminates the experiences of a community that has often been marginalized and misunderstood and whose stories have been neglected or distorted. I embarked on this study to give voice to Zeke's trials and triumphs, and to pose questions regarding ways in which teachers and other mentors may choose to engage in social action that disrupts oppressive social paradigms. As described by Chase (2005), I approached data collection more organically,[1] rather than adhering to a structured or even semi-structured interview scheme typical of most qualitative studies. Thus, I sought to capture what Bamberg (2012) described as an empirical view of a person "in interaction and under construction" (p. 105). As the study progressed, I found that my experiences and background as a southern gay man, albeit from an older generation, made the free sharing of ideas quite natural (Clandinin, 2006).

Zeke's Story

Zeke is a stocky man in his mid-20s with heteronormative mannerisms that do not typify gay male stereotypes. He shared, "The biggest reaction that people have when I tell them I'm gay, they'll say, 'I never would have guessed it.' I'm thinking, 'Well, if I had a dime every time I heard that (laughs).'" Naturally extroverted, his deep baritone voice and southern drawl complement his warm smile and direct eye contact to exude a friendly alpha male persona that seems well suited to a career in musical leadership. Although Zeke's masculine demeanor has provided social capital, his story illuminates identity negotiation struggles within social and professional contexts.

The Rise

Zeke described his hometown of Godley, Alabama, as a mixture of Southern hospitality, religious fervor, and blatant racism more reminiscent of the 1950s than current times. He explained, "Where I was born and raised, the Black people did not go to school with the White people . . . at all. The Black people did not go to the same funeral home that the White people go to." He continued, "About two or three White people go to a public school of about 700 or 800 people; all of the White people go to the private school. And the whole purpose of the private school was a response to the integration of schools. So that tells you just a little bit of the town that I grew up in." Commenting on educational quality, Zeke shared, "We had two types of teachers in either school: those who were starting out and couldn't find a job elsewhere—*very* green. And on the flip side of that, we had the teachers that had 20–25 years in the public school systems. They had retired from the public school systems, and they were just dead tired.

And so of course, we suffered. I suffered educationally in a lot of areas—how to write, reading comprehension, math skills. I felt like I suffered quite a bit because we were at a disadvantage." He also noted that his private school did not have music classes. Any and all music education came from church settings.

For Zeke, the church was a lifeline, not only for music education but also for a sense of safety, belonging, and social capital. This sense of trust and belonging among fellow Christians permeated Zeke's social world. Lines were drawn between believers who could be trusted and others who might be viewed more warily.

> As a kid growing up, if I would go to a friend's house and my mom really didn't know exactly who that friend was, she would say, "Well, who are his parents, and what church do they go to?" So it's very much I guess a southern thing. You know, "What church do they go to?" Wants to make sure they go to church because they don't want the influence of non-church atmosphere.

Zeke's grandparents, whom he described as staunch Southern Baptists and prominent figures in the town, shared similar sentiments. He was raised in a single-parent household along with his older brother and younger sister. Being divorced in Godley, Alabama, was still somewhat scandalous, but his grandparents were wealthy, prominent figures in town who commanded community respect. Although close to his mother, Zeke described his grandparents as surrogate parental figures who continually championed his musical talents, both emotionally and financially. Zeke's description of early memories provided insights into the intersection of faith, family, and music that impacted his sense of identity. He shared,

> This is a huge thing for me. My grandmother taught me a hymn on the piano when I was 4 years old. It was both hands, and it was my crab claws, you know? [Zeke sings], 'What can wash away my sins, nothing but the blood of Jesus.' [Zeke stops singing] Of course I was like, "Oh, I want to play piano."

Through the years, these bonds of faith, family, and music grew stronger, solidifying a sense of family, faith, and music that continues to be indelibly intertwined.

> My grandparents have always been my biggest fans. My grandmother and I sing all the time. When I go home, we sit for at least an hour, flipping through the old Baptist hymnal, and we sing them together. We do that every single time I go home, even right now. That's what we do. She pulls up a chair, and we sit there and we sing, and I play. And my grandfather once said, "I want you to play a song for me," and I said, "What song is that?" And he said, "Floyd Cramer's 'Last Date.'" I learned that for him, so that was huge for them because that was

their song. That song was played at his funeral too; they loved that song so much. Every time I would go home while he was still living, I would play pieces for them, because nobody plays except for me.

Throughout his childhood, Zeke's grandparents championed his musical talents. This support cannot be underestimated in a town that often prized athletic prowess over musical ability. Zeke offered:

Everyone growing up fit into a mold. And if you did not fit into that mold, then obviously, you were an outcast. For boys in particular, you started pee-wee football in 4th, 5th, and 6th grade. If you didn't do that, then something was wrong with you. But in my case (chuckles), I started taking piano from a private piano teacher at the school at the age of 6. I got picked on a lot. Of course they'd call me gay and all that kind of stuff. You know like girls are supposed to be the ones that play the piano. Not boys.

Although Zeke's musical interests made him socially suspect, his family and faith provided a sense of belonging and validation. The warmth of faith that Zeke experienced within his family became more personal as he approached his pre-teen years. During this time, Zeke entered a period of self-discovery in which he embraced a personal, declaration of faith congruent with Southern Baptist expectations of the age of accountability.

I went up to my pastor and said, "I want to become a Christian," and he said, "Tell me what you think it means to become a Christian." I told him. So we prayed, and I was baptized at the end of July of 1999. It became real for me. I knew what my heart was telling me. That was also a key moment, too, because it was like I was so innocent. I felt so innocent, and I felt so proud of myself.

As he approached his teen years, faith and musical identity became even more intertwined. At the age of 12, Zeke's grandmother took him to the annual Christmas Cantata production at his piano teacher's church. Immediately, Zeke was struck when the conductor, Dr. George, appeared at the front of the congregation.

I saw the conductor come out, and I was just fascinated because you know . . . he had this white hair (chuckles). It was just beaming, and I was just like, (hushed tones) "Gosh, I want to do that! I want to conduct so bad!" And of course I asked my teacher about him, and she was like, "Well you know, he's a retired college professor of 39 years, and he's very well-known throughout the state of Alabama, especially in the Baptist world." Because not only was he a college professor—he also had a church where he had been at for a long time—very well-known throughout the state. He impacted a lot of lives, musically.

A few months later, Zeke walked into Dr. George's office, introduced himself, and declared that he wanted to take voice lessons. Dr. George not only agreed to teach him voice lessons but later offered to provide them free of charge in exchange for Zeke's participation in his church choir. In this role, Dr. George not only became a musical role model, but also served as a surrogate father/grandfather figure.

> *Having a doctor teach me! That was phenomenal. He really inspired me. Not only was I hit with voice, but I was hit with theory and conducting and music history, and (pause) I felt very honored to be in this position that I was in, and taking from him. And not paying a penny! That changed my heart completely, when I realized, "Gosh, I'm getting all this stuff from such an awesome, awesome teacher. And for nothing. What can I give and pay?" So I was singing in choir with him. And I'd say, "Hey Doc, do you need anything done around here? I'll be happy to." And of course he saw I had a good work ethic. When I started driving, he was like, "Well, you know, I have a bunch of stuff—yard work in my home. Why don't you come over on a Saturday and have lunch with me and my wife, and you and I will work out in the yard?" And so I did that from 15 . . . and I'm still doing it when I go home. So he and I have a very close relationship.*

Even as Zeke was developing musically and spiritually in church settings, his enthusiasm set him apart from peers with other interests, and he often felt alone. He shared:

> *I kind of had the Eeyore personality (chuckles, then imitates Eeyore's voice) "All alone!" You know, (laughs), so I kind of had that type of personality. At least that's how I perceived myself to be. And of course, my friends and even some of the parents, would say, "You need to go out there and play football. And you need to start making contact. It'll build a man out of you."*

When asked if his demeanor met expected gender norms, he replied:

> *Yes and no. I'm masculine. So that part was a gender norm. But the boys that I grew up with were so redneck. I always watched my hands because I played piano. So I think they kind of threw up the little flag for some people, like, "Why is he so different?" or "Why is he so involved in church? Why is he so churchy?" It was acceptable that I was hanging out with Dr. George. But it was like, "Well, shouldn't he be playing football—or shouldn't he be playing video games instead of being at church?"*

In many ways, Dr. George provided an acceptable lifeline for Zeke to pursue his artistic and spiritual needs, and the church provided validation for his efforts.

He explained, "I felt like that my calling was music. You know, immediately, like that was my purpose in life."

Had Zeke identified as a heterosexual male, his spiritual and professional trajectories may have progressed without interruption. In contrast, as adolescence progressed he found himself attracted to other males, which challenged everything he had been taught about social mores. Messages from the pulpit were as damning as the homophobic slurs he began to witness among his peers. Gay boys more effeminate than Zeke received the worst brunt of ridicule, but bullying made him cringe inwardly. At times, his own sense of masculinity created confusion, explaining, "The word 'gay' was associated with *really, really* effeminate people. Like *very* effeminate people. And so of course I was like, 'Well, I don't act like that.'" Zeke grew up without any gay role models whose lives mirrored his own interests and values.

During this time, he remained deeply in the closet and began dating girls in the hope that he might learn to live the dream others had chosen for him. "I was trying to lead a life and play certain roles that I knew I couldn't play. I was almost engaged to one girl. I would declare 'Homosexuality is wrong.' And I would throw up HUGE walls." He began his college education by attending a community college with a strong choral program and thrived on its rigor. By the age of 20, Zeke took Dr. George's suggestion and found a job as a choral director in a small church. This early leadership experience confirmed his skills as a natural leader and inspired him to continue his studies. All was going well until he transferred to Alabama University to complete his education at a four-year institution.

During this time, he began to struggle more and more with his own sexual orientation, which led to distractions in his studies that threatened his academic success. The toll of living an inauthentic life became more and more burdensome, even as he continued to thrive in church settings, obtaining a new choral position at a larger church. On the one hand, he and his girlfriend performed at churches throughout the area. On the other hand, he felt tremendous guilt and conflict as he began to understand his own innate sexuality more clearly. During this time, he began exchanging innocent, yet mutually flirtatious, texts with a young man in his congregation. When the minister of the church discovered the texts, Zeke knew he had to speak with the pastor to put his mind at ease. Little did he know just how dramatically his life would change in a matter of hours.

The Fall

When Zeke arrived to the church for what he thought would be a private meeting, he was confronted by an entire room of church leaders who had all been given copies of the text messages.

> So I walked in there, and the minister proceeded to chew me out saying, "I cannot believe you did this. Not only did you embarrass the face of this church, but you

*embarrassed the whole Baptist church music department" and all this other kind of
stuff, because everybody knew who I was. The deacons were in there, and the
committee of committees were in there, and the personnel committee was in there.
And one guy said to me, "There's so many things that I want to say to you right
now, but I can't say it because I'm in church."*

After being publicly humiliated, Zeke was summarily fired from his position
as choir director. In addition, the minister had given Zeke's girlfriend a copy of
the text messages. Her father was a leading figure within Alabama public schools,
which also threatened Zeke's aspirations to teach in public schools. He recounted:

*I felt like my entire secret had been let out. And that was my deepest, darkest secret,
ever. And it's been revealed for the whole world to see. I was embarrassed and
humiliated. And I felt ashamed. And I just felt like I was completely unworthy of
everything.*

Upon returning back home, Zeke came back to face his mother, who was highly
distraught and confused. He had not come out to her, and now he feared that
his secret would have a severe impact on her as well as himself. He feared she
would be perceived as a bad mother and that social attitudes toward her could
even impact her career. He shared:

*Out of the three kids, I'm the most successful so far. And so she has this huge
vision for me. And me being a gay man is not on her radar. It wasn't part of the
plan. And my mom's mentality is 'I raised these three kids myself. And I'll be
damned if my kid turns out differently because I want people to know that I was
strong and raised my three kids.'*

Sharing his humiliation was more than he could bear, and the emotional
walls he had already constructed became more deeply embedded in his psyche.
Those who loved him most were not able to provide the support he needed. In
addition, almost everyone in his church turned their backs on him, and he lost
many friends. Feeling rejected by his support group, Zeke made the decision to
abandon music, explaining that, because church and music were so indelibly
entwined in his mind, he did not feel worthy of pursuing music. He felt like
damaged goods. Within 2 weeks of the event, Zeke decided to relocate to a
metropolitan city in Texas to study a new career at a trade school.

Prodigal Son

After moving to Texas, Zeke cut off most contact with people in Alabama and
began focusing on a new career. At the same time, he began attending a gay church
and exploring gay life in a major metropolitan city. Experiences in gay settings

were both enlightening and disturbing. On the one hand he was relieved to find
gay men who were successful in their careers.

> It seems like every gay man in the area is successful . . . Almost. You know, like
> they're driving around in a BMW, and they're driving around in a Lexus. They're
> really good at saving money. And you know stuff like that. That is a little bit of
> what I saw. But then I also saw people who acted normal and were gay. Of course,
> I didn't know much about these people, but it just seemed like they were normal.
> I think that was positive.

Conversely, he found others whose lives revolved around bars. The church
he attended provided a view of all walks of life and, within that setting, he began
to find messages of hope and resolution. Within these spaces, he resonated with
sermons that challenged Biblical condemnations of homosexuality. Moreover, he
found informal conversations with church leaders and other church members to
be even more enlightening as he sorted through his own particular issues. Life
was beginning to make sense again; however, he found that he still yearned to
pursue the musical career he had originally planned. Although Zeke missed his
family, he recognized that distance allowed him to reflect on his own life goals
without fear of judgment.

Fear of judgment also led Zeke to avoid any contact with Dr. George and his
wife. Losing that association was devastating, yet he was too ashamed to initiate
contact again. After 8 months, his grandmother told him that a family friend had
asked Dr. George about Zeke, to which Dr. George hung his head and sighed,
"Zeke's gone." Zeke related:

> When I heard that, I was just like, "Oh my gosh! I'm killing him. And he's
> killing me." It was like so emotional. So for like 2 weeks, I was like, "(sighs) I've
> got to call him. I've got to call, I've got to call, I've got to call."

After gathering courage to make a phone call, Zeke dialed the number and
heard Dr. George's voice.

> I just started boo-hooing. I boo-hooed for over an hour. I was just crying and saying
> how sorry I was. "Please don't hate me." It was very, very, very emotional. He
> was very quiet, and said, "Ma and I look to you like a child, and we love you like
> one too. And that's not going to change. I just want to know one thing. Why in
> the world did it take you so long to call me?" And of course I was like crying
> uncontrollably. So he said, "When are you coming back home?" I went home that
> next weekend. I think God works in mysterious ways because the week I went to
> see him was the last time I saw my grandfather before he went into the hospital.
> So he and I had a good visit. And of course Dr. G. and Mrs. G. and I had a
> good visit. They never asked, "Are you gay?" They never asked, "What the hell's
> going on with you?" or anything like that. They received me with open arms.

During Zeke's visit, he recognized that he needed to be home to help his family cope with his grandfather's illness and impending death. He moved back to Godley, Alabama for several months and served as a stabilizing force of support and kindness. Although he attended church with his family, he had never considered returning to church music. He felt too unworthy. But before leaving to return to school, Dr. George challenged his shame. Zeke explained:

> When I was fired, I thought I would never ever be able to work in a church ever again. Growing up, I was very much the kid, I never did anything unless you told me to. I never did anything without that person's permission. Meaning like I almost became satisfied with the fact I would never ever be in church music again. About a month or so before I left to come to Texas, Dr. George sat me down and said, "Well, I want to ask you a question. Why haven't you arranged to have a church job yet?" And I said, "What?!" He says, "Why haven't you arranged to have a church job?" And I said, "Well what do you mean?" And he said, "Well—are you not a church musician?" And I said, "Well yeah." And he says, "Have you not felt that call that we've discussed so often?" And I said, "Well yeah, I still feel it." He says, "Well, I want to know why you're sitting on your laurels." And I said, "Oh OK." And so I immediately began searching. I guess with his permission, I was like "Let's go back to church music." And I was all gung ho about it, and still am.

This turn of events also inspired Zeke to reconsider his educational pursuits. Upon returning to Texas, he made the decision to audition for a four-year university to complete his studies in choral music education.

Rebirth: Mentorship and Acceptance

Much to his surprise, Zeke was accepted to an esteemed university without question. Within the first few days of school, Zeke was approached by Dr. Stone, a professor who was highly successful in his field and deeply committed to students' success. Zeke shared:

> Dr. Stone said, "Now, I know you're new here. But I want you to know that you need to stay in touch with me because I don't want you to get in trouble in any way with your classes. When my door's open, just stop by." Well, I stopped by once. I said, "Hello Dr. Stone. How are you? Have a good day." Now when I stop in to visit, our conversations can run as long as 30–40 minutes.

These conversations became immensely important to Zeke, both professionally and personally. His previous experience in church choirs allowed him to explore concepts on a deeper level than most students, and he had someone with whom he could discuss advanced choral concepts, as he had with Dr. George. Of equal importance, Zeke was able to open up to Dr. Stone and share his previous experiences with coming out. Dr. Stone was highly sympathetic to Zeke's situation, having also grown up in the Deep South. He spoke the same language and could relate to Zeke's faith commitments. Zeke explained that he was considering a career in church music as well as public schools, and Dr. Stone was able to help him navigate the need to express identity authentically. He noted that Dr. Stone was a master at directing conversations in ways that protect one's privacy and came to the conclusion that "what goes on in your personal life is your personal life, and it's under your control whether you want somebody to be let into that or not."

While at his new school, Zeke began to thrive with new friends who shared his vocational passions and whose positive attitudes toward LGBTQ issues were expressed directly and indirectly. He was shocked to discover that students with strong evangelical backgrounds embraced him with open arms in a way that he had never experienced.

I held back from three guys for a long time. Two of them are pretty faith-based. Coming from a very faith-based family, I realized there was a possibility I would lose their friendship. And I felt like everybody knew around them. I finally said, "Look, I know there's a possibility I'm going to lose your friendship, but if you're my true friend, it won't matter. I need to share with you that I'm gay." And every one of them—every one of them said, "What's that matter? You're always going to be my friend no matter what."

Zeke credited these new friendships, in part, to the positive environment Dr. Stone fostered in classes. In addition to in-class projects requiring group cooperation, Dr. Stone engaged students in outside projects that gave them an opportunity to work together toward meaningful goals.

Every year, Dr. Stone has celebration parties at this house. And we do things in groups all the time. Meaning, "I need seven people to do this project for me." I need ten people to do something else. We're around each other and we mingle. It doesn't bother Dr. Stone to have a little bit of chitter chatter in our ensemble. What has been formed there creates relationships that will be long lasting. In my other ensembles, I sing next to people but know almost nothing about them.

Dr. Stone did not discuss his sexual orientation among students and, yet as an unmarried man, he represented a diversion from expected norms in southern society. For Zeke, Dr. Stone's mentorship was a lifeline. He explained:

I look up and I'm like, well he seems normal, and he's successful. And I look up to him, and so I'm thinking "OK, he does exactly what he wants to do. And he can still (pause) he still is happy at the end of the day." So I look at that and I'm thinking, "That does give me a little bit of hope." I just wish that I personally (pause) like I appreciate our talking very openly (pause), but I also want to hear more of that even from other successful people as well, just to know that there's more than one person out there who's successful and is willing to talk about it or be a role model. Like maybe you should talk about this, maybe you should think about this before you make that decision (pause) as a gay man.

At the end of the semester, Zeke had finished coursework and was about to begin his student-teaching semester the following fall. Although he acknowledged and celebrated the rapidly changing social attitudes as reflected in recent LGBTQ legislation, he also recognized that positive attitudes toward LGBTQ individuals were not universal. Having experienced outright rejection as well as open acceptance, he understood that his career path would include many strategic decisions in emotional, spiritual, and professional realms.

In addition, Zeke faced additional decisions about disclosing his orientation to family in Alabama. He began dating a young man with whom he could envision sharing a life, and that led him to consider how much of his life he felt was safe to discuss with others. After being fired from church service in Alabama, he constructed enormous emotional walls that he has slowly begun to dismantle. Yet, as much as he wants to open up to others, he fears rejection, both personally and professionally. Zeke recognizes the challenges, but also acknowledges the triumphs made thus far and hopes that by sharing his story others might have a deeper understanding of the experiences of a gay, Christian musician and educator.

Commentary

It may come as no surprise that gay men have served as choral leaders in both church and school settings, but for years, their voices have been silent. The purpose of this study was to break their silence and to examine ways that educators may help students negotiate intersections of faith, musicianship, and vocation. This story is not intended to provide definitive answers, but rather to generate personal reflection and questioning. What can teachers learn from Zeke's experiences, and how might his story inform our teaching practices?

Congruent with previous research (Love et al., 2005), Zeke's story provides a window into the power of belonging that Christian churches can provide for LGBTQ individuals during childhood and adolescence. As reported in both secular (Adderley et al., 2003; Arasi, 2006; Countryman, 2009; Hylton, 1981; Parker, 2010, 2014, 2016; Sweet, 2010) and religious settings (Krause & Wulff, 2005), choral participation continued to validate Zeke's musicianship and personal worth in a community where his peers valued athletic prowess over artistic talent. Symbiotic relationships between religious and musical identities, as documented in previous studies (Rohwer, 2010; Seago, 1993), were further solidified through grandparents and mentors who championed his artistic interests within religious environments. Intersections between faith and musicianship may be complementary and empowering for boys whose lives conform to heteronormative ideals, but for Zeke, emerging awareness of his attraction to men interrupted this validation. Messages condemning homosexuality from church and home threatened his sense of place, which led him to build emotional walls for protection. When ultimately condemned by church authority figures, his sense of belonging vanished, and with it, his validation as a musician. With any sense of resiliency gone, he sought escape.

Researchers have reported that individuals grappling to integrate religious and sexual identities may not only encounter rejection from the church but also may lack support among other LGBTQ friends who have rejected organized religion (Love et al., 2005). In a study of 105 lesbian, gay, queer, and questioning (LGQQ) adults between the ages of 18 and 24 years old, Dahl and Galligher (2009) reported that, although 87 percent had identified as religious during childhood, 52 percent identified as agnostic or atheist after coming out. Yet some who no longer identify as religious continue to identify as deeply spiritual, seeking personal growth in venues outside of organized religion (Dahl & Galligher, 2009; Tan, 2005). Individuals who remain committed to their faith often seek a deeper understanding of scripture, which can lead to the reinterpretation of religious texts (Ganzevoort et al., 2011; Walton, 2006). Some may feel at home in congregations that cater specifically to the LGBTQ community, such as the Metropolitan Community Church (Rodriguez & Ouellette, 2000). Still others may remain in their faith communities by distinguishing a difference between God and the church—if rejected in one congregation, they continue to maintain a sense of personal relationship with God as they seek out worship opportunities in more affirming congregations (Walton, 2006).

Several researchers have described the process of LGBTQ faith integration in terms of resiliency (Foster, Bowland, & Vosler, 2015; Kubicek et al., 2009; Lapinski & McKirnan, 2013; Levy, 2012), requiring new cognitive meaning-making processes and intentionality. Traditionally, investigators examining resilience have focused on innate qualities of individuality and hardiness (Masten, 2007), but proponents of relational cultural theory (RCT) have viewed these descriptions as limited. Rather than focusing on ever increasing levels of separation and independence as a means of strength, RCT advocates have posited that mutual empathy and growth-fostering relationships are a vital source of resilience that should not be ignored (Jordan et al., 1991; Hartling, 2008). Hartling (2008) explained, "RCT would propose that relationships are a primary source of one's ability to be resilient in the face of personal and social hardships or trauma. Furthermore, relationships are a primary source of experiences that strengthen the individual characteristics commonly associated with resilience" (p. 54). Hartling further emphasized that "all relationships are constructed within, and are highly defined by, the social and cultural contexts in which they exist. A cultural context can facilitate or obstruct one's opportunities to participate in relationships necessary for strengthening one's ability to be resilient" (p. 55). Although first conceived as a means to describe women's experiences, Miller (1991) acknowledged that RCT serves as an appropriate means to examine the experiences of men, racial and ethnic minorities, and sexual minorities. Likewise, Comstock et al. (2008) declared:

> RCT complements the multicultural/social justice movement by (a) identifying how contextual and sociocultural challenges impede individuals' ability to create, sustain, and participate in growth-fostering relationships in therapy and life and (b) illuminating the complexities of human development by offering an expansive examination of the development of relational competencies over the life span. (p. 279)

Congruent with tenets of RCT (Jordan et al., 1991; Hartling, 2008), at least two key people, both educators, served to help Zeke rediscover a sense of belonging and place in musical communities. In alignment with Froehlich's (2007) call that teacher educators need to take "seriously the individual worth and learning habits" (p. 7), they served as "gate-openers" rather than "gate-keepers" to the complexity of music teaching. Dr. Stone's open-door policy with all students was especially valuable for Zeke as he explored intersections of faith, sexual identity, and vocation. Although Dr. Stone did not reveal his own sexual orientation, he made an effort to establish commonality with Zeke as an unmarried man whose marital status had sometimes defied social expectations of his time. Scholars have reported that gay pre-service teachers often yearn for help to navigate access (Donahue, 2007; Paparo & Sweet, 2014; Holmes & Talbot, 2016), but that LGBTQ topics are often absent in pre-service programs (DeJean, 2010; Holmes & Talbot, 2016). Furthermore, some older gay educators may fear negative repercussions if they dare to reach out to others who share their orientation (Kissen, 1996). By acknowledging his own unmarried status, Dr. Stone found a way to convey understanding. In addition to establishing connections with his students, Dr. Stone worked to build community between students in his classes through a series of group projects in and outside of class that might foster camaraderie based on their vocational goals as public school teachers. These connections provided Zeke with valuable social foundations and a sense of belonging that he had lost in previous academic settings. As I contemplated Dr. Stone's influence on Zeke, I considered several questions. To what extent are our doors open to students, and how do we establish commonality with their experiences? Moreover, how do we help students establish commonality with each other? For those in higher education, how might we structure activities that encourage students to meet outside of class in the pursuit of shared vocational goals? And to what extent are our offices and classrooms safe places for students to discuss intersections or personal and vocational identities? Furthermore, how willing are we to open our own lives as examples?

Dr. George also played a pivotal role in Zeke's life. Losing a sense of belonging in church ministry had been quite painful. As a highly revered figure in Southern Baptists circles, and a straight male, Dr. George provided the validation Zeke sought to reconstruct musical and spiritual connections within a ministerial context. Considering the social mores of his region, Dr. George's support was not without social and professional risk. Yet framed within a Christian narrative, his actions could be seen as part of his Christian duty, analogous to the father who welcomed the wayward prodigal son back into the flock. Smith (2015) acknowledged similar risks within the teaching profession that might be offset by framing LGBTQ support as "good teacher" behavior. In both religious and school settings, Dr. George's example inspires contemplation regarding the role that allies may play in LGBTQ students' lives. In what ways can allies provide students with access to music and a sense of belonging in musical communities? How might open support of the LGBGTQ community change the way others perceive allies, and what risks might be encountered when standing as advocates in schools, church, and at home? Moreover, how might such a stand provide leadership for other potential allies who might share similar sentiments but would benefit from community support?

Zeke's story almost begs the question, "Why would a gay man seeking escape from a judgmental, conservative environment in Alabama choose *Texas* as his mecca?" Furthermore, why did he abandon music education? Why not just transfer to another university to become a music educator in a more liberal state like Massachusetts or New York? When I posed these questions, Zeke explained that he was not necessarily looking for a more liberal area; he was just seeking the most expedient exit from home. He had an aunt in Texas close to a school where he could start anew, and the move seemed logical in a time of chaos. When I pressed further to ask why he abandoned music education, he shared:

> *The stress of being in college in Alabama and trying to adjust and trying to find myself—honestly, my grades weren't that good. I suffered a lot academically, so I think that contributed to my decision to go to a trade school. It was a quick out.*

He then began to reflect more deeply about the role of music and faith in his life, sharing:

> *It's just like I get up in the morning and put on my socks and shoes. That is just as simple for me as it is going to church and having the relationship between my musical skills as well as my spirituality. They just go hand in hand. Growing up, we didn't have a music program in our school, so the formal music training that I did get was through leaders in my church.*

He went on to acknowledge that his musical and faith identities were so completely intertwined, that he felt unworthy to pursue music any further, recalling:

When I left Alabama, I stayed clear of music as well as church—until I started going to a gay church several months later.

Scholars investigating intersectionality among LGBTQ people of faith have discussed these intertwining identities and the ways in which individuals strive to manage the social complexities of authentic identity formation (Addison & Coolhart, 2015; Mair, 2010; McQueeney, 2009; Rahman, 2010; Rosenkrantz et al., 2016; Wadsworth, 2011). In many ways, Zeke's story aligns well with my own at his age. We were both born into communities in which virtually everyone was assumed to be a Protestant Christian. As Wadsworth (2011) noted, "Even Americans in the religious majority are typically *born into* religious communities, and thus into identities, which inform their ideology, political treatment, and social realities independent of their will, at least initially" (p. 203). Our sense of safety, belonging, and personal dignity was deeply tied to the practices of our faith. To this day, we continue to embrace the values of honesty, integrity, and honor instilled in our childhood, and we both value monogamy and the institution of marriage. In many ways, these values align well with McQueeney's (2009) observations of normalizing strategies and "good Christian identities" (p. 169) among gay and lesbian people of faith who have sought communities in which their integrity as gay men and lesbian women was validated. Consistent with studies examining the positive aspects of faith and LGBTQ intersectionality (Addison & Coolhart, 2015; Rosenkrantz et al., 2016), Zeke and I both agree that we emerged as stronger within our belief systems, more empathic with others, and more accepting of ourselves. During our coming out process, we were both sometimes dismayed by exaggerated, negative stereotypes of both gay men as well as Christians and sought to establish an authentic sense of identity that captured the multiple complexities of our own experiences. Although Zeke and I hail from Christian roots, scholars examining intersections of faith and sexuality within Sikh (Mair, 2010) and Muslim (Rahman, 2010) traditions have also reported similar challenges among men of other faiths. Like Zeke and me, the men detailed in these works rebelled against hedonistic stereotypes of gay men but found that autocratic descriptors of their own faith failed to provide effective narratives of their lived experiences. Both authors (Mair, 2010; Rahman, 2010) suggested that rather than seeking to fit into existing paradigms, men might embrace a queer approach to interrupt binary conceptions of faith, race, gender, and sexuality.

Zeke and I were both forced to reconsider and reevaluate the theological positions we had embraced and, although our journeys have been far from easy, we have each found peace. I now identify as agnostic and strive to respect the individual journeys that each person endures in their own search for truth. Zeke maintains a strong Christian identity, striving to live the tenets of his faith through his talents as a musician and an educator.

Schools often serve as neutral zones where the separation of church and state is supposed to be acknowledged; however, educators must remember that our students do not come to us as blank slates. Zeke's story provides an opportunity for educators to understand more fully how intersections of faith and musicianship can affect LGBTQ students. While educators are not in a position to provide religious counsel, knowledge of the journey may provide deeper insights into their students' experiences. Acknowledging the struggle that LGBTQ individuals of faith sometimes encounter, Bowland, Foster, and Vosler (2013) posited:

> Spiritual struggles inherent in the coming out process need to be uncovered through sensitive questioning by practitioners who are attuned to the centrality—especially for many conservative Christians—of both their families of origin and their religiosity. Because these are so highly valued in conservative culture, the coming out process becomes even more complex and potentially destabilizing. (p. 330)

Finding that literalist interpretations of scripture no longer resonated authentically, Zeke and I both sought theology that would uphold the high moral standards of our youth, yet dignify our identity as gay men. In many ways, our struggles mirrored tenets of queer theology, which acknowledges the value of individuals who disrupt heterosexist norms. Stuart (1997) explained:

> While western theology and society as a whole have tended to view difference as problematic and dealt with it by creating hierarchies which allow some people's understanding of the world and of God as truth and that of others as unimportant or wrong, queer theologians (along with others) celebrate difference as an insight into truth rather than a threat to it. This is not to say that anything goes. Queer Christians are not content simply to allow one another a completely free rein. We are Christians because we believe that Christianity provides us with the rules, the language, the grammar to make sense of our lives. (pp. 3–4)

Similarly, Hays (2015) used queer theory to challenge pastoral counselors to deconstruct and critically assess assumptions about the LGBTQ community:

> . . . in order for pastoral counselors to engage in ethically and theologically grounded counseling with queer-identified persons, we must queer our own practice. In other words, we must disrupt, frustrate, and turn upside–down the embedded heterosexist assumptions within our practices that lead us to conclude that gender is fixed, that sexuality is fixed, or that identities are fixed. I am confident that doing so will be difficult and uncomfortable and will demand that we enter into intentional relationships of professional accountability to do so. It is, however, possible. (p. 346)

As Zeke discovered, disruption can come at the price of gainful employment. He recognized that those who challenge the status quo might need to tread lightly while gently urging members to consider theological alternatives. His conclusions align with suggestions made by Creed, DeJordy, and Lok (2010):

> . . . this paradoxical combination of institutional maintenance and disruption may be . . . the only viable option for actors who wish to remain embedded or become more central in institutions that marginalize them. (p. 1359)

Conclusion: Going Forward

Zeke continued to succeed in his pre-service studies and is now thriving in his first years of teaching. A year after data collection, I asked Zeke to consider what he would like people to take away from his story. What could he offer students who might be struggling with the same issues he encountered? Likewise, I wanted to know what advice he might offer gay teachers as well as straight teachers. For other music students who may be enduring similar struggles, Zeke's message was as follows:

> God doesn't make mistakes. If you were given the gift of music, then by golly, you should use it. If you feel called, follow your passion because that's where your happiness lies. It's so evident that I am supposed to be in music and to be in academia. So many more doors have opened because I am a musician than if was to ever be in another field. It's a God thing. It really is, and I firmly believe that. If you don't use it, that's like taking a whole chunk of your life away. It's your identity. When I was fired from the church in Alabama, I was scrambling around searching for answers about "Is this really who I am? Is this just a phase? Is this something I can pray through?" And yeah, it is something you can pray through. Not to pray out of but to pray through and how we can improve our spiritual life with Him. I questioned whether my relationship was right with God. I did not lose my faith nor did I ever, ever consider turning away from it.

Regarding advice for other gay teachers, Zeke encouraged his colleagues to build connections from shared experiences. He observed:

> I know a handful of teachers off the top of my head who are gay, and because they are gay, they put on a certain air to keep kids at arms' length. I think gay teachers need to be open and be approachable. I know there's a way, because I'm experiencing this currently. There is a way to be that approachable, loving, and caring figure in the classroom and teacher in the classroom but not get personal. And I have kids tell me stuff all the time, like "I need some relationship advice. I think this person likes me, but I'm not really sure." And I have lots of lesbians in one of my classes.

But it's not one of those things that I say, "Let's talk about being gay today" or "Let's talk about being lesbian today." I make myself available, and if they want to talk to me about something, I'm going to listen to them for what they have to say, and take it as that and give my opinions without necessarily revealing myself. You can keep your personal life distant, but it's very important to build that relationship and build that connection to teach students, no matter if they're gay or lesbian or what they're dealing with.

When asked about advice for straight teachers, Zeke continued to stress the importance of relationship building in much the same way he offered for gay teachers. He emphasized the value of neutrality and safe space:

I think it's important that if your values or thoughts on homosexual topics are different than the student's, remain neutral. If that student wants to talk to you, it's because they look up to you and feel comfortable. If a straight teacher says something judgmental, then they're going to shut down, and they're going to end up feeling even more depressed. I think a lot of our job just entails listening. I think it goes back to the relationships that we start with from day one. I told the choir, "We're part of a large group of people, but we're also a family within each choir. And if we have things that we have to discuss or things that we should discuss, then we're going to discuss them." And I did use the word "safe." "This is a safe space. And you need to know that anything you feel led to say or anything you feel concerned about, please know that I'm not looking over you; please know that I care. I want to hear." And of course, it was a big deal for me during my first several weeks of school to make sure I build a relationship with each one of my students. I see them in the hallway, and I always stop and talk to every one of my students. And that's what makes students feel like they're humans. They're not just a number. They're a person. And with that, does come baggage, but I'm willing to work through the baggage. Meaning, someone wants to talk to you about their cat that died last week that's been in the family for the last 16 years. So we talk about the cat. It has nothing to do with choir, but I have built a relationship with them enough that they want to talk about their freakin' cat that died. It's a big deal. I feel privileged to be able to talk about that with my students. Each relationship with each student is authentic. That's how we can create a safe environment and have people feel like humans.

As educators, it behooves us to take stock of the socio-political environments in which we teach and to recognize that our students' backgrounds may vary tremendously. Zeke's story illustrates the powerful impact that dedicated teachers can make. By breaking his silence, he hopes to generate thoughtful reflection that may lead to positive social change and greater understanding in our field.

Discussion Questions

1. LGBTQ students need LGBTQ mentors to provide models of success and understanding, but many may be hesitant. How might you support LGBTQ teachers in your environment?

    a. How might your race, class, appearance, language, and demeanor affect the ways in which your support is perceived?

2. How might open support of the LGBTQ community change the way others perceive you in school, at home, and within faith communities?

    a. To what extent are you willing to take risks to support LGBTQ students?

3. How might your LGBTQ support provide a model of leadership for other potential supporters who might be fearful to take a stand?

Notes

1. After obtaining approval from the Institutional Review Board at my university, I invited Zeke to tell me his story in a series of one-hour, weekly meetings throughout the spring 2015 semester. All conversations were recorded using the Voice Memo application on an iPhone 5 and were later transcribed in a total of 174 pages using Express Scribe software. Pseudonyms were used for all individuals and locations. Throughout the writing process, Zeke made significant contributions. He chose his own pseudonym, reviewed transcripts, added detail to previously explored stories, and edited varying editions of the final product.

References

Adderley, C., Kennedy, M., & Berz, W. (2003). "A home away from home": The world of the high school music classroom. *Journal of Research in Music Education, 51*(3), 190–205.

Addison, S. M., & Coolhart, D. (2015). Expanding the therapy paradigm with queer couples: A relational intersectional lens. *Family Process, 54,* 435–453.

Arasi, M. T. (2006). *Adult reflections on a high school choral music program: Perceptions of meaning and lifelong influence* (Doctoral dissertation). Retrieved from digitalarchive.gsu.edu/cgi

Bamberg, M. (2012). Narrative practice and identity navigation. In J. A. Holstein & J. F. Gubrium (Eds.), *Varieties of narrative analysis* (pp. 99–124). Los Angeles, CA: Sage.

Bergonzi, L. (2009). Sexual orientation and music education: Continuing a tradition. *Music Educators Journal, 96*(2), 21–25.

Bowland, S., Foster, K. A., & Vosler, A. N. (2013). Culturally competent and spiritually sensitive therapy with lesbian and gay Christians. *Social Work, 58,* 321–332.

Carter, B. A. (2013). Nothing better or worse than being black, gay, and in the band: A qualitative examination of gay undergraduates participating in historically black college or university marching bands. *Journal of Research in Music Education, 61,* 26–43.

Chaparro, D. F. (2012). *Preferences in the hiring of music leaders within Southern Baptist and United Methodist churches in America* (Doctoral dissertation). Available from ProQuest Dissertations and Theses Global. (UMI No. 3542206).

Chase, S. (2005). Narrative inquiry: Multiple lenses, approaches, voices. In N. K. Denzin & Y. S. Lincoln (Eds.), *The SAGE handbook of qualitative research* (3rd ed., pp. 651–679). Thousand Oaks, CA: Sage.

Chase, S. E., (2011). Narrative inquiry: Still a field in the making. In N. K. Denzin & Y. S. Lincoln (Eds.), *The Sage handbook of qualitative research* (4th ed., pp. 421–434). Thousand Oaks, CA: Sage.

Clandinin, D. J. (2006). Narrative inquiry: A methodology for studying lived experience. *Research studies in music education, 27*(1), 44–54.

Comstock, D. L., Hammer, T. R., Strentzsch, J., Cannon, K., Parsons, J., & Salazar, G. II. (2008). Relational cultural theory: A framework for bridging relational, multicultural, and social justice competencies. *Journal of Counseling & Development, 86*, 279–287.

Countryman, J. (2009). High school music programmes as potential sites for communities of practice: A Canadian study. *Music Education Research, 11*, 93–109.

Creed, W. D., DeJordy, R., & Lok, J. (2010). Being the change: Resolving institutional contradiction through identity work. *Academy of Management Journal, 53*, 1336–1364.

Dahl, A. L., & Galliher, R. V. (2009). LGBTQ young adult experiences of religious and sexual identity integration. *Journal of LGBT Issues in Counseling, 3*(2), 92–112.

DeJean, W. (2010). Courageous conversations: Reflections on a queer life narrative model. *The Teacher Educator, 45*(4), 233–243.

Donahue, D. M. (2007). Rethinking silence as support: Normalizing lesbian and gay teacher identities through models and conversations in student teaching. *Journal of Gay & Lesbian Issues in Education, 4*(4), 73–95.

Foster, K. A., Bowland, S. E., & Vosler, A. N. (2015). All the pain along with all the joy: Spiritual resilience in lesbian and gay Christians. *American Journal of Community Psychology, 55*, 191–201.

Froehlich, H. (2007). Institutional belonging, pedagogic discourse and music teacher education: The paradox of routinization. *Action, Criticism & Theory for Music Education, 6*(3), 7–21.

Ganzevoort, R. R., van der Laan, M., & Olsman, E. (2011). Growing up gay and religious: Conflict, dialogue, and religious identity strategies. *Mental Health, Religion & Culture, 14*, 209–222.

Harrison, D. (2009). Southern gospel sissies: evangelical music, queer spirituality, and the plays of Del Shores. *Journal of Men, Masculinities and Spirituality, 3*(2), 123–141.

Hartling, L. M. (2008). Strengthening resilience in a risky world: It's all about relationships. *Women & Therapy, 31*(2–4), 51–70.

Hays, J. (2015). Pastoral counseling and queer identities. In E. A. Maynard & J. L. Snodgrass (Eds.), *Understanding pastoral counseling* (pp. 327–352). New York: Springer.

Holmes, E., & Talbot, B. C. (2016, May 18). Towards a more inclusive music education: Experiences of LGBTQQIAA students in music education programs across Pennsylvania. Paper presentation at the 3rd Symposium for LGBTQ Studies in Music Education, Urbana, IL.

Hylton, J. B. (1981). Dimensionality in high school student participants' perceptions of the meaning of choral singing experience. *Journal of Research in Music Education, 29*, 287–303.

Jordan, J. V., Kaplan, A. G., Miller, J. B., Stiver, I. P., & Surrey, J. L. (1991). *Women's growth in connection: Writings from the Stone Center.* New York: Guilford Press.

Kissen, R. M. (1996). *The last closet: The real lives of lesbian and gay teachers.* Portsmouth, NH: Heinemann.

Krause, N., & Wulff, K. M. (2005). Church-based social ties: A sense of belonging in a congregation, and physical health status. *The International Journal for the Psychology of Religion, 15,* 73–93.

Kubicek, K., McDavitt, B., Carpineto, J., Weiss, G., Iverson, E. F., & Kipke, M. D. (2009). "God made me gay for a reason": Young men who have sex with men's resiliency in resolving internalized homophobia from religious sources. *Journal of Adolescent Research, 24,* 601–633.

Lapinski, J., & McKirnan, D. (2013). Forgive me father for I have sinned: The role of a Christian upbringing on lesbian, gay, and bisexual identity development. *Journal of Homosexuality, 60,* 853–872.

Levy, D. L. (2012). The importance of personal and contextual factors in resolving conflict between sexual identity and Christian upbringing. *Journal of Social Service Research, 38,* 56–73.

Love, P., Bock, M., Jannarone, A., & Richardson, P. (2005). Identity interaction: Exploring the spiritual experiences of lesbian and gay college students. *Journal of College Student Development, 46*(2), 193–209.

Mair, D. (2010). Fractured narratives, fractured identities: Cross-cultural challenges to essentialist concepts of gender and sexuality. *Psychology & Sexuality, 1,* 156–169.

Masten, A. S. (2007). Resilience in developing systems: Progress and promise as the fourth wave rises. *Development and Psychopathology, 19*(3), 921–930.

McQueeney, K. (2009). We are God's children, y'all:" Race, gender, and sexuality in lesbian-and gay-affirming congregations. *Social Problems, 56,* 151–173.

Miller, J. B. (1991). Women and power. In J. Jordan, A. Kaplan, J. Miller, I. Stiver, & J. Surrey (Eds.), *Women's growth in connection.* New York: Guilford Press.

Nichols, J. (2013). Rie's story, Ryan's journey: Music in the life of a transgender student. *Journal of Research in Music Education, 61*(3), 262–279.

Paparo, S., & Sweet, B. (2014). Negotiating sexual identity: Experiences of two gay and lesbian preservice music teachers. *Bulletin of the Council for Research in Music Education, 199,* 19–37.

Parker, E. C. (2010). Exploring student experiences of belonging within an urban high school choral ensemble: an action research study. *Music Education Research, 12,* 339–352.

Parker, E. C. (2014). The process of social identity development in adolescent high school choral singers: A grounded theory. *Journal of Research in Music Education, 62,* 18–32.

Parker, E. C. (2016). The experience of creating community: An intrinsic case study of four midwestern public school choral teachers. *Journal of Research in Music Education, 64,* 220–237.

Rahman, M. (2010). Queer as intersectionality: Theorizing gay Muslim identities. *Sociology, 44,* 944–961.

Rodriguez, E. M., & Ouellette, S. C. (2000). Gay and lesbian Christians: Homosexual and religious identity integration in the members and participants of a gay-positive church. *Journal for the Scientific Study of Religion, 39,* 333–347.

Rohwer, D. (2010). Church musicians' participation perceptions: Applications to community music. *Research and Issues in Music Education, 8,* 1.

Rosenkrantz, D. E., Rostosky, S. S., Riggle, E. D. B., & Cook, J. (2016). The positive aspects of intersecting religious/spiritual and LGBTQ identities. *Spirituality in Clinical Practice, 3,* 127–138.

Seago, T. (1993). *Motivational factors influencing participation in selected Southern Baptist church choirs.* (Doctoral dissertation). Available from ProQuest Dissertations and Theses Global. (UMI No. 9320319).

Smith, M. J. (2015). It's a balancing act: The good teacher and ally identity. *Educational Studies, 51*, 223 243.

Squire, C., Andrews, M., & Tamboukou, M. (2008). What is narrative research? In M. Andrews, C. Squire, & M. Tamboukou (Eds.), *Doing narrative research* (pp. 1–21). Thousand Oaks, CA: Sage.

Stuart, E. (1997). *Religion is a queer thing: A guide to the Christian faith for lesbian, gay, bisexual and transgendered people.* Cleveland, OH: Pilgrim Press.

Sweet, B. (2010). A case study: Middle school boys' perceptions of singing and participation in choir. *Update: Applications of Research in Music Education, 28*(2), 5–12.

Tan, P. (2005). The importance of spirituality among gay and lesbian individuals. *Journal of Homosexuality, 49*(2), 135–144.

Valentine, J. (2008, May). Narrative acts: Telling tales of life and love with the wrong gender. In *Forum Qualitative Sozialforschung/Forum: Qualitative Social Research, 9*(2), Art. 49. Retrieved at http://nbn-resolving.de/urn:nbn:de:0114-fqs0802491.

Wadsworth, N. D. (2011). Intersectionality in California's same-sex marriage battles: A complex proposition. *Political Research Quarterly, 64*, 200–216.

Walton, G. (2006). Fag church: Men who integrate gay and Christian identities. *Journal of Homosexuality, 51*(2), 1–17.

10

A CASE STUDY OF TWO MUSIC EDUCATION MAJORS WITH VISUAL IMPAIRMENT

Elizabeth C. Parker, Amy E. Spears, and Tami J. Draves

I made a campus visit [to another school] and you know, usually when you make a visit you get to meet with a professor in the department that you want to major in, and I went into the Music Department at that school with one of the heads of the department, and I was told that if I wanted to be successful I would have to change my major. They didn't think I would be successful in music ed as a blind student. So that was kind of tough . . . I grew up in a smaller town and went to a smaller high school where everybody knew each other and were supportive and that's how it is here. So that was the first time that I had been out of an environment where I had always been encouraged and it was discouraging to be told we don't think you can do this, and that is really how I chose to come here. I knew I would get support and be encouraged rather than not be helped when I needed it.

Christopher[1]

People say, so you're blind and you're a teacher, does that mean you want to work at a school for the deaf and blind? . . . They're assuming that the only thing that you're good for or should do is work with other blind people because you're blind! . . . If that's something that I wanted to do, I would do it. However, I've been trained to work with sighted people, so I can work with sighted people. Why should I limit myself? It just shows how judgmental people are.

Lindsey

Introduction

Christopher and Lindsey's experiences reflect attitudinal barriers and potential legal violations that individuals with visual impairment face on a regular basis.

In educational research, the most considerable challenge for teachers with impairments included attitudes and assumptions about disability from members of the school community (Bowman & Barr, 2001). Pre-employment inquiries often involved questions regarding the capability of the applicant to perform a particular job (Anderson, 1998). Attitudinal barriers and inquiries discouraged teachers with impairments to seek accommodations because the appearance of needing assistance was perceived as damaging to one's overall capability to perform job functions. Brock noted (2007), "A simple fact of life with a disability is that often a request for help causes more problems than you started with" (p. 11). For teacher candidates, the decision to disclose an impairment was complex as it might affect obtaining and retaining a P-12 teaching position. Administrators were unsure whether teachers were able to perform the essential functions of the position, and were without a working definition of essential functions from the Council for the Accreditation of Educator Preparation (CAEP). Defining one's ability to perform essential functions was often left to the individuals themselves (Papalia-Berardi, Hughes, & Papalia, 2002; Parker & Draves, 2016).

In music education, practitioner-based articles have focused on providing resources and strategies for educators working with students with visual impairment (e.g., Goldstein, 2000; Kerchner, 2004). Only a few research studies have centered on the musical experiences of students with visual impairment in P-12 music classrooms (Abramo & Pierce, 2013; Moss, 2009) and university settings (Parker & Draves, 2017). Researchers have highlighted the negative experiences in inclusive public school music classes for students with visual impairment. Participants noted teachers' heavy reliance on notation with late or unavailable braille scores, and their failure to sufficiently modify the curriculum (Abramo & Pierce, 2013; Moss, 2009; Parker & Draves, 2017). Additionally, participants reported poor treatment by their peers (Abramo & Pierce, 2013), and felt responsible for their own accommodations (Moss, 2009). Within an instrumental ensemble, Moss (2009) found that students with visual impairment used memorization as the most common tool and braille as a means of "mediation" between aural and visual learning. The timing of the braille scores was a considerable issue for participants and often they would have memorized their scores before braille music was available.

The challenge of braille scores also resonated with Parker and Draves (2017) who collected narratives of two choral pre-service music teachers during their student teaching semester. The pre-service teachers encountered similar challenges to those reported by Abramo and Pierce (2013) and Moss (2009) with regard to accessible music and self-accommodation. Rather than strengthening participants' evolving teacher identities, student teaching may have weakened them. Collisions of the expectations of teachers in schools, learning music aurally without timely availability of braille notation, and interactions with cooperating teachers, university supervisors, and colleagues contributed to both participants' decisions to pursue choices other than public school teaching following graduation.

Extant literature represents an important foundation toward greater under-standing of the experiences of music students and education majors with visual impairment yet there is much more we need to know. As the rise of individuals registering with impairments on college campuses continues (Valle et al., 2004), and prominence and attention toward individuals with impairments in P-12 schools grow (Jones, 2014), teacher and music teacher educators must begin to more fully address pre-service teachers with impairments, and specifically in our experiences, music education majors and pre-service music teachers with visual impairment. Understanding the experiences of music education majors with visual impairment is vital toward embracing inclusive and supportive practices for all students in our care. The purpose of our case study was to explore the experiences of two music education majors, one undergraduate, and one graduate, with visual impairment or blindness. We asked what it was like for an individual with visual impairment to major in music education and how one's musician-teacher-researcher identity evolved through the degree program.

Social Model of Disability

We have come to know the fundamental truth that blind people are nothing more than normal people who cannot see, and that, if we receive proper training, including appropriate attitudinal adjustment, we can participate fully in society and compete on terms of absolute equality with our sighted colleagues. (Omvig, 2009, para. 11)

Omvig (2009) unpacked societal perceptions between those who are considered "normal" or able-bodied and those who are "abnormal" or disabled. In the 1970s, broad attention to societal perceptions of abled and disabled began with a disability rights organization called the Union of the Physically Impaired Against Segregation (UPIAS) (Mertens, Sullivan, & Stace, 2011). UPIAS fought to separate disability from impairment, arguing that what individuals have are impairments and society has created disability. Known as the social model, the New Zealand Ministry of Health (2001) and the United Nations' Convention of Rights of People with Disabilities (2006) followed by stating that society erects barriers that prevent those with impairments from full participation. Davis (2002) stated, "Disability is more about the viewer than about the person who may use a cane or wheelchair" (p. 50).

This redefinition of disability and impairment helped to change the conscious-ness of individuals, particularly those with impairments (Shakespeare & Watson, 2001), and challenged the prevailing medical model of disability. Disability did not reside in bodies or minds, rather it was framed as a social issue, and one that society must work to ameliorate. The disability studies movement identified that the "medical model" focused on rehabilitating and curing the individual—

disability was a personal problem that must be cured (Siebers, 2008). The medical model continued to perpetuate the notion of disability as a responsibility of the individual. Mutua and Smith (2006) and Thomas (2002) argued that special education depended on the medical model to reproduce disability, and special education has been "impervious to disability studies' argument that society plays a key role in the construction and production of disability" (Mutua & Smith, 2006, p. 123).

Critics argued the social model, while originally a good idea, "became ossified and exaggerated into a set of crude dichotomies" (Shakespeare, 2014, p. 17). When the pendulum swung from medical to social, the focus on society negated the individual and physical experiences of those with impairments. Rather than striving to attend to the psycho-emotional dimensions and working to meet individuals' needs and hearing their experiences, the goal of the social model was to remove structural barriers (Thomas, 2002). Shakespeare and Watson (2001) proposed that disability and impairment represented a continuum; disability need not be associated with a medical condition, it also need not be reduced to social barriers. For many with impairments, impairment is a real and daily struggle that requires greater attention and understanding.

As our study focused on music education majors with visual impairment, it is important to briefly frame the social and medical models within music schools. The language that musicians use speaks to their beliefs (Lerner & Straus, 2006). Terms such as sight-singing or sight-reading situate sight as a necessity for musicians. Lubet (2004) argued that Western music, in particular as reproduced in music schools and higher education spaces, reifies the notion of ableism—the dependence on written notation and a visible conductor may deprive employment for musicians with visual impairment. Other worlds of music, such as blues, jazz, and popular music, do not define visual impairment as an issue. Lubet (2011) asked an essential question for music educators: "By whom are identities socially constructed?" (p. 20). We extended his question with our own provocation. Within the context of a university music school, how do undergraduate and graduate participants with visual impairment construct their identities as music education majors?

Aligning with UPIAS and the United Nations' Convention on the Rights of People with Disabilities, we embrace a transformative paradigm that engages our participants and focuses our inquiry as one of social justice (Mertens, Sullivan, & Stace, 2011). We believe:

- Reality is a social construction where some individuals hold greater power than others.
- Individuals have impairments and not disabilities.
- A close collaboration between ourselves as researchers and participants helps to build trust and critically engage our own experiences.

As teachers in the field of music education, we ask how we can contribute to social justice and how we may further human rights for all people. In this study, we used the lens of the social model as we collected the perspectives, experiences and discussed important and possible futures for music education majors with visual impairment. We share the experiences of two music education majors with visual impairment—Christopher and Lindsey—in this chapter.

Case Study

We have an intrinsic interest in Christopher and Lindsey's cases (Stake, 2005) not only because they were our students, but also because we are committed to developing teachers that represent the diversity of our schools and society, including teacher candidates with visual impairment. We did not seek generalizability, rather believed in the "power of the particular" (Pinnegar & Daynes, 2006). Stake (2010) supported a closeness to the case studied when he said, "but the collection of features and the sequence of happenings are seen by people close at hand as (in several ways) unprecedented, a critical uniqueness" (p. 31). We sought to view Christopher and Lindsey's cases closely as they represented important experiences that we must listen to as we co-constructed knowledge and potential pathways for all teacher candidates.

Our "cases" were individuals, Christopher and Lindsey, and hence our interpretation of each case necessitated a relational understanding and acceptance of individuals' distinctiveness. We employed an established rapport (Seidman, 1991) with Christopher and Lindsey, as two of us were their music education professors. We also shared data collection and analysis among the three authors to strike a balance between unique and global perspectives. We established context sensitivity through our situated understanding of specific universities and music teacher preparation programs in the study, and our individual backgrounds in music education.

Higher education music schools and music education programs are complex contexts and we seek greater understanding of their complexities (Mertens, 2010). Our case study of Christopher and Lindsey focused on their experiences as music education majors; Christopher was beginning his first undergraduate year and Lindsey her first graduate year. The data collection consisted of two interviews with Christopher and Lindsey for approximately 60 minutes each in January and February, respectively, at the beginning of their second semester of academic study. Because Amy (author) taught Christopher in introduction to music education and Tami (author) taught Lindsey in qualitative research, Elizabeth (author) conducted the one-on-one interviews. In the first interview, she asked Christopher and Lindsey why they chose to enter a music education program, what they wished to do with the degree when completed, what they had learned, and if there had been any challenges toward progress.

After the first interview, we openly coded the data separately, and discussed what additional perspectives were needed and what additional interview questions we wished to ask. The second interview with Christopher and Lindsey focused on a field experience placement for Christopher, and Lindsey's experiences in a graduate music education program as compared to her undergraduate program. In both cases, we sought to probe the participants' developing musician and teacher identities as they related to their current degree progress. To triangulate and add dimensionality to the data collection, we collected one additional interview each with three faculty members who taught the participants: two of Christopher's professors (a theory professor and a music education professor) and one of Lindsey's (a music education professor). Amy and Tami also collected field notes from experiences in coursework with Christopher and Lindsey (Creswell, 2013; Stake, 2010).

Our data analysis included open and focused coding (Hatch, 2002). We met several times to come to an agreement of the code list and then focused our codes in order to identify what was unique and common across cases, thereby conducting cross-case analysis (Bresler & Stake, 1992; Creswell, 2013; Miles & Huberman, 1994). We viewed the data globally and considered Denzin's (1989) epiphanies, which were larger moments including decisions to enter a music education program, and then eruptions or reactions (p. 129) to occurrences that have happened. We also considered immediate moments during the semester we interviewed the participants that may have had greater meanings later as Christopher and Lindsey continued within music education programs.

We begin with thick, rich description (Geertz, 1973) of Christopher and Lindsey's cases to situate the uniqueness of each participant's experience (Stake, 2005). We then reveal our analysis of cross-case themes. It is important to note themes may be stronger for one participant or another, as case study employs flexibility to reveal different patterns when under study (Yin, 2009).

Christopher

Christopher, who was visually impaired beginning at birth, began taking piano lessons at the age of five and playing the clarinet in the fifth grade. A versatile and highly active musician, Christopher transitioned to bass clarinet in the sixth grade and added saxophone to play jazz charts. As he continued making music in high school, Christopher became even more involved in music by marching in the marching band, playing in the top jazz band, and performing in All-State Band for 3 years. He also sang in two choral ensembles, accompanied the annual variety show on piano, and was elected president of the Tri-M music honor society.

Christopher credited his development of ear playing to his early piano teacher because they worked out a system for him to learn: she would play his pieces, and then he would memorize them and learn them for himself. He said, "I really hadn't developed a good way to learn by ear, and so just the repetition of what she would play . . . helped me develop my ear and to be able to start playing by ear." Christopher's aural learning continued through high school with his solo and ensemble clarinet music. He would listen to recordings and memorize the music, gleaning as much as he could, including stylistic aspects, tempi, dynamics, and articulations. Christopher remembered moments where learning braille music was discussed, however his teacher for students with visual impairment did not know how to read music and found it especially challenging to teach another person. When she introduced braille music, Christopher was confused by the note patterns and braille music concepts. He said, "we just didn't feel like we had a good system in place and I was already doing alright learning by ear, so we just didn't pursue it."

In high school, particularly during sight-reading exercises in choir, Christopher noted, "I would just sit there and not do anything until they would start the music that I listened to, so that motivated me a little bit to have some kind of a system." Christopher's choral teacher was also motivated to help Christopher learn braille music and they devised a creative system that served temporarily to give him enough information to follow along with the class. After Christopher became focused on majoring in music education, his choral teacher researched braille vocal music and began to assist Christopher's transition to standard braille scores.

Christopher decided to become a music teacher in his junior year of high school. Once he embraced music education as his future, he realized the many skills he would need, including a facility with braille music and conducting. He became a teacher's assistant for the middle school band his senior year and conducted a piece with the Seventh and Eighth Grade band at their concert. Teaching middle school students was a fulfilling and pivotal experience. To facilitate his middle school assistant role, the school system had the piece he conducted brailled—he described it as "my first real experience seeing braille music in that format. It was pretty overwhelming." As a senior, Christopher's experience as a teacher's assistant increased his desire to teach middle school band, provide a solid foundation, and advance the musicianship of students who "still have so much they can learn."

Early in Christopher's senior year, he organized a college campus visit to ensure the university and faculty would be able to accommodate his visual impairment. He was pleasantly surprised, "I really got the feeling they were really excited and had some really good ideas . . . I got a good feeling about the support I would get." Over the summer, he engaged in meetings about theory with the theory professor, took a few lessons with the clarinet professor, and met with other professors to ensure his books would be in accessible format. As a full-time student in university, Christopher noted that visual media, including documents and scores, had to be planned for in advance. The coordinator from the Office of Services of Students with Disabilities hired work-study students to assist with transcribing scores and class materials. Christopher felt the office "always thinks ahead about what I will seek next, what the next steps are, and what I need to do to become a better learner. They are always thinking ahead for me, which is really good."

He was learning to be proactive in communicating with future professors what they might need to do to help him in future classes. He alluded to a concern that if professors did not get information to the Coordinator in enough time, he would not be able to fully participate in class readings, activities, and discussions.

As Christopher initially acclimated to the university music school, an early and important decision included how he was going to learn his musical scores, which caused him some stress. He described his first semester as a combination of braille and audio learning. Though he knew how to read the notes, he struggled with chords, intervals, and sight-reading in theory class. Braille music has limited dot combinations and uses literary braille but in conceptual patterns rather than literal translation (e.g., a D in literary braille is not a D in braille music). Completing homework was difficult because communicating chord progressions from software to sighted score readers was often inconsistent. Christopher worked closely with his theory professor throughout the semester in individual meetings, and doing this seemed to alleviate some of his worry regarding how he would learn the material.

Over the winter break, Christopher located, enrolled in, and completed three levels of braille music courses from the Hadley School for the Blind. As a second semester student, he stated he was "finishing up that transition" of learning band music from braille. Because he was used to using only recordings to learn his pieces, the experience of using primarily braille music was intimidating. Yet, as Christopher became more involved in his music education program and developing his musicianship, he highlighted the importance of score reading. He felt that his facility with braille music reading was quickening, "I've been exposed to so much of it and [because I am] using it a lot, my reading speed is going up." In his private clarinet lessons, Christopher also expressed that he began to "get off of using recordings so that I'm making my own interpretation and [not] relying on what's recorded."

As a future music educator, Christopher realized his new facility with braille music not only required him to read the score but also explain to his students what they were seeing. He stated, "We had to make sure, and plan in [theory] class that I was understanding how it worked for me . . . but also understanding what was going on visually [for others]." Christopher's theory professor stated that Christopher was helping other students in class and that was a big point of encouragement. Because Christopher was able to assist his peers with their work, this interaction seemed to help him develop good rapport and feel more connected to them. The professor said, "Well I think the reason is because his number one interest is that he wants to be a music educator, and so it's showing to him that '[he] can actually do this.'"

In his second semester, Christopher was assigned his first field experience placement at a local middle school. When he went to the school and met the students, they showed a lack of curiosity about his blindness. Christopher wondered if the field experience teacher told students about his visual impairment before he entered the school setting—their apparent lack of questions as they interacted with him made him apprehensive. Christopher expressed feeling eager to share himself with these middle school students in a similar way that he had when he was a student assistant at the other middle school: those students blatantly asked him about being blind, and Christopher was happy to talk to them about it because it provided a natural way to circumvent some of the awkwardness that may have existed had they not acknowledged it. He hoped there would be such an opportunity to discuss it with these middle school students later, since initially they did not seem to acknowledge his blindness, but the opportunity never presented itself. Although he did not have the opportunity to share his experiences with visual impairment with the students, he remained excited to work with "real students" and took every opportunity to grow, as he perceived middle school band as his future teaching career.

Christopher stated his number one goal as a university student was to learn, and that his relationships with professors and cooperating teachers were essential to meet his goal. He described the stress that resulted from relying on others and stated the importance of communication and relationship building. As a university music student he found that learning was more time consuming than he expected. "All the other people are saying, 'Oh that took me 20 minutes,' but that doesn't mean I will get it done that fast, so it's just something I have to get used to." Christopher anticipated next year's conducting course by discussing collaborative plans in which he and faculty were engaging, and his eventual student teaching placement.

Lindsey

Before student teaching, Lindsey[2] planned to teach choral music in a public school and to perform as a vocalist. During her student-teaching semester, however, she decided that if she was to teach in a public school, she would need the accommodation of an aide to work alongside of her. She also believed that "due to budget cuts in the fine arts, principals want to hire one person who is going to do all the teaching and etc., etc. as opposed to two people" (Parker & Draves, 2017, supplementary material, p. 10). This line of thinking led her to decide that a well-funded private school or a community college setting would have the type of support and environment that she would need to be successful. Lindsey identified individuals, such as professors and peers, and experiences, such as working in a musical theater company and research classes, as impacting her work as a music education major and her musician-teacher-researcher identities.[3]

After completing her bachelor of music education degree, Lindsey decided to attend graduate school. She considered matriculating at a different university for a master's degree in musical theater, but ultimately decided to start her master's degree in music education full-time at her undergraduate institution. The master's degree program included applied lessons, ensemble, and graduate-level music education and research classes. At the time of this study, Lindsey was enrolled primarily in music education research classes. She also continued her work as a music director at a local theater company where she had many responsibilities, including choosing, arranging, and performing all of the music for the shows. Unfortunately the theater closed in November of her first graduate school semester. Though she worked and went to school for her first semester as a graduate student; during the second semester, Lindsey no longer worked and chose to focus entirely on her graduate degree.

Lindsey's experiences with her undergraduate and graduate professors played a major role in shaping her professional decisions. She compared the two, noting that she did not feel her graduate classes required as many accommodations and modifications from her professors as her undergraduate classes. In her undergraduate classes, she needed music brailled for most classes and took her second semester of conducting as a private lesson; in her graduate classes, she needed accessible reading materials and journal articles. Though Lindsey perceived the modifications were fewer for graduate study than when she was an undergraduate, one of her professors noted she felt she had to make more accommodations. There was a Disabilities Services Office, but due to the density of content and amount of materials, most of which were visual such as textbooks, journal articles, and PowerPoint presentations, the professor developed modifications for most aspects of the course. In the master's degree program, Lindsay stated "the music education faculty have been really helpful" and that she had not encountered unhelpful teachers as of yet.

In addition to professors, Lindsey's job at the theater company played an important role in her life, specifically in shaping her musical and teaching identities. Though she only worked there for a few months, Lindsey focused a great deal on it in her interviews. As a musical director, Lindsey led in a creative capacity, making decisions and working with others on their acts. She stated, "That was my control sort of thing, like where I got to make a lot of decisions that were solely my decisions to make musically . . . it was my music." It was very difficult for Lindsey when the theater company closed their doors, but she admitted that she was also glad that it ended that way, "Well let's just say that the only two reasons why I would have left the theater company would have been if the theater closed or if I was offered a job where I was doing the same thing."

Upon further reflection, Lindsey noted that working at the theater company showed her she was capable of many things on her own because it represented "a multifaceted position as doing arranging, teaching, casting, doing the hosting of the show, playing for two and a half hours straight, underscoring . . . I'm capable of that." She admitted "being blind, you really don't have much control over anything in your whole life." At the theater company, she was able to be in control of many things that were very important to her.

Graduate coursework presented several challenges, specifically the focus on research. When working on quantitative research in her introduction to research methods course where charts, graphs, and numbers were involved, Lindsey had trouble understanding the layout of the numbers and formatting. A friend helped her complete the homework, and she claimed that if she had to do the work by herself, she "would have died." She enjoyed qualitative research better because she liked to tell stories. Her study for the qualitative research class focused on "how other blind/visually impaired music students surmount the trials and tribulations that come either from a high school music program or college." Though she spoke excitedly about her study, Lindsey wished her project was not about being blind, but she could not think of another topic that was as personal.

In November of her first semester, Lindsey decided to submit a different research project she had completed with one of her professors to the state music conference. Lindsey was excited upon her poster acceptance but the state music conference took place a few hundred miles away from her home. She expressed that she did not consider riding with another individual who might attend the conference; rather she would need to find someone to drive her. In the end, Lindsey was unable to attend her poster session because she could not find a ride, a situation that frustrated her. However, because Lindsey sang in the university choir that was performing at the conference later the same day, she traveled with the group and was able to sing in the performance. Upon seeing and talking with her mentor teacher at the conference, Lindsey realized that she could have come earlier with a group of people rather than relying on having to ride on the choir bus.

> Well I just didn't think about that two sighted people would go together, and it's usually—the way I understand it—it's one sighted person and they each go separately. I never imagined—for whatever reason—I never imagined two teachers going together for the sake of going together.

The combination of the closing of the musical theater company and the challenge of graduate coursework began to take its toll. Lindsey confessed that she seemed to be on a "downward spiral" and that she was losing interest in going to school and completing her coursework. When working at the theater, Lindsey stated:

> It was obvious that I, as a person, as well as the work that I was doing, was valued and I was seeing the benefits of that effort. Whereas in an undergraduate program and a master's program you don't see that until after you graduate, and I think I'm kind of that type of person that needs to see it right away.

During the midpoint of the semester, Lindsey stated she did not have the "mental energy" to do all the things she needed to do and admitted, "needing to find reasons to come to school." Lindsey hoped once this semester was over, she would be able to "focus on the real music education master's stuff, like comps and the projects."

Cross-Case Themes and Discussion

Our cross-case analysis revealed four themes that reflected Lindsey and Christopher's experiences as music education majors. They included (1) continually revealing my impairment, (2) connecting with others, (3) experiencing relevance, and (4) reaching beyond impairment. We begin by describing each theme, and then interrogate it in relationship to the social model of disability and extant literature.

Continually Revealing My Impairment

Christopher and Lindsey described a constant necessity to address their impairment with those around them, especially individuals new to their lives. Revealing oneself as an individual with visual impairment was even more important when Christopher and Lindsey relied on others for accommodations, arranged logistics, or needed others' support. As a new student to the university, Christopher was motivated to educate others. He scheduled meetings with each professor to ensure they understood his visual impairment, his drive to be successful, and his desire to make plans early in the process, even semesters before beginning in the instructor's course. The theory professor stated:

> I know for sure that if he feels like a professor isn't aware of what it's going to be for him to succeed, that really stresses him out. If it doesn't appear to him they're going to make sure to stay on top of it, that stresses him out . . . So he is very proactive with his professors, going semesters ahead sometimes to make sure that people are aware of what might be needed, and he is very much willing to engage in almost a training part on his side: a "what do I need to tell you so you can help me"-type of a discussion.

Regarding his field experience, Christopher noted a similar process:

> . . . getting [the middle school band director] comfortable with having a blind student you know in the classroom for an educational observation, and making sure that I have access to things, so if he wants me to help with the sectional or help a student that's struggling I need to have access to that music . . . I think that will take some working through to know the best way to work with that teacher and make sure that I have everything I need without making it too much extra work for him.

Lindsey revealed her impairment to others less than Christopher because she attended the same institution as her undergraduate program and was working with many of the same instructors. She communicated her needs by emailing or speaking with her professors in class or during office hours. Though Lindsey perceived that she needed fewer accommodations in her graduate program than she did in her undergraduate program, she imagined "that there would be a

situation where some major project was going to have some form of accommodation that's going to be required" or that she might need to "be exempt
from altogether because of the impracticality of that for me." As noted previously,
a professor who taught Lindsey in both undergraduate and graduate school felt
she was developing even more accommodations for Lindsey in the graduate
program.

In previous research (Brock, 2007; Hazen, 2012), pre-service and in-service
teachers with impairments tried to be inconspicuous and were reluctant to ask
for accommodations. Christopher and Lindsey's experiences reflected a desire to
be acknowledged as "able" music education students with visual impairments.
Unlike previous research, they appeared unafraid to ask for accommodations and,
at some points, may not have been aware of the accommodations offered. For
example, Lindsey seemed unaware of the accommodations her graduate school
professor was spending a great deal of time developing so that she could be
successful in the course. Christopher's desire to educate others spoke not only to
his confidence, but also to his realization that he must help break down barriers
between those who have and do not have visual impairments. Both Christopher
and Lindsey chose to reveal themselves to create an open dialogue and to
proactively address issues that might arise.

Christopher's need to make the middle school band director "comfortable"
with his impairment is important. As a second semester student, Christopher sought
to build relationships with others toward his future success. He viewed key
constituents as professors, teachers, and students. Though not an exact parallel to
a reluctance to ask for accommodations in Brock's (2007) study, his language
suggests he felt responsible for his own accommodation. The medical model
continues to replicate the notion that those who are impaired are responsible
for overcoming challenges themselves. Lindsey's language represents a foil to
Christopher's language as she discussed potential exemption from requirements
because of their "impracticality." As a graduate student, Lindsey may have placed
responsibility squarely on society, in this case, her professors and the institution,
to make modifications necessary for her success.

Connecting with Others

"Connecting with others" emerged from Lindsey and Christopher's perceptions
of how others viewed them and how they viewed others. Christopher was very
aware of how his new professors, his cooperating teacher from his field experience,
and students at his practicum site perceived him. In his field experience, he wanted
others to feel at ease when interacting with him and longed for the students to
"be interactive" so he could build relationships. He said, "I'm looking forward
to working with the students, you know, either one-on-one or eventually in the
group just to get to know them and make them more comfortable." Christopher's
challenge connecting with the students may have been precipitated by the

teacher's revelation of his visual impairment before Christopher entered their classroom. Christopher was not given the opportunity to introduce himself and the teacher's communication with his students may have represented a barrier to connection. Though Christopher was disappointed by this limitation with his field experience students, he felt confident from his previous high school experiences as a teaching assistant. Lindsey created meaningful connections with select undergraduate professors, but she did not have the same experiences with her undergraduate peers. She noted when she transferred from a community college to begin her undergraduate degree, she felt like she was "alone, swimming in shark-infested waters" because, while people "didn't go out of their way to be mean, they didn't go out of their way to be friendly, either." Lindsey also discussed how she did not feel valued or validated by others when she would speak in class. However, in graduate school, she was finding that people were more mature and listened to and valued her thoughts—she was able to contribute to class discussion more:

> I think as a graduate student I'm more on an even playing field in terms of—I don't know how else to say it—I contribute something and they like what I've said or they want to piggyback off it, you know, as opposed to undergrad.

To Bowman and Barr (2001), the most difficult task for individuals with impairments was overcoming others' attitudes. Lindsey and Christopher experienced difficulty making human connections, perhaps due to others' perceptions. As a transfer student to the university as an undergraduate, Lindsey's entry in her sophomore year may have additionally impacted her integration into the music education community. It was also unclear how much Lindsey collaborated with her peers as an undergraduate, though she described important collaborations in the graduate research class. In Christopher's case, the theory professor's encouragement and mentorship provided pathways toward meaningful relationships.

Lindsey and Christopher's experiences support the notion that intergroup contact positively influences attitudes toward individuals with impairments and helps to decrease prejudice (Jellison & Taylor, 2007). Peers and professors embraced a positive attitude toward Lindsey and Christopher as they grew relationally. These connections were largely facilitated by in-class activities and purposeful actions of instructors. Perhaps others can provide more opportunities and pathways for those with visual impairments to establish meaningful connections with those around them.

Experiencing Relevance

"Experiencing relevance" was situated within participants' expectations and evolving identities and emerged as Lindsey and Christopher described their progress in their respective music education programs. In the following sections we begin with expectations, and then move into musical and teaching identities and for Lindsey specifically, as a graduate student, her researcher identity development.

Expectations. Christopher and Lindsey expected their degree programs would pave the way toward their intended careers. For Christopher, he placed trust in his university to provide him with the necessary experiences including an array of courses and practicum placements to successfully prepare him for a career in teaching middle school band. Christopher's program expectations matched his desire for stronger musicianship and his motivation to develop critical thinking as a music educator. Another important piece of Christopher's expectations was the accommodations the university provided. He responded positively to the university's purposeful planning, stating the university's resource center "has been really good at making sure that everything has worked out as far as me having access to what I needed." For example, because of limited public transportation, the university arranged or reimbursed for taxis based on Christopher's needs to attend his practicum placement.

Though Christopher embraced high expectations for his degree program, he also articulated several stressors regarding things he could not control, particularly as they related to future faculty and cooperating teachers that would support or potentially impede his progress. At the time of data collection, he was positive about those he had as instructors and felt the small music school atmosphere would help as the faculty shared best practices for working with his visual impairment. He expressed confidence in meeting challenges as they arose, and that once current challenges were worked out, new experiences would bring new challenges to face.

Lindsey decided to pursue a master's degree because she believed it would provide greater opportunity for a teaching position at a community college where she could teach a variety of things, including voice, music theory, and music theater, in an environment where she was not legally responsible for the physical safety of her students. She chose this degree program over others such as music theater and theory because of her expectation that it would better prepare her and offer more career stability. Though Lindsey embraced a clear goal of teaching in a community college, she experienced disillusionment in her second semester of coursework as familiar challenges, such as transportation, and new challenges, such as research coursework, presented themselves.

Karp, Anderson, and Keller (1998) described key points in the professional lifespan for individuals with and without impairments including admissions to college and the education preparation program, successful completion of degree programs including practica and student teaching, becoming certified, and securing employment. Lindsey and Christopher discussed key points in their professional lives, but were situated at different locations in their development. Christopher believed in building the skills needed for the future and facing challenges as they arose. His intentions were strong toward becoming a middle school music educator. Lindsey articulated the importance of degree completion toward her goal of teaching at a community college.

Music–teacher–researcher Identities. Christopher and Lindsey both expressed strong musical identities. Christopher described his highly developed aural and performance skills as significant pieces of his identity. He had been invited recently to play on an honors recital and experienced both surprise and pride at the invitation. Lindsey was preparing for a tour to France to sing solo with a community choir. She expressed confidence in her theory capabilities, calling herself an "amateur theorist." At university, Christopher considered music course-work and participation in instrumental and vocal ensembles and lessons as important parts of his musical identity in preparation for his future in music education. He was working tirelessly not only on his braille music reading for theory, but also for his clarinet lessons and private vocal study. Lindsey's multi-faceted musician identity had always been strong, however in her master's degree she experienced less of a focus on her musicianship development as compared to her undergraduate program. The emphasis shifted to her development as a researcher, which was challenging because she did not see the relevance in her future. A lack of relevance translated into a dichotomous view of research and what she considered the "real work" of her master's degree. One example of this was Lindsey's poster for the statewide music conference. Though she submitted a research project to present a poster, the poster session is an exclusively visual medium; she had little involvement in the development and design of the poster itself and, due to lack of transportation, she was unable to be present for the poster session. These challenges prevented Lindsey from full involvement and thwarted a key opportunity toward her construction of her researcher identity.

Lindsey has yet to develop a strong researcher identity, which suggests the possibility that she had not been mentored to understand the value of research as a musician or teacher, or she has not discovered for herself the potential of research to inform her musician and teacher identities. Conway, Eros, and Stanley (2009) found that individuals' motivations for pursuing a master's degree varied and included desire for more of a music focus or desire for more of a reading and writing focus. They expressed concern "about the balance between the agenda of music education coursework (creating critical thinkers and independent music education scholars) and the need to address the practical needs of graduate students who are working in public schools" (Conway, Eros, & Stanley, 2009, p. 140). In summer masters programs, Conway, Eros, and Stanley (2008) found that some summers-only students missed the musicianship development that was more readily available in the academic year. Lindsey's apparent music focus may have contributed to her lack of researcher identity construction and the lack of relevance she perceived in her program. Her desired focus for her master's degree seemed to be one of practitioner rather than scholar.

Reaching Beyond Impairment

Lindsey and Christopher described important individuals who were able to see beyond their impairment, witness their talents, enjoy their personalities, and build relationships with them, both personally and professionally. However, they also both described individuals that had openly disputed their potential as music educators. From our data analysis, we suggest that Lindsey and Christopher desired to reach beyond their impairment to realize a self where impairment was not a part. Lindsey referenced society's limitations to look beyond blindness in order to embrace the employment of a teacher with visual impairment. To Lindsey, society also placed limits on institutions where teachers with visual impairment should teach stating that it "pisses [her] off" that individuals suggested she work at the school for the deaf and blind.

Lindsey wished to "move beyond the blind thing." She discussed individuals with visual impairment teaching private voice lessons out of their own homes, writing music, and producing recordings. In her research, she described a desire to study perspectives outside of visual impairment, stating, "I kind of wish that it wasn't about blind people." Later, she stated she felt she spoke about disability too much.

Christopher articulated eagerly seeking strategies to work beyond his impairment. He described his and others' preparation, organization, and proactive communication as key elements toward his success as a music teacher. He was most concerned about how his impairment was perceived by others, especially those who were new to him and stated how stressful he found relying on others to be. Christopher felt supported in his university context—the only limitations that he perceived were individuals who were not willing to fully accommodate his needs.

Lindsey and Christopher actively combatted disabling conditions constructed by society. In Lindsey's case, she enjoyed her work at the theater company and wanted to contribute her creativity to the music education of others through teaching them to read, to perform, and to experience the fullness of their musicianship. Christopher was progressing in his music education major and fully intended to teach middle school band. Yet, they both shared a fear and a frustration: that of others' stereotypes and misconceptions (Oren & McLeod, 2011). Oren and McLeod state the greatest challenge lies "in those who are sighted that choose not to peer into my world of blindness" (p. 519). Christopher and Lindsey were able to overcome disabling conditions when others placed themselves in a space of understanding. However, when others did not, they felt forced into the disability end of what Shakespeare and Watson (2001) call the "continuum between disability and impairment."

At some points, Lindsey and Christopher described society's disabling conditions and, at other times, the experience of impairment. For Lindsey, perhaps her most considerable frustration was that she could not push beyond impairment and fly off of the continuum. Lindsey's description of a lack of control in several aspects of her life indicated her desire to have more agency in her own world, agency she felt she might achieve in a community college career. Though Lindsey found a more supportive community of peers in her graduate program, her frustration was evident because few contexts contributed to a sense of independence in her life. She stated, "I have been climbing up a hill for years, and think I just want to stop." Lindsey may have been reflecting Thomas's (2002) criticism of the social model as it focused too heavily on societal barriers and not on the lived experiences of those with impairments. Thomas (2002) argued that impairment is personal, and there are psycho-emotional dimensions that must be attended to. Furthermore, to Thomas (1999), the world of those with impairment is tied to social processes. Within their inner world, those with impairments are affected by the "ablebodied," influencing the individual with impairment's beliefs and ultimately, their decisions. Lindsey's case highlighted the frustration and desire to reach beyond impairment while fully acknowledging her own perception in the eyes of others.

In her second interview, Lindsey seemed to believe that she was unable to build a professional home, one that would reflect her creativity, her musicianship, and her desire to give back through teaching others. Christopher's description of his stress in both interviews may have reflected his fear and anticipated challenges toward building a professional home in public school music education. He appeared to manage his stress by what Ferri, Keefe, and Gregg (2001) term "overdoing" in order to ensure his success. Patterson and Hughes (1999) state, "any body that is excluded from making a contribution to the construction of the social world cannot find a home in it" (p. 604). Though our interpretations of Lindsey and Christopher's experiences are only one possibility, we are unsure of their futures until we witness more of their paths.

Final Reflections

Christopher and Lindsey's experiences highlight the continual reliance on sight in education and music education. Lubet (2004) articulated that Western classical music presents impediments to full participation for those with visual impairment because of dependency on music scores. P-12 schools and higher education music schools, as institutions that continue to replicate Western classical music practices, represent spaces where full participation is not consistently possible. In Christopher's case, as a P-12 student, he did not learn braille music because it was a cumbersome system (Moss, 2009). Unlike participants in Abramo and Pierce (2013), however, Christopher enjoyed positive experiences in public school music education. His choral teacher, in particular, worked diligently to include him by devising a form of braille music, though his lack of reading braille music did not prepare him for higher education music school. Christopher's tireless efforts to learn multiple forms of braille music and adjust to how sighted students read music are examples of his desire to overcome the sightedness of his profession and educational institutions. The accommodations put in place by the coordinator from the Office of Services of Students with Disabilities and additional support from professors seem to be providing him a way to positively participate in his courses at a high level. Cases like Christopher's are ones that should be studied more closely as individuals look to support students with visual impairments in university music schools.

In Lindsey's case, music education research is also heavily sighted with considerable focus on visual media such as posters, figures, and tables. Lindsey appeared to be using strategies such as relying on classmates but also was working to build an identity outside of those media, one that she perceived has greater flexibility. Lindsey's experiences encourage researchers and music teacher educators to build researcher identities through mentorship with multiple epistemologies, such as philosophical, interpretive, and action research that suits the student and her career goals. Students will benefit from a flexible program that allows them to anticipate and access what they perceive as needs for future teaching and learning contexts.

In conclusion, we challenge the reader and continue to ask ourselves how this research can further human rights. Siebers (2008) argued that society must acknowledge both the embodied nature of impairment and societal barriers, proposing the concept "disability as human variation" (p. 25). Shakespeare and Watson (2001) supported the embodied nature of impairment when they stated, "No one's body works perfectly consistently, or eternally. We are all in some way impaired" (p. 24).

Though we may all be in some way impaired, we are not all limited by society because of our impairment. Lindsey and Christopher are but two examples of many within our field who are highly competent, passionate, and caring individuals with bright futures. They are also individuals who face potential violations toward employment because of their perceived abilities (Anderson, 1998). Teachers with visual impairment are critically needed in our P-12 schools, community colleges, and university classrooms because they support and represent a bridge for multiple identities and are representations for individuals with other types of impairments too (Kielian-Gilbert, 2006). We must model inclusion with our colleagues and our students to foster a more realized society.

Discussion Questions and Activities

1. Consider Shakespeare and Watson's (2001) continuum of impairment and disability. What aspects of music and music teaching may transform a visual impairment into a disability? What about other impairments such as sensory, mobility, chronic medical, mental health, or intellectual? How might each differ based on the music teaching setting and content?
2. What does Lindsey and Christopher's considerable success as musicians, based primarily on aural learning, suggest about how we teach and learn music?

3. Consider your own attitudinal barriers toward music teachers with visual impairments. What would be your concerns? Pair up with classmates to develop ideas for unpacking and addressing those concerns.
4. How do some of the challenges faced by Lindsey and Christopher also present challenges for full inclusion by other music education students? In answering this question, research and consider *universal* or *inclusive design*—an approach meant to produce experiences and environments that are inclusive and accessible to all individuals—and develop approaches to these challenges that would allow for full participation by all students.
5. In small groups, develop a list of *essential functions* for music teachers. You may use National Association for Schools of Music guidelines and CAEP or other resources. How might an individual with visual impairment meet your list of essential functions?
6. The presentation and dissemination of music education research rely primarily on visual means such as posters and keynote or PowerPoint presentations. Develop ideas for presentational formats that are inclusive of individuals with visual impairment.
7. In music, practitioners use non-inclusive terms and language such as *sight-singing* and *sight-reading* to refer to common practices. What are other examples of non-inclusive terms and language used in the music lexicon? What about other examples educators use in their teaching? For further discussion with regard to visual impairment and language use, see Bolt (2005).

Notes

1. Christopher is a pseudonym; Lindsey prefers to use her real name.
2. Like Christopher, Lindsey's visual impairment began at birth.
3. For more detail of Lindsey's undergraduate experiences, see Parker, E. C., & Draves, T. J. (2016b).

References

Abramo, J. M., & Pierce, A. E. (2013). An ethnographic case study of music learning at a school for the blind. *Bulletin of the Council for Research in Music Education*, *195*, 9–24.
Anderson, R. J. (1998). Attitudes toward educators with disabilities. In R. Anderson, C. Keller, & J. Karp (Eds.), *Enhancing diversity: Educators with disabilities* (pp. 180–190). Washington, DC: Gallaudet University Press.
Bolt, D. (2005). From blindness to visual impairment: Terminological typology and the social model of disability. *Disability & Society*, *20*(5), 539–552.
Bowman, C. A., & Barr, K. (2001). Conversations from the commissions: Negotiating the tensions in the preparation of teachers with disabilities. *English Education*, *33*(3), 252–256.
Bresler, L., & Stake, R. E. (1992). Qualitative research methodology in music education. In R. Colwell (Ed.), *Handbook of research on music teaching and learning* (pp. 75–90). New York: Schirmer Books.

Brock, B. L. (2007). The workplace experiences of educators with disabilities: Insights for school leaders. *Educational Considerations, 34*(2), 9–14.

Conway, C., Eros, J., & Stanley, A. M. (2008). Summers-only versus the academic year master of music in music education degree: Perceptions of program graduates. *Bulletin of the Council for Research in Music Education, 178,* 21–34.

Conway, C., Eros, J., & Stanley, A. M. (2009). Perceived effects of the master of music in music education on P-12 teaching practice. *Research Studies in Music Education, 31*(2), 129–141.

Creswell, J. W. (2013). *Qualitative inquiry & research design: Choosing among five approaches.* 3rd ed. Thousand Oaks, CA: Sage Publications.

Davis, L. J. (2002). *Bending over backwards: Disability, dismodernism, and other difficult positions.* New York: New York University Press.

Denzin, N. (1989). *Interpretive interactionism.* Thousand Oaks, CA: Sage Publications.

Ferri, B. A., Keefe, C. H., & Gregg, N. (2001). Teachers with learning disabilities: A view from both sides of the desk. *Journal of Learning Disabilities, 34*(1), 22–32.

Geertz, C. (1973). *The interpretation of cultures: Selected essays.* New York: Basic Books.

Goldstein, D. (2000). Music pedagogy for the blind. *International Journal of Music Education, 35,* 35–39.

Hatch, J. A. (2002). *Doing qualitative research in education settings.* Albany, NY: State University of New York Press.

Hazen, M. (2012). Is classroom management possible for disabled teachers, with or without accommodation? *Multidisciplinary Studies Theses.* Retrieved from http://digital commons.buffalostate.edu/multistudies_theses/4/.

Jellison, J. A., & Taylor, D. M. (2007). Attitudes toward inclusion and students with disabilities. *Bulletin of the Council for Research in Music Education, 172,* 9–23.

Jones, S. K. (2014). Teaching students with disabilities: A review of music education research as it relates to the Individuals with Disabilities Education Act. *Update: Applications of Research in Music Education.* Retrieved from: http://journals.sagepub.com/doi/pdf/10.1177/8755123314548039.

Karp, J. M., Anderson, R. J., & Keller, C. E. (1998). A guide for decision making and action. In R. Anderson, C. Keller, & J. Karp (Eds.), *Enhancing diversity: Educators with disabilities* (pp. 272–280). Washington, DC: Gallaudet University Press.

Kerchner, J. (2004). Singing visions: Metaphors for teaching students with visual impairments. *The Choral Journal, 45*(5), 26–36.

Kielian-Gilbert, M. (2006) Beyond abnormality—dis/ability and music's metamorphic subjectivities. In N. Lerner & J. Straus (Eds.), *Sounding off: Theorizing disability in music* (pp. 217–234). New York: Routledge.

Lerner, N., & Straus, J. N. (2006) *Sounding off: Theorizing disability in music.* New York: Routledge.

Lubet, A. (2004). Tunes of impairment: An ethnomusicology of disability. *Review of Disability Studies: An International Journal, 1*(1), 133–46.

Lubet, A. (2011). *Music, disability, and society.* Philadelphia, PA: Temple University Press.

Mertens, D. M. (2010). *Research and evaluation in education and psychology: Integrating diversity with quantitative, qualitative, and mixed methods.* 3rd ed. Thousand Oaks, CA: Sage Publications.

Mertens, D., Sullivan, M., & Stace, H. (2011). Disability communities transformative research for social justice. In N. Denzin & Y. Lincoln (Eds.), *Sage handbook of qualitative research* (4th ed., pp. 227–241). Thousand Oaks: Sage Publications.

Miles, M. B., & Huberman, A. M. (1994). *Qualitative data analysis: An expanded sourcebook.* 2nd ed. Thousand Oaks: Sage Publications.

Moss, J. (2009). *Quality of experience in mainstreaming and full inclusion of blind and visually impaired high school instrumental music students* (Doctoral dissertation). University of Michigan, Ann Arbor.

Mutua, K., & Smith, R. M. (2006). Disrupting normalcy and the practical concerns of classroom teachers. In S. Danforth & S. Gabel (Eds.), *Vital questions facing disability studies in education* (pp. 121–132). New York: Peter Lang.

New Zealand Ministry of Health (2001). *New Zealand disability strategy.* Wellington, NZ: Author.

Omvig, J. H. (2009). Why use the word "blind"? *Braille Monitor, 52*(1). Retrieved from: https://nfb.org/images/nfb/publications/bm/bm09/bm0901/bm090107.htm.

Oren, T., & McLeod, R. (2011). The marker is empty: Lessons learned from a student teacher who is visually impaired. *Journal of Visual Impairment & Blindness, 105*(9), 516–520.

Papalia-Berardi, A. P., Hughes, C. A., & Papalia, A. S. (2002). Teacher education students with disabilities: Participation and achievement favors. *Teacher Education and Special Education, 25*(1), 23–31.

Parker, E. C., & Draves, T. J. (2016). Tensions and perplexities within teacher education and P-12 schools for music teachers with visual impairments. *Arts Education Policy Review.* Advanced online publication.

Parker, E. C., & Draves, T. J. (2017). A narrative of two preservice music teachers with visual impairment. *Journal of Research in Music Education, 64*, 385–404.

Patterson, M., & Hughes, B. (1999). Disability studies and phenomenology: The carnal politics of everyday life. *Disability and Society, 14*(5), 597–610.

Pinnegar, S. & Daynes, J. G. (2006). Locating narrative inquiry historically: Thematics in the turn to narrative. In D. J. Clandinin (Ed.), *Handbook of narrative inquiry: Mapping a methodology* (pp. 35–75). Thousand Oaks, CA: Sage.

Seidman, I. E. (1991). *Interviewing as qualitative research.* New York, NY: Teachers College Press.

Shakespeare, T. (2014). *Disability rights and wrongs revisited.* 2nd ed. New York: Routledge.

Shakespeare, T., & Watson, N. (2001). The social model of disability: An outdated ideology? In S. Barnartt and B. Altman (Eds.), *Exploring theories and expanding methodologies: Where we are and where we need to go* (pp. 9–28). Oxford, UK: Elsevier Science, Ltd.

Siebers, T. A. (2008). *Disability theory.* Ann Arbor: University of Michigan Press.

Stake, R. E. (2005). Qualitative case studies. In N. Denzin & Y. Lincoln (Eds.), *The SAGE handbook of qualitative research* (3rd ed., pp. 443–466). Thousand Oaks, CA: Sage Publications.

Stake, R. E. (2010). *Qualitative research: Studying how things work.* New York: Guilford Press.

Thomas, C. (1999). *Female forms: Experiencing and understanding disability.* Philadelphia: Open University Press.

Thomas, C. (2002). Disability theory: Key ideas, issues, and thinkers. In C. Barnes, M. Oliver, & L. Barton (Eds.), *Disability studies today* (pp. 38–57). Cambridge: Polity Press.

Union of the Physically Impaired Against Segregation (UPIAS). (1976). *Fundamental principles of disability.* London: Author.

United Nations (2006). *Convention on the rights of persons with disabilities.* Retrieved from: http://un.org/disabilities/convention/conventionfull.shtml.

Valle, J., Solis, S., Volpitta, D., & Connor, D. (2004). The disability closet: Teachers with learning disabilities evaluate the risks and benefits of "coming out." *Equity & Excellence in Education, 37,* 4–17.

Yin, R. K. (2009). *Case study research: Design and methods.* 4th ed. Thousand Oaks, CA: Sage Publications.

CONTRIBUTORS

Sarah J. Bartolome is an Assistant Professor of Music Education at Northwestern University. A children's music and choral specialist with an interest in world music for the classroom, she has completed music fieldwork in Ghana, Sierra Leone, South Africa, Zimbabwe, Panama, and Lithuania. Her scholarship in music education has been published in journals such as the *Journal of Research in Music Education*, the *Journal of Music Teacher Education*, and the *International Journal of Community Music*. Her research interests include children's musical cultures, ethnomusicology and music education, effective music teacher preparation, and issues of diversity and inclusion in music education.

Vanessa L. Bond is an Assistant Professor of Music Education at University of Hartford's The Hartt School where she teaches undergraduate and graduate courses in music education. She specializes in early childhood/elementary general music education, choral music education, and world music pedagogy. Her research interests include the musical lives of young children (with special interest in the application of Reggio Emilia early childhood approach principles to music education), culturally responsive teaching, and the choral experiences of under-represented populations.

Carlos Castañeda Lechuga is a leading mariachi music educator, performer, and advocate in the Greater Phoenix area. Former lead mariachi teacher at Rosie's House—a music academy for children—and Director of CALLE de Arizona's music workshops, he currently teaches middle school orchestra for the Kyrene School District, co-leads the Arizona State University (ASU) mariachi ensemble, serves a mariachi educational consultant for the Isaac School District and Arizona Musicfest, and is mariachi director for the Harmony Project Phoenix and South

Mountain Community College. He has earned bachelor's and master's degrees in music education from ASU.

Tami J. Draves is an Associate Professor of Music Education at the University of North Carolina at Greensboro where she teaches undergraduate and graduate music education courses and advises masters and doctoral students. Her research interests include pre-service and in-service music teacher preparation and support, with an emphasis on identity. Her publications appear in the *Journal of Research in Music Education, Bulletin of the Council for Research in Music Education, Journal of Music Teacher Education, Music Education Research, Research Studies in Music Education,* and *Arts Education Policy Review* and she has presented her research nationally and internationally.

Karin S. Hendricks is Co-Director of Undergraduate Studies in Music and Assistant Professor of Music Education at Boston University. A regular presenter of research papers and practitioner workshops, Karin has served as an orchestra clinician and adjudicator throughout the United States and abroad. She currently serves as national secretary of the American String Teachers Association. Dr. Hendricks conducts research in music psychology, student motivation and engagement, and social justice, and has published papers in professional and peer-reviewed journals and books. She is author of *The Compassionate Music Teacher*, co-author of *Performance Anxiety Strategies*, and co-editor of the forthcoming book *Queering Freedom*.

Joyce M. McCall serves as a Postdoctoral Resident Scholar/Visiting Assistant Professor of Music Education at Indiana University Jacobs School of Music. Her research focuses on examining issues of race, class, and culture as well as using digital platforms to create spaces that will further expand the possibilities of student engagement and music composition. McCall has presented sessions and research at various conferences and symposiums, nationally and internationally. Toward awakening the consciousness of the music education profession, she actively pursues opportunities to stand alongside her peers to speak and act on issues of access, diversity, equity, and inclusion.

Elizabeth C. Parker is an Associate Professor of Music Education at the Boyer College of Music and Dance at Temple University where she instructs under-graduate general music and choral methods, and graduate history and philosophy courses. Prior to her work at Temple University, Parker taught general and choral music education at the Schwob School of Music at Columbus State University, GA and P-12 general and choral music in New York, Nebraska, and Georgia. Her research interests include the social, vocal, and philosophical development of adolescent choral singers as well as pre-service music educator identity.

Deejay Robinson is an early childhood general music teacher. He has authored two editorials and co-authored two chapters. Currently, Deejay is engaged in a large-scale research project. The project hopes to reveal the ways in which Black and Latino/a music teachers have dealt with and overcome issues of social/educational marginalization in music and music education because of race. Deejay has written curriculums for Boston's Handel and Haydn Society and the Massachusetts Department of Elementary and Secondary Education. Deejay has degrees in vocal performance from Millikn University (B.M.), Longy School of Music of Bard College (M.M.), and an Ed.M. in Music Education from Boston University.

Margaret Schmidt is a Professor of Music Education and Assistant Director of the School of Music at ASU, where she teaches courses for future and current music educators. She is director of the ASU String Project, supervising over 25 music education and performance majors teaching more than 200 area children. For 14 years, she taught elementary and junior high strings in Austin (Minnesota), Albuquerque (New Mexico), and Naperville (Illinois). Prior to her appointment at ASU, she taught at St. Cloud State (Minnesota) University. She earned degrees from the University of Michigan, State University of New York at Stony Brook, and Lawrence University.

Colleen A. Sears is an Associate Professor and the Coordinator of Music Education at The College of New Jersey where she also leads curriculum development for the *Institute for Social Justice in the Arts*. Her research focuses on issues of equity and access in music education. Her current projects engage students and educators with issues of social justice through music performance and interdisciplinary esthetic experiences. She holds a Bachelor of Music from The College of New Jersey, a Master of Arts from the Eastman School of Music, and a Doctor of Education in music education from Teachers College, Columbia University.

Amy E. Spears is an Assistant Professor of Music Education at Nebraska Wesleyan University. She holds a Ph.D. in Music Education from ASU. Her previous teaching experience includes secondary school instrumental and general music classes in Alabama and Arizona, and music education courses at Florida Atlantic University and ASU. Dr. Spears is a regular presenter at national and international conferences including the National Association for Music Education (NAfME) and its various state affiliate conferences, Society for Music Teacher Education (SMTE), Instrumental Music Teacher Educators Colloquium (IMTE), Association for Popular Music Education (APME), and Midwest Band and Orchestra Clinic.

Melanie E. Stanford is currently working as a head choral director at a junior high school outside of Houston, Texas. She earned her Bachelor's degree in Music Education from Louisiana State University and eventually would like to pursue graduate degrees in the field of music education. She has taken on leadership roles in numerous LGBTQ advocacy and activism organizations. These leadership opportunities furthered her desire to help music educators include and provide support for transgender students in the music classroom. To protect herself from employment discrimination, she writes under a pseudonym.

Brent C. Talbot is an Associate Professor and the Coordinator of Music Education at the Sunderman Conservatory of Music at Gettysburg College, where he teaches various courses in music education and supervises student teaching. Brent is artistic director of the Gettysburg Children's Choir and founding director of Gamelan Gita Semara. His research examines power, discourse, and issues of social justice in varied settings for music learning around the globe. Brent has published in professional and peer-reviewed journals and books. He is editor of this book, author of *Gending Raré: Children's Songs and Games from Bali*, and associate editor of *Action, Criticism & Theory for Music Education*. For more, visit www. brentctalbot.com.

Don Taylor teaches undergraduate and graduate courses in music education at the University of North Texas. Serving as the Coordinator of Ph.D. Studies, his primary area of instruction is elementary general music, and his research interests focus on social justice issues in music education. Prior to a career in higher education, he taught elementary music for 9 years in San Antonio, Texas. His work has been published in a variety of journals, including the *Journal of Research in Music Education*, the *Bulletin of the Council for Research in Music Education*, the *Journal of Music Teacher Education*, and *Music Educators Journal*.

Darrin Thornton is an Assistant Professor of Music at the Penn State School of Music and teaches music education foundations, methods, and techniques courses at the undergraduate and graduate levels while advising undergraduate music education students and serving on graduate thesis committees. His research focuses on pre-service and in-service teacher development, educational access and outreach in music and music education, learning in ensemble settings, and lifelong music engagement. Dr. Thornton remains active as a performing percussionist, conductor, church musician, adjudicator, clinician, guest lecturer, and consultant.

INDEX